The greatest is charity

Andrew Reed
Reproduced by courtesy of Reed's School, Cobham, Surrey

The greatest is charity

The life of Andrew Reed, preacher and philanthropist

Ian J. Shaw

EVANGELICAL PRESS

EVANGELICAL PRESS
Faverdale North Industrial Estate, Darlington, DL3 0PH, England

Evangelical Press USA
P. O. Box 825, Webster, New York 14580, USA

e-mail: sales@evangelicalpress.org

web: http://www.evangelicalpress.org

First published 2005

British Library Cataloguing in Publication Data available

ISBN 0 85234 593 3

Printed and bound in Great Britain by Creative Print & Design Wales, Ebbw Vale

To Christine,
with my love

Contents

Illustrations

Foreword

The name of Andrew Reed means very little to most evangelical Christians today; a fleeting recognition may acknowledge him as one of the many evangelical philanthropists of the nineteenth century, in an age when three quarters of all charitable organizations were founded by Christians with clear evangelical convictions. It is such names as Spurgeon, Booth, Barnardo, Müller and Quarrier that come first to mind — but Andrew Reed is scarcely known.

That the name of Andrew Reed should be better known will be obvious to all who read Dr Ian Shaw's excellent biography. It is at once an enthralling read, a moving account of compassion for those at the bottom of society and a valuable social history — especially including the struggle for equality by Dissenters against the narrow-mindedness of nineteenth-century Anglicanism. Here is the story of one of the truly great preachers of the Victorian age, who built up a church of under a hundred to one regularly numbering around two thousand, during his half century as pastor of New Road Chapel (later rebuilt and renamed Wycliffe Chapel) in Stepney, London. He also maintained a world vision for gospel work across the rapidly opening continents. Above all, Andrew Reed is to be remembered for his vital work in establishing three orphanages, two homes for those with what we call today 'learning disabilities' and a 'hospice' for those with severe physical disabilities. Four of the charities Andrew Reed founded still continue their work today, although in changed form.

Unlike George Müller of Bristol, Andrew Reed was never reluctant to enlist the support of public figures to advance his work: a dozen or so Members of Parliament, the 'iron' Duke of Wellington and Prince Albert were among his greatest supporters. At one meeting, the Duke of Wellington rose to speak and, pointing to Reed, announced: 'I am here tonight at the request of that great man, whose wishes to me are law.' By the time of his death in 1862, this Mr Great Heart — described in his day simply as 'the orphan's friend' — had provided homes for 6,400 children and adults from among the forgotten of society.

It was the two asylums for 'idiots' — not then a pejorative term but a recognized medical description — that drew my greatest respect. 120 years before the formation of the modern charity Prospects — a national charity supporting adults with learning disabilities to live their lives to the full in a caring environment — Andrew Reed had ventured into this complex world. His was an age when those with 'learning disabilities' were either totally ignored or became the object of amusement, yet Reed and his workers established a home with a modern-day wisdom and insight: not a rigid, soul-destroying institution, but a happy, loving, active and progressive family. It was all quite remarkable for any day, but most of all for the nineteenth century.

Misunderstood by friends, ridiculed by opponents, betrayed by those he trusted and hampered by narrow bigotry, Andrew Reed was a giant in faith and self-discipline who passionately believed that *every* individual had value simply because they had been created in the image of God — and that nothing would be impossible if he reached out for the hand of God.

In a day when British society is in serious danger of forgetting or neglecting its Christian roots, this book is an exceptional reminder that our heritage of care and compassion has excellent models based upon the highest principles and motivation. Everything about the life and work of Andrew Reed was intended for the glory of God, and in that, as in all that he did, this Victorian preacher and philanthropist was unquestionably successful.

I must pay tribute to the careful research, historical accuracy and valuable reference notes that are typical of the author and historian, Dr Ian Shaw. No one will read this book without being moved, enlightened and inspired to greater compassion for those at the bottom of society, and greater confidence in their God. There is still much being done today for our society by a host of care organizations in the evangelical tradition, but the scope for more is unlimited. The story of Andrew Reed will provide a stimulus and an incentive to go forward.

Brian H. Edwards
Surbiton
July 2005

Acknowledgements

Although Andrew Reed's name was once mentioned in the same breath as those of William Wilberforce, Lord Shaftesbury, or Thomas Barnardo, his remarkable ministry has now sadly passed from public notice. My first encounter with him came in the course of PhD research I was undertaking at the University of Manchester into the work of ministers holding Calvinistic doctrine in nineteenth-century cities. Iain Murray of the Banner of Truth Trust commended him to me as a candidate well worthy of study. A short section of the book that followed, *High Calvinists in Action* (Oxford University Press, 2002), considers Andrew Reed's ministry. That research showed that there was far more to discover about him and highlighted the great need for a full-length biography of this important figure.

A key source for the life of Andrew Reed, particularly concerning his inner spiritual life, is the *Memoirs* compiled by his sons Charles and Andrew immediately after their father's death. They made much use of their father's 'Journal', and an extensive collection of letters that he kept. Sadly, despite the endeavours of the Reed family to locate these original items, they could not be unearthed. However, there remains a wide range of other material upon which to draw, including the archives of the church of which Andrew Reed was the minister, and the records of the charities which he formed.

Four of the five charities he founded still exist, although in changed form, and for them Reed's remarkable work remains important to their ethos. In researching this book the assistance, encouragement and enthusiasm of individuals associated with these charities has been invaluable. Amongst many who have

helped, special mention should be made of Jackie Sullivan and
Alan Bott of Reed's School, Jean Watkins and Richard Link of
the Reedham Trust, and Rosemary Brotherwood of the Royal
Wanstead Children's Foundation. The kind assistance of the
Royal Hospital for Neuro-disability, Putney, is acknowledged,
particularly that of Robert Sproats, who facilitated access to the
hospital's archives and kindly commented on part of the text.
The descendants of Andrew Reed have also been most supportive of the writing of this book, and particular mention should
be made of the great assistance and encouragement of Douglas
Reed. Others have given of their time and wisdom in reading
and commenting on parts of the text, and for this particular
thanks are owing to Dr Brian Stanley (of the University of
Cambridge), Dr John Jeacocke (of International Christian
College) and the Rev. Brian Edwards, who has kindly supplied
a foreword.

I am deeply grateful that Marianne Thorne (Honorary
Archivist to the Royal Wanstead Children's Foundation) and
Derrick Smith (historian of the Reedham Old Scholars' Associa-
tion) have not only commented on parts of the text, but also
shared with me the fruits of their own researches into aspects of
Andrew Reed's life. The staff of many libraries have been of
great help, particularly the Metropolitan Archives, London
(formerly the Greater London Record Office), Redbridge
Central Library, Ilford, the Guildhall Library, London, the
Surrey History Centre, Woking, and the library of International
Christian College, Glasgow. Much of the research for this book
was undertaken while on sabbatical leave from my post as
lecturer at International Christian College, Glasgow, and thanks
is due to them for making this time available. I am also grateful
to Evangelical Press for their willingness to embrace a work on
Andrew Reed's life, when others rejected the idea on the
strange logic that people will only read books about individuals
who are already well known.

Thanks are above all due to my wife, Christine, for her
enduring love and encouragement. To her I dedicate this book.

1.
Beginnings

For Andrew ... these were ... years that helped shape his future Christian faith, and his convictions as to what would constitute a healthy and happy upbringing for children.

1.
Beginnings

As the nine-year-old boy stood quietly in St Paul's Cathedral, London, holding his mother's hand, he looked intently at the newly unveiled statue of the prison reformer and philanthropist John Howard.[1] Moved by his deep Christian convictions, Howard had devoted himself to the cause of prison reform, publicizing the degrading and inhuman conditions experienced by many prisoners in Britain and throughout Europe. Who knows what went through the mind of young Andrew Reed as he stood and thought of the life and work of the famous and heroic philanthropist? Little would any observer of that simple scene have imagined that on that boy's death sixty-six years later, he too would be revered as one of the greatest of English philanthropists.

His parents

There was nothing in the humble home life and upbringing of young Andrew Reed to indicate that such an illustrious future lay ahead of him. His father, also called Andrew, was born in 1748, one of six sons born to John and Mary Reed, of Maiden Newton, Dorset. The Reeds were renowned in the area as devout Christians and, although Nonconformists, for a number of years they attended the local parish church, where the rector faithfully preached the gospel. However, his successor did not continue this evangelical ministry, and so the family took to walking some ten miles each Sunday to the Independent Chapel in Bridport to meet with like-minded believers. John Reed and his six sons all became involved in local lay preaching around the Dorset area and in supporting the itinerant work of other ministers. Their witness in Maiden Newton was so successful that it led to the eventual establishment of an Independent congregation in the village.

John Reed's fourth son, Andrew, was set to learn the craft of watchmaking and, at the age of twenty-one, he moved from his father's home to work in Weymouth, where there were more opportunities for his trade. Here he developed his skills and reputation, but Andrew had greater things in mind. When he had gathered sufficient savings, he walked to London to set up in his own business as a watchmaker. Six feet tall, sturdy, yet gentle and kindly in character, he joined up with a local Independent church and took on the responsibility of visiting the sick and the needy in some of the poorest parts of the capital. On one such visit, to a hovel near Drury Lane, he overheard someone praying in an adjoining room and, going quietly in, he saw a young woman kneeling by the bedside of a lady who was seriously ill. That meeting was to change his life.[2]

Mary Ann Mullen had suffered much tragedy in her young life. Her mother had died when Mary Ann was young and, although her father had remarried, he died not long afterwards. The family of her stepmother then conspired to deprive Mary Ann of any inheritance, and left her penniless. She had managed to eke out a living by teaching a small class of children to read and write in her own home. Her own childhood suffering had opened her heart to the needs of others and, with a deeply compassionate nature, she spent her spare time visiting and nursing the elderly and sick in the area where she lived.[3]

Brought together in this providential meeting, and united by a common love for the poor and needy and by their deep Christian faith, it was not long before Andrew and Mary Ann

Beaumont House
The birthplace of Andrew Reed

were married. Filled with youthful hope, they happily set up home in a rickety old house in Butcher Row, St Clement Danes. Yet their early years of marriage were to be marked by great sadness. In the London of those times, infant mortality was appallingly high. It is hard to imagine the agony the young couple must have endured in those years, but their story was all too common in the dreadful urban living conditions in the late eighteenth and early nineteenth centuries. Three times Andrew and Mary Ann rejoiced at the birth of a child; three times tragedy struck soon afterwards. Perhaps they wondered whether they would ever know the blessing of seeing a child live to adulthood. Then on 27 November 1787 a fourth child, Andrew, was born; his parents rejoiced as he lived on through infancy. They poured their hopes and dreams into him; Mary Ann bestowed on her son the fulness of her maternal heart in a way she had been cruelly denied in her own childhood.

Parenthood in urban Britain in the dying years of the eighteenth century was filled with bright hopes and all-too-real fears; every childhood illness was a cause for justifiable alarm. Poor sanitation, poor hygiene and poor diet left people prey to the frequent epidemics that swept through the crowded streets. Childbirth was a desperately dangerous time for both mother and baby. The lives of infants who survived that trauma could then be snatched away by highly infectious diseases in a matter of hours, with little meaningful medical assistance and no antibiotics or effective medicines to help. Scarlet fever, cholera, typhus and diarrhoea were all killers of children. Such conditions prevailed throughout much of the nineteenth century. Of those buried in the graveyard of Wycliffe Chapel, Stepney, as late as 1849, almost half were children, and nearly one in five were under the age of one.[4]

The early years

More sadness was to follow, as Andrew and Mary Reed lost other infants too frail to survive the rigours of London's polluted environment. Their anguish was eased nearly six years after Andrew's birth, when another surviving child, Martha, was born. Andrew was devoted to his sister, with her blue eyes and rosy cheeks. A few years later came another son who survived, Peter.

There is little doubt that those early years, lived in a home touched by the frequent shadows of mourning for lost children punctuated by fleeting moments of joy, rendered Andrew particularly sensitive to the suffering of others, especially that of mothers and young children. When at the age of four he heard the news of the death of one infant brother, he was inconsolable: 'I felt as if I had lost everything in losing him.'[5]

In an attempt to find a healthier spot in which to bring up the children, their parents hired a cottage in the village of Mitcham, where Mary was able to look after them while her husband continued with his watchmaking trade in London. The little fair-haired children were inseparable, attending the village school and enjoying the freedom to play in the cornfields, meadows and woods of rural Surrey. At weekends their father was with them, and Sunday was a particularly happy day. After the evening service their big, gentle father would take the children on his knees, ask them questions about the day's services and encourage them in their childlike answers. Then they would sing a hymn together, and he would take them in his strong arms and say, 'God Almighty bless ye, my children.'

For Andrew, Martha and little Peter these were idyllic, laughter-filled, childhood years. To Andrew the period brought a developing love of nature and a conviction of the importance of fresh air for a healthy existence. They were years that helped shape his future Christian faith, and his convictions as to what would constitute a healthy and happy upbringing for children. From infancy the children were taught how to pray and read the Bible. At the age of seven Andrew was given by his mother a copy of the *Westminster Shorter Catechism*, the learning of which helped mould his religious thinking.[6] When the eight-year-old Andrew neglected to say his prayers one evening, it was his little sister who rebuked him: 'Remember, brother, God sees you!'[7] Secure in the knowledge of their parents' love and prayers, and shaped by their clear and consistent example, the children thrived.

Of course, it could not last for ever. Andrew was believed to have great academic potential, and so his parents resolved to give him the best start in life possible, and to stretch their meagre resources to pay for him to receive a higher level of education. It would be 1870 before state education began in England, and in the early years of the nineteenth century most schools charged some fees. For the majority of children the only education they received was at Sunday school; many were given none at all. Andrew Reed was given opportunities that many from his social background were never to benefit from, and for two years he received a classical education at a school in Islington. To pay for this, the family returned to live above the watchmaker's shop in St Clement Danes, and Mary Ann resumed teaching her small class of children in the largest room of their house. His enlightened parents also ensured that Martha received a proper education. However, the Reed family's finances were eventually exhausted, and the decision was taken that Andrew should follow his father's trade. The bright young lad quickly took to the work, and proved highly proficient in making and mending watches and clocks.[8]

Andrew Reed's father, who became well known as a lay preacher in the London area, knew many of the leading Independent ministers in the capital, and these men were frequent visitors to the little back parlour behind the watchmaker's shop. He took his son Andrew to the meeting in 1799 at which the interdenominational Religious Tract Society was founded. Interested in overseas missions, he was also friendly with some of the founders of the London Missionary Society. The children were reared on accounts of the famous Great Ejection of 1662 when, on grounds of religious conscience, some 2,000 ministers were removed from the Church of England for refusing to compromise their conscience, and became Nonconformists. The family attended the New Court Chapel, Carey Street, in central London, and sat under the ministry of Richard Winter, but after the death of the venerable pastor, they began to attend the New Road Chapel at St George's-in-the-East, Stepney.

Here there was a new minister, Samuel Lyndall, who was noted for his warm and powerful preaching. It was a walk of three and a half miles, but the family were happy to make the effort.

Most Sundays were spent by Andrew's father in preaching in village chapels around the London area. He worked with the London Itinerant Society, founded in 1796, and the Congregational Society for Spreading the Gospel in the Dark Parts of England, the name of which was simplified in 1803 to the Village Itinerating Society. The genial watchmaker had enjoyed only a limited education as a boy, but some of his London neighbours recognized his latent ability: one lent him volumes of theology from his personal library; another gave him instruction free of charge in Hebrew and Greek, so that he might read the Old and New Testaments in their original languages. Mary Ann Reed devoted all the surplus income from teaching her pupils to the purchase of theological books, mainly volumes from Puritan authors such as Thomas Manton, Richard Baxter and Matthew Poole.

At the age of fifteen, young Andrew was apprenticed to another clockmaker, and moved from his parents' home into that of his new master. Suddenly he encountered a very different atmosphere from that carefully nurtured by his parents: new temptations came his way, particularly through his employer's son, who was about his age. Together they went several times to the theatre, something totally forbidden by Andrew's parents. There began a struggle in his heart as to the type of life he would lead. The pull of the world, with its attractions, was very strong. His parents pleaded with him, warning him about the choices he was making, but he remained undecided.

Conversion and early Christian experience

Then one Sunday Samuel Lyndall preached a sermon of warning from the parable of the wise and foolish virgins, in Matthew 25:10, emphasizing the fate of the foolish: 'And the door was shut.' This deeply troubled Andrew, and that night he thought and prayed much. The next day he attempted to put these thoughts behind him and to stifle his convictions. However, that evening he went to his parents' home, where he happened to pick up a pamphlet by the eighteenth-century hymn-writer Isaac Watts which his mother had been planning to send to him. As he read, Andrew Reed began to feel deeply aware of his own sinfulness, and the need for personal faith in Jesus Christ. Now greatly concerned about his spiritual state, he began to read another work with a title that seemed suitable to his need, *Alarm to Unconverted Sinners* by the Puritan writer Joseph Alleine. He spent a night in earnest prayer. Then the matter was resolved as he surrendered his life to Jesus Christ. He wrote out a personal covenant with God, which he signed on 8 June 1803. He was fifteen years old.[9]

This commitment was made in full knowledge of what were to be serious consequences, both immediate and future. He searched his life, seeking to make decisions that would help him to honour God in his everyday conduct. Most important was a resolution to break completely with the teenage associates who had been leading him astray, especially the son of his employer. To achieve this Andrew decided that there was no alternative but to leave his master's house and abandon his formal crafts-man's training. It was a huge step, for a completed apprentice-ship would have secured him employment prospects and good wages, with privileges within the City of London. Also, his indentures could not be cancelled without considerable ex-pense. However, his devoted parents, seeing the reasons behind their son's decision, came to his aid and made further sacrifices on his behalf. Somehow the required premium was paid off and Andrew returned to the security of his parents' home.

Andrew spent hours in private prayer, often walking to Highgate Woods to meditate. He resolved to repay his parents the considerable expense to which they had been put, by working hard for his father in the latter's watchmaking business.

But such a resolution was easier in theory than in practice, and other hopes were already stirring in Andrew's heart. Often as his mother tidied up her son's workbench at the end of the day she would find amongst his tools works of theology which had become of more interest to him than completing the task in hand. His wise parents did not scold him, but allowed him freedom to explore the big religious questions that were forming in his mind.[10]

The influence of Mary Ann on both her husband and her son was profound. When she saw people being blessed by her husband's preaching and prayers, she realized it was impossible that he could ever train to become a minister so late in life. Yet, with a clear spiritual discernment and a willingness to make deep personal sacrifices, she resolved that if by the labours of her own hands she could earn enough money to free him from giving all his time to watch and clockmaking, he would be able to take on more preaching engagements. The family had a deep interest in mission, and if she and her husband were too old to go to the South Pacific islands, where the workers of the London Missionary Society had begun pioneer missionary work, why not go to the villages around London where there were few chapels and churches? The powerful example of his parents, both in Christian and parental devotion, was hugely influential on young Andrew. He soon began to accompany his father as he went each Sunday to preach in what were then still villages around London, such as Barking, Woodford, Lewisham and Dulwich. Together they discussed the day's messages as they walked, Andrew turning up the references in the Bible as his father called them out to him. On their weary way home, often after three services, they sang hymns to each other to help the journey pass more swiftly.[11]

Then the Reed family received unexpected blessings. A small legacy enabled Mrs Reed to give up teaching her small class of pupils, and when the City of London authorities decided to press ahead with long-considered plans to undertake street improvements in the Strand, which entailed knocking down the watchmaker's premises in St Clement Danes, a significant sum of compensation was paid. The family relocated to Chiswell Street, Finsbury, where Mrs Reed carried out a long-cherished plan of opening a shop selling Staffordshire pottery. After a few years she proved so successful that Andrew Reed senior was able to give up watchmaking and devote himself fully to lay preaching. In this capacity he was able to give a further twenty years of faithful service.[12]

First steps in Christian service

Young Andrew Reed was also seeing his gifts in Christian service develop. He became a Sunday school teacher at Ponder's End, Enfield, one of the small chapels his father visited. Yet he struggled with a profound lack of confidence in public speaking. The first time he was asked if he would pray in a service, he was so worried at the prospect that he did not attend for several weeks. Gradually, however, he overcame his fears and began to bring short messages, which the superintendent at Ponder's End greatly approved of. As the number of Sunday school pupils increased, he encouraged friends from the New Road Chapel to help him in the work, even though it meant leaving home soon after seven o'clock on a Sunday morning. Together they started a small prayer meeting and began to visit the parents of the children regularly. With his teenage friends he started a Sunday evening service in a cottage nearby, at which they read the Bible and *Pilgrim's Progress* to those who attended, since none of the boys felt in any way qualified to preach.[13]

As his gifts developed, Andrew gave more and more time to study. He helped his mother in the pottery shop when needed during the day, doing the accounts in the evening, but his thirst for studying theology grew. He started to join his father at the Greek and Hebrew classes he was attending and, ever possessed of a practical streak, taught himself to write shorthand.

He debated serious theological and philosophical questions at length, until his mother feared his energies would be wasted in theoretical speculations. She promptly went out and bought him Luke Tyerman's *Life of George Whitefield*, which she left on his desk, praying that her son might live to be 'like that man'. Once again his mother's deep spiritual wisdom proved its worth. Andrew devoured the volumes and resolved to be more devoted, more humble and more zealous in God's service.

Without ever telling Andrew, his mother had begun to pray that her son might be called into Christian ministry. For a period of months this seemed unlikely, as Andrew became deeply introspective and was troubled by temptation and doubt. He found that prayer was no longer easy and the services at church seemed disappointing. His faith was being profoundly tested.[14] He faithfully persevered with his Sunday school teaching, but his enthusiasm seemed to be waning. Again, it was something his mother did that was to prove decisive for his future philanthropic career: the act of helping others lifted him from this period of spiritual discouragement.

Ever filled with compassion and kindness, when Mary Ann came across a little girl who had recently been orphaned, she refused to allow the child to be sent into an orphanage, fearing that she would find little there in the way of love, and instead offered her shelter with her own family, where she stayed for many years. As Andrew helped to teach the little girl to read and write, the joy of seeing her happiness, and her ability to learn so quickly, liberated him from the depths into which he had fallen. He saw afresh how much he had been blessed in his own family life, in comparison with this little girl. Again he was able to cast himself unreservedly on the grace of God. The healthy relationship between a life of faith and a life of active service to God was clearly formulated in his mind.

Andrew applied to join the New Road Chapel and on 31 January 1806, at the age of eighteen, he was accepted as a communicant member. The ties with a watchmaking career were finally broken that same year when he sold the tools he had bought for his apprenticeship in the trade. The money raised went on a small library of theological books, which Andrew studied deeply. His mother's constant prayer was: 'Suffer my dear boy to depend on no learning or ability, but on Thyself alone.'[15]

Other habits were also being formed. The love of nature learned amidst the green fields of Surrey deepened. Andrew would frequently walk out to Hampstead Hill, or Highgate. Sometimes he took longer trips, to Harrow, or Beckenham, drinking deeply of the wide views from the open hills out across the lush green of the woods and fields of the Home Counties. In years to come, when in need of time to reflect or relax, he would head away from the town to these quieter rural spots. The exercise gained helped sustain his constitution during periods of great stress.[16]

The sadnesses of early childhood, strong, supportive, family influences, a love of learning, an appreciation of the beauties of the natural world, and a deep sense of duty to help those who suffered — all worked together in the moulding of Andrew Reed's character. Now added to this was an intensely personal, and growing, Christian commitment, which had been severely tested, but had emerged strong, and shaped in such a way that it would be expressed earnestly and practically. It seemed that the prayers of his father and mother, that he would grow not only to love God, but also to serve him, were beginning to be fulfilled.

2.
The call to the ministry

Although the level of education Andrew Reed received was higher than that of many other children at the time, it was still fairly limited. His experience was typical of many artisan families, who found that in the early nineteenth century opportunities for good-quality schooling were rare, and libraries were few. For many children, Sunday school was the only education they would ever receive. In 1806 Andrew Reed and the friends he had gathered around him to help him in Sunday school teaching at Ponder's End made an attempt at self-improvement when they joined together to form 'the Society of Contending Brethren'. These friends were similarly artisan and working-class by background: they included a shoemaker, a clerk, a frame-maker and a currier. Andrew was eighteen at the time, and he and this group of aspiring young men were determined to develop their minds. They wrote essays on subjects such as 'The authenticity of the Bible', 'The Origin of Evil' and 'Pulpit Eloquence', which they read to each other. Deeper subjects were not avoided: influenced by their reading of the eighteenth-century American theologian Jonathan Edwards, the subject of 'Degrees of Glory' appeared on the agenda for debate. Books such as the Baptist theologian John Gill's *Body of Divinity* were read aloud and discussed paragraph by paragraph. Alongside theology they studied grammar and composition, Latin, Greek and even Hebrew.[1]

A meeting of the Society of Contending Brethren

The class led by Matthew Wilks

Theology remained the subject dearest to Andrew Reed's heart, and his path towards the Christian ministry began to open up when he was invited by Rev. Matthew Wilks to join a small class of young men studying theology under his guidance. This was a significant step, for Wilks was from 1780 to 1829 the minister of the Moorfields Tabernacle, built in the eighteenth century for the great evangelical preacher George Whitefield. As one of the leading Nonconformist preachers in London, Wilks provided a direct link to the religious revival of the eighteenth century and to Whitefield, Andrew Reed's great hero. Having benefited from

training at the Countess of
Huntingdon's college at
Trevecca in Wales, the
minister of Moorfields
Tabernacle did all he could
to encourage young men
who showed signs of apti-
tude and calling for the
ministry. He ran a small
class for young men who
wished to study theology
more deeply, and oversaw
their progress in fatherly
fashion. Matthew Wilks was
also connected to many of
the leading, and recently
launched, evangelical institutions of the day, such as

Matthew Wilks

the London Missionary Society, founded in 1795, and the
Religious Tract Society. He sought to promote itinerant preaching, and had met Andrew and his father through their work with
the Village Itinerating Society.

Keen to impress Wilks, Andrew offered to compile a cata-
logue of his library, and for several weeks he perched on a
ladder deep in the minister's books, unearthing and listing the
treasures hidden there. After he had been attending the small
class for six months, Wilks summoned him to his study. Anxious
to know if he had done something wrong, Andrew was quickly
reassured when he found this highly respected man wished to
discuss with him the possibility of his training for the Christian
ministry. Andrew acknowledged that he had felt drawn to the
ministry but, remembering his struggles even to pray in his early
days at the Ponder's End Sunday School, he expressed his
belief that he lacked the required abilities. The senior pastor,
however, indicated that he had observed in Andrew gifts which,
with further study, prayer and maturing, might be useful in the

cause of Christ. Asking him to think the matter over, Wilks sought permission to talk to his parents. Samuel Lyndall, Andrew Reed's minister at New Road Chapel, was thrilled to see such possibilities opening up for the young member of his congregation.[2]

Hackney College

Within a week the matter was settled. Andrew Reed was to apply to study at Hackney College as soon as possible, under the care of the principal, Rev. George Collison. Before he could be accepted Reed was required to appear before the ministerial committee, where he gave a fifteen-minute address on the words from Genesis 6:9, 'And Noah walked with God,' and answered a series of questions. He keenly felt his youthful inadequacy when speaking before such senior clergy, but he met with warm acceptance.

On 13 March 1807, aged nineteen, Andrew Reed entered Hackney College as a ministerial student. In his journal he poured out his heart: 'Oh! That the Lord may disappoint my many fears, and enable me both to fill my new situation to His glory, and to put more confidence in his supreme goodness.'[3] The pressure of coming to this decision brought on a reaction typical of the sensitive nature of Andrew Reed: for a few days he found himself enveloped in a cloud of depression, feeling that he was not only unfit for Christian ministry, but also unworthy to be considered a Christian at all. He was convinced that if God were to use him it would be 'a most marvellous display of Divine goodness'.[4] His wise parents were not deterred and called a meeting of friends for prayer and praise at their home, seeking the Lord's particular favour on their son's future ministry. Still the doubts lingered in Andrew's mind, and when he preached in Buckinghamshire in July he felt so miserable that he found it difficult to put his sentences together at all.[5]

Although daunted by the prospect of training for the ministry, he was in his own mind somewhat overestimating the
intellectual ordeal ahead of him. The programme of study,
while thorough, was not designed to present any great academic challenge. Hackney College was a theological academy
founded in 1803 in connection with the Village Itinerant Society
for Spreading the Gospel in England. The committee chose for
president of the newly founded college George Collison, then
aged just thirty-one. He was to stay in post until his death in
1847, combining the role until 1837 with the pastorate of Marsh
Street Chapel, Walthamstow. He was a warm-hearted, diligent
and devoted teacher, but he was no profound scholar or
original thinker and because of his pastoral work was unable to
devote all his time to his students. None the less, during the
forty-four years of his presidency some 150 students were
trained for the ministry at the college.[6] Hackney avoided the fate
of many other Dissenting academies, which lacked continuity
and could fail with the death or removal of the leading tutor.
Lack of resources, and students of limited ability and spirituality,
frustrated the efforts of some tutors. William Steadman of the
Horton Baptist Academy in Bradford lamented that most of his
students were 'illiterate, their talents small, their manners dull
and uninteresting, their systems of divinity contracted ... and
their exertions scarcely any at all'.[7] Hackney College was also
small, with limited resources, and many of its students lacked
the abilities and application to study that were shown by
Andrew Reed.

Then, newly started on his ministerial training, a further
challenge was placed in his way. In late July 1807 he was
approached by Dr Blair of Woodford, who had heard Andrew
preach and had seen considerable ability in the young man. He
presented the young student with prospects that were far more
intellectually stimulating and attractive than those offered at
Hackney. Dr Blair offered to secure Andrew's entry into Cambridge University, and to place him under the support and
pastoral care of Charles Simeon, the leading evangelical

Anglican minister of the day. Simeon was minister of Holy
Trinity Church, Cambridge, and also Fellow of King's College,
and played a vital role in the theological training of many
evangelical students at the university. The contrast between the
homely pastoral tuition of Hackney College, where the small
number of students lived in the college house, making the most
of the limited library resources, and the classical education
available at Cambridge, could not have been more pronounced. As a Nonconformist it was not possible to study at
Oxford University, but Cambridge was more sympathetic.
Nonconformists could study at the university, but until 1856
were not allowed to graduate with a degree unless they were
willing to conform to the Church of England. As a Nonconformist, Reed had conscientious objections to doing so, but he could
still have benefited from the course of study. Alternatively he
could have buried his principles and become an Anglican,
allying himself with a system where opportunities for ministerial
usefulness and progress would have beckoned.

It took Andrew a week to decide, but when it came, the
response to Dr Blair was in the negative. The prospects of
Cambridge were declined on principles of conscience, a sacrifice many other able young men were constrained to make.
When Matthew Wilks and George Collison realized the dilemma
Reed faced, and the sacrifice he had made, they sought to
encourage their young protégé with the proposition that, after
his period at Hackney, he should study for a further two years
at Glasgow University, where since the eighteenth century a
steady stream of English Dissenters had studied.[8] This proposal
somewhat softened the blow, but the plan was never executed,
largely because Reed was in such demand as a preacher by the
time he had finished his studies. There remained a sense of
frustration in Andrew Reed that the discrimination against the
Nonconformists of his day had denied him access to education
at the highest level. In his heart was formed a steely resolve to
do something about the privileges enjoyed by the Church of

England, but denied to those who could not subscribe to the Established Church and its teachings and practices.

Paying for study at Hackney College was no easy matter. Andrew Reed lived in the college house, and for this accommodation and his study he was required to find around £30 per year.[9] Most of this came from his parents, who made huge sacrifices to provide him with the opportunity, although gifts from friends and ministers were also forthcoming. Andrew Reed proved worthy of their efforts. The habits he had formed in his parents' home served him well. He rose early and studied hard, preferring to devote himself to his books even in times available for recreation. Those around him began to observe the interest he took in ordinary people. When he discovered a servant in the college who could not read, he took on the task of teaching her and gave her a copy of Philip Doddridge's *Rise and Progress of Religion in the Soul* as a reward for her success.

His first summer vacation was spent preaching in the market town of Selby in Yorkshire. Here he worked with a group who were attempting to establish a Congregational church in the town. Initially meeting in the Assembly Room, and then in a barn, the group responded very warmly to young Andrew's ministry. Congregations numbering 120 in the morning, and 220 in the evening, were attracted. During his stay with them they resolved to build their own premises, and so much did they appreciate his ministry that the congregation urged him to consider abandoning his studies and becoming their pastor. This was a pressure frequently placed on students at the Dissenting academies, where there was no formal qualification at the end of the course. The offer was declined, but Reed was greatly encouraged by the warmth of response from this congregation. He went to Yorkshire still uncertain over his sense of call, but returned convinced that God was willing and able to use him.[10]

The studies at Hackney College were continued steadfastly, although Reed soon outstripped the abilities of the president, George Collison, and did much study on his own. He mastered Latin and Greek, and developed an effective prose style. The influences of Collison and his college studies helped refine his theological views. Samuel Lyndall's ministry had been appealing to Reed, and had led to his conversion, but the minister of the New Road Chapel was a high Calvinist and, while believing very much in the reality and necessity of Christian experience, he strongly emphasized the sovereignty of God in the salvation of the believer. This made him reluctant to freely invite all unbelievers to respond to the gospel message. At Hackney College Andrew Reed's theological views moved away from those of Lyndall, in the direction of evangelical Calvinism, emphasizing not only the sovereignty of God in predestination, but also the responsibility of the sinner to believe in Christ for salvation, and the duty of the church to proclaim the gospel to all. His views moved into line with those of George Whitefield and his successor Matthew Wilks.[11] Andrew Reed became firmly convinced of the rightness of evangelical Calvinism, stressing the need to proclaim the gospel to all, as he later urged his own son: 'If the few only are taught, what is to become of the million?'[12] This progression in doctrinal views mirrored that of George Collison, who had also been converted under Lyndall's ministry in Yorkshire. On moving to study in London, Collison's views had broadened into an evangelical Calvinism.[13] Perhaps it was the similar trajectories of their theological development that drew the principal of Hackney College and Andrew Reed into particularly close friendship.

Invitations to preach

On his twenty-first birthday Andrew took time to reflect on his life, giving two hours to private prayer and praise. His sense of call was now clear; his longing was to 'preach the gospel with abundant success'. Such periods of self-examination were to become characteristic throughout his life.

His pattern of intense study was disrupted by a period of illness lasting several months, and for a while he believed his life would be short. However, with his recovery came a series of invitations to preach which indicated the growing regard in which he was held. On his twenty-second birthday he delivered a sermon in Whitefield's Tabernacle, Moorfields, and he was invited to preach every three months in the New Road Chapel, where he was a member. His summer vacation from college was spent on a preaching tour of Independent churches which took in Plymouth, Ireland and Scotland. The crossing from Liverpool to Dublin was in the midst of a fierce storm that broke the boat's bowsprit and seemed about to sink the vessel. Amidst the chaos Andrew felt a remarkable sense of calm, able to surrender his fate freely to God, quite at peace as to whether he should perish with the ship, or reach port safely. It was a calm he was to feel when buffeted by terrific pressures in the future.[14]

Where that future was to lie remained uncertain. Invitations to settle as their minister flowed in from churches as far afield as Cheltenham, Dublin and Plymouth, together with an invitation to assist Matthew Wilks at Moorfields Tabernacle. Then came a most unexpected opportunity. Samuel Lyndall, whose preaching had led Andrew to faith in Christ, resigned from the pastorate of the New Road Chapel. The congregation voted overwhelmingly to invite Andrew Reed to be their minister. He felt he had little choice but to accept. This was the church to which he owed so much — his conversion, his nurture in the Christian faith and the encouragement to enter training for Christian service. Yet his choice was in other ways not the most obvious one — he was turning his back on offers from prosperous churches with large congregations, to accept a position in one that had fallen into serious decline.[15]

Ordination to the ministry

The ordination service was held on 27 November 1811, Andrew Reed's twenty-fourth birthday. Some of the leading figures of London Congregationalism took part: Robert Winter,

John Clayton of the King's Weigh House Chapel, and George Collison of Hackney College. Matthew Wilks offered the ordination prayer. In the service Reed declared his convictions as to the rightness of Independent church government, principles which had led him to forgo prospects of studying at Cambridge University. He set out the reasons why he dissented from the Church of England: the union of church and state was 'inimical to that kingdom which is "not of this world" '; its rites and ceremonies were opposed to the 'simplicity' of the gospel, and its mode of selection of ministers was 'a violation of the rights of conscience'.[16] Reed united himself heart and soul to his people; for them he promised to 'study assiduously; over them will I watch tenderly; to them I will break the bread of life constantly. Their souls and their joys, their perplexities and their fears, their anxieties and calamities, shall be mine.' For them he would spend and be spent. In the service he solemnly consecrated to Jesus Christ his talents, his energies and his influence.[17]

The service proved an almost overwhelming experience for Andrew Reed, with nearly one hundred ministers and students present and the church packed to overflowing. The seriousness of what he had undertaken weighed heavily on him, and privately he prayed, 'Great Father of the people! Send rich supplies from Thy right hand.' Conscious of his human limitations and frailties, he was convinced that if he was to be 'of any great service to the cause of God and man, it will be nothing less than a miracle of Divine grace'. He realized that the excitement and encouragement of the ordination day would soon be past, and he noted in his journal, 'I am desirous, not merely of *beginning* well, but of *running* well. *Setting out* is something, *holding out* is more. Jesus is sufficient for all things.'[18] Such commitments were resolutely kept, and his prayer answered. Every year for the next fifty years Reed and his congregation held an anniversary service on the day of his ordination, 27 November, until the year of his jubilee brought his retirement — he not only began well, he ran well.

3.
Stepney

By 1818, the sixty members had increased to over 400. It was becoming clear that Andrew Reed's ministry in Stepney was going to be a remarkable one.

3.
Stepney

The New Road Chapel, to which the twenty-four-year-old Andrew Reed was called, was situated in the East End of London, an area that was to change drastically over the next fifty years of his ministry. In 1811 the chapel was in a prominent situation just off the Commercial Road. Reed initially rented a small house in St George's Place, off Cannon Street Road, a busy thoroughfare running from the Commercial Road down towards the London Docks. In 1815, the year before his marriage, Reed took the lease of a property on the same road as the chapel. 32 New Road[1] was a small, but genteel, three-storey town house with cellars, and a small walled garden behind it. It had previously been occupied by a surgeon and his wife and the rent was set at £42 'of lawful money of Great Britain'.[2]

The area

Outwardly the immediate area of Stepney and Whitechapel appeared modestly prosperous, the main thoroughfares lined with shops, villas and the respectable houses of merchants and tradesmen. Yet behind the pleasant and busy main streets, and unnoticed by the eye of many observers, pockets of poor-quality housing were developing, packed closely together, small, ill-ventilated and overcrowded. Over the course of the nineteenth century, as the local population rose rapidly, these

hidden-away areas spread and standards of living rapidly
declined. In the worst areas, approachable only through dingy
courtyards and alleyways, were filthy and dilapidated slums
where countless families fought a battle for existence. With little
drainage or clean water, and the presence of virulent disease, it
was a battle many lost. At the end of Batty's Garden, a court-
yard approached through a small arch, was a rubbish heap on
which the residents dumped their household refuse, including
rotting waste food and human excrement. The stinking heap
was so large and wet that it saturated the walls of the hovels
around. The privies[3] in the area were filled to overflowing and
totally unusable.

By 1848 poverty was widespread; the average weekly wage
in the area was just £1. 0s. 2d. Most men were employed as
labourers, but there were significant numbers of shoemakers,
carpenters, tailors and costermongers. With the London docks
nearby, the families of many sailors and dock workers lived in
the area. Women working in the local clothing industry were
often paid a pittance for their needlework skills. Others worked
in match and matchbox making, or sewing sacks, and were
similarly ill-paid.[4] As the nineteenth century wore on, the East
End became notorious for its 'sweated labour', with impover-
ished and debilitated workers struggling to earn a living wage in
the wretched garrets of Spitalfields, Shoreditch, Stepney and
Bethnal Green. St George's-in-the-East, where the New Road
Chapel was located, experienced some of the worst poverty.

Along the Radcliffe Highway was a notorious 'rookery' with
houses filled with professional thieves, public houses packed
with raucous sailors, while outside prostitutes plied their trade
accosting strangers as they passed by. When Hector Gavin
visited nearby Bethnal Green in the late 1840s, he noted down
his impressions of the streets along which he walked: Cross
Street he described as 'utterly beastly'; Pleasant Place, he said,
was signally misnamed, being 'utterly filthy and abominable'.
Down Digby Street was a manure heap 'in every stage of
offensive and disgusting decomposition', alongside which were

deep lakes of 'putrefying *night soil* ... dammed up with the more solid dung and refuse'. He counted up the earth-closet privies: often only one for every fifty of the population. The poor, he angrily wrote, were 'left to rot in their filth'.[5]

Life expectancy was largely determined by a family's degree of affluence and their housing conditions. In Whitechapel the average age of death for a professional gentleman and his family was forty-five years old, whereas for a tradesman it was twenty-seven years, and for labourers and their families a mere twenty-two years. As Andrew Reed's parents had tragically found, the highest death toll was amongst children: almost half of all deaths were of children before they reached the age of five.[6]

These problems with poverty, bad housing and disease were present at the beginning of Reed's ministry, but in the following years they became more commonplace, and more pronounced. By the time of his retirement in 1861, on the jubilee of his ministry, the social needs of Stepney were acute. It is no surprise that just four years later, in 1865, on an old Quaker burial ground off the Commercial Road, a few hundred yards from the chapel building where Reed had ministered so long, William Booth pitched his tent and began his famous work of open-air evangelism. Booth became General Booth, and the work became the Salvation Army; his aim was to reach the most needy in the lowest social groups of society.

The New Road Chapel

The New Road Chapel of 1811 was well situated, facing onto the busy thoroughfare from which it took its name, and surrounded by a large burial ground — death was never far from everyday life in the early-nineteenth-century city. The building was long and narrow, capable of seating 800 people, and lighted by impressive brass chandeliers filled with candles which needed to be trimmed in the middle of each service, much to the disturbance of the congregation. The beginnings of this place of worship were believed to date back to 1642, the time of the Civil War, when, as one of the early Independent congregations, it met at Haydon's Yard, Minories, Aldgate. It was then thought to have moved to Smithfield, before relocating to Stepney. The New Road Chapel was opened in 1780. In 1785 a schoolhouse was built for the purpose of educating poor boys, and in 1790 a Sunday school was opened. Samuel Lyndall became the minister of the chapel in 1799. A Lancastrian brought up in Yorkshire, Lyndall proved an extremely able and popular preacher, and during the early years of his ministry the congregation grew to number over 500. However, he was not able to sustain this growth, and during the years leading up to his retirement in 1811 numbers in the congregation began to fall away dramatically. In the months after his departure the membership had shrunk to just sixty. There was also an enormous debt of £2,000 outstanding on the building.[7]

New Road was not the only Independent chapel in the area, with the historic Stepney Meeting and Old Gravel Lane both nearby, together with other Baptist and Methodist chapels. In the eighteenth century eleven new Anglican churches, including St George's-in-the-East, had been built in the East End of London, funded by grants from the government. A further spate of Anglican church-building was to follow in the nineteenth century, inspired by the efforts of the Bishop of London, Charles Blomfield. For all this investment in buildings, when a religious census was taken in 1851 it found that, of a population of 110,775 in Stepney, only around 19,756 attended church in the morning, and a further 15,505 in the evening. However, many attended more than one service, so there would have been a degree of overlap between these figures, and it has been calculated that in all just 25% of local residents attended church.[8] The ignorance of Christian truth in many parts of the East End of London was deepening as churches struggled to make an impact on the masses, who showed few signs of obvious interest in the gospel message. In 1858, the vicar of St

Andrew's, Bethnal Green, described his unsuccessful ministry as 'what I might venture to call mental torture'.[9] Andrew Reed faced an enormous challenge, not only in restoring the fortunes of the New Road Chapel from the low ebb to which they had fallen, but also in trying to win as many as possible of the local residents to the faith he held so dear. On this his ministry was to stand or fall.

Martha

He did not face the task alone. When he moved to live in the area of the New Road Chapel, his parents decided that it would be good for his sister Martha to stay with him to act as his housekeeper. The little girl who had roamed the fields of Surrey with Andrew was now a young woman of eighteen. She had grown up in the love and faith of her parents, and by the age of twelve was assisting in Sunday school teaching. Martha had a strong affinity to children, and imbibed from her mother great facility in teaching them.

In her mid-teens Martha had passed through a period of deep spiritual searching and self-examination and was troubled by a sense of unworthiness before God. As with her brother Andrew, her conversion was accompanied by a time of intense conviction of sin. Eventually she came to a point where she knew she could trust in Jesus Christ alone for salvation. She felt a great sense of peace and joy sweep over her, as her brother remembered: 'It was the joy of penitence — the joy of hope — the joy of love — the joy of gratitude — the joy of Heaven!'[10]

A person of great gentleness and humility, she was to prove an immense strength to Andrew in his early years of ministry. Yet her life was to be marred by suffering. At the age of sixteen she caught a severe cold after attending a funeral on a snowy day, and developed a persistent cough which could not be shaken off. A few months later she ruptured a blood vessel during a coughing fit, and began to cough up blood. It became clear that Martha's lifespan might well be curtailed, and that she would constantly need spells of rest and recuperation. She decided to offer to God her remaining days: 'All that I am, and all that I have, the faculties of my mind, and members of my body, my worldly possessions, my time, my influence over others, I consecrate to Thee. In Thy service I desire to spend the remainder of my time upon earth.'[11] The thought of an early death did not depress her, but brought an earnestness and urgency to her concern for others. Her time was devoted to visiting the needy, the infirm and the elderly. The little money she had was spent on gifts, messages of hope and religious tracts for those who were suffering. Her letters to Andrew always included challenges: 'Act for eternity'; 'Prepare for eternity.' If she was to be denied a lifetime of Christian service, she did all she could to ensure that Andrew would make up for her unfulfilled potential. Her determination to live absolutely for God led her to turn down an offer of marriage, because she was not convinced that her suitor was serious in his Christian faith.

In addition to helping to run Andrew's house and overseeing the household budget, Martha also asked him to set her a course of theological reading to equip her further for the work at New Road Chapel. Together they studied portions of the works of John Owen and Richard Baxter and then Jonathan Edwards. They turned to areas of moral and political philosophy and church history. On 3 January 1812, just over a month after Andrew was inducted as the pastor of the New Road Chapel, Martha also became a member of the church. She soon had a leading role in the Sunday school, taking an infants' class, and also running a Bible study for older teenage girls who were considering making a commitment to church membership. She took responsibility for their pastoral care, visited them when they were ill and encouraged their spiritual growth. On a weekday evening she started a class for older girls and helped teach them to sew and learn other skills that would make it easier for them to gain work or run a home. Martha undertook extensive visitation around the area, visiting the sick and the

bereaved, and calling two or three times a week upon a bedridden elderly female member of the congregation. One family she
visited had fallen on desperate times. The father, a master
mariner, had lost his job when his shipping company had failed,
and he was unable to find other employment. He now lay ill in
bed with a fever. His wife had sold the furniture to buy food for
herself and the children, and when Martha called their supplies
had run out and there was no fuel for the fire. Martha was
spurred into action: she found money to meet their immediate
needs and helped nurse the father. Later she was able to help
the mother to find work.[12]

The early years at the church

There is no doubt that the call to Andrew to serve as the minister of New Road Chapel was issued by a church in considerable
difficulties and with a large debt. He was well known to the
church, but was young and inexperienced. Yet youthfulness
brought with it vision and enthusiasm, and he was deeply
committed in his devotional life. He was also an exceptionally
gifted preacher, and there was soon clear evidence of the
success of that ministry. His well-prepared, evocative and
earnest preaching proved popular with the congregation. His
messages came with a clear challenge to action, whether of
commitment to Christ, or to obedient Christian service. The
fortunes of the church began to recover. The first church
meeting after his induction saw fourteen new members added
to the church, and the additions at following church meetings
continued this steadily encouraging trend. Some of this was due
to the return of members who had drifted away in disillusion-
ment towards the end of Samuel Lyndall's ministry, but month
by month new additions to the church membership were noted
in the church record book.

By late 1814, as Andrew Reed started the fourth year of his
ministry at New Road, the membership had grown from sixty to

180, and there were signs of the congregation becoming more active and energetic. Yet the title of his sermon on the third anniversary, 'Brethren, pray for us', revealed how deeply conscious Andrew Reed was that any such progress was attributable to the hand of God. He looked outside the church and saw thousands indifferent to the claims of Christ, and he looked into his own heart and saw weakness and frailty: 'Still, nothing is done. Oh! Had I a thousand lives, I would devote them all to my Lord. But I have only one, and that a frail one. Blessed Saviour, receive what I have... Let my bosom be purged from every debasing feeling. Let it become the temple of the Holy Ghost; and let me preach and act, and think and live, beneath his inspiration.' Ever since as a young Christian he had read the life of George Whitefield, the great evangelist of the eighteenth-century revival had been his inspiration. Now he wrote, 'How I pant for Whitefield's ardour, talents and success! But, alas! I often seem his perfect contrast. I look for light, and behold darkness; and for life, but lo! Insensibility and torpor prevail.' Andrew Reed was deeply committed and zealous in his work, yet he greatly feared that in all the activity into which he threw himself, it was possible to lose sight of God himself. He lamented, 'Oh! It is possible to lose the spirit of religion even in the services of religion. There is nothing I fear so much.'[13]

Martha Reed took an important role in the work of the church, encouraging others to join with her in the tasks she undertook. Devoted to prayer, Bible reading and the service of others, she was to prove to her brother a vital female pastoral assistant amongst the women and children of the church.[14] But there were growing concerns about Martha's health. Already physically delicate, she began to suffer from headaches and there were advancing signs of tuberculosis, accompanied by occasional bouts of depression. Her family urged her to slow down, to which she responded that it was 'better to wear out than rust out'. Her father's wise reply was: 'Fairly to wear out, but not to *tear out.*' Martha took a short period of rest at Broadstairs, but quickly returned to the work she so loved, declaring, '*I must make up lost time*. Soon the scene of action will be past. O that I could always act for eternity.'[15] There is little doubt that Martha's gentle pastoral ministry complemented that of Andrew while he was a young single man, as the fortunes of the church began to recover after the later troubled years under Samuel Lyndall. Andrew knew this only too well: 'How far she assisted to promote the peace and prosperity of my charge, must be revealed by the light of a brighter day... She was raised up by the hand of Providence, as a most opportune and valuable blessing.'[16] Martha was also to play a role in a decision that was to launch Andrew Reed in his work as a philanthropist.

The wider pastoral ministry

In addition to the focus on preaching and pastoral work, three other strands were important to Reed's approach to the religious needs of the Stepney area.

Making the Scriptures available to all

He did all he could to ensure that families in the area had access to copies of the Bible, or portions of it. He wanted to impress on the local people that 'the Bible is their book'. He encouraged other members of the clergy to join with him in starting an East London auxiliary of the Bible Society. The project ran into surprising opposition from High Church Anglicans such as H. H. Norris, the High Church rector of South Hackney, who objected to working together with Nonconformists, even when it was only in distributing the Scriptures. However, steadfast support came from evangelical Anglicans such as William Champneys, Rector of St Mary Matfelon in Whitechapel. Champneys' highly successful ministry attracted congregations of over 1,500 and he was actively involved in educational work, the care of orphan children and rescue work amongst prostitutes. In addition to making the Scriptures available in the East End of London, the Bible Society auxiliary also sought to distribute translations of the Bible in other languages amongst the crews of the ships from other nations which called at the London docks.[17]

Work among children

Work with children was also crucial to Reed's urban ministry. He had gained vital early experience in Christian work as a Sunday school teacher, and was convinced of the benefits of this approach. With little education available for most children from poorer homes, Sunday school was often the only opportunity many of them had of learning the rudiments of reading and writing. Reed appreciated the importance of this, but was concerned that the spiritual content of Sunday school lessons could all too easily be lost. His solution was to throw efforts at providing basic education into the day school attached to the church during the week, and to keep lessons on Sunday for biblical teaching, thereby maintaining both emphases. As with the local Bible Society auxiliary, he also saw the value of working together with other evangelical churches in forming an auxiliary to the Sunday School Union. By this means churches could pool resources in providing training and materials for the children, and work together in starting Sunday schools in areas of most need.

The Sabbath as a day for the poor

The third strand of Reed's ministry was a simple one: 'to impress upon the poor, that the Sabbath is their day'. This emphasis united his social and religious vision. Those who had laboured through the week at a trade or on the London docks needed a day of rest, but such rest was not merely to be physical. Rest from everyday work gave time to seek God.[18]

Steady growth

The encouraging progress of the early years at New Road became steady and sustained. By 1818, the sixty members had increased to over 400. It was becoming clear that Andrew Reed's ministry in Stepney was going to be a remarkable one. He believed that most of the 354 members welcomed into the church since his induction were converts under his ministry, 'my joy in the Lord', as he called them. The New Road building was becoming crowded on Sundays, as visitors and enquirers made their way to hear the gospel preached. A further legacy of the unhappy past was put behind the church that same year as the troublesome £2,000 debt on the building was finally cleared; it was the first time the chapel had been free of debt for forty years. The members were also able to reward their pastor, who by then was aged thirty and supporting his own young family, with a salary increase from a meagre £125 to a more comfortable £250 per year.[19] This brought significant relief to him, freeing his mind from worry about household expenses and giving him liberty to give spontaneously to the charitable needs he frequently encountered. He resolved to live as economically as possible, and give any surplus to charity.[20]

Through his pastoral visitation, and the testimony of those who came to see him in the chapel vestry or his study, Reed learned of lives being transformed through his preaching. A young man of considerable talent, who had made a Christian profession several years previously in his home city of Edinburgh, had gone back on his religious commitment on coming to London, but struggled deeply with depression. Beset by frequent temptations to commit suicide, he happened to hear Reed preach on Genesis 19:17: 'Escape for thy life.' The sermon spoke to him in his mental turmoil, and sent him to Andrew Reed's door. With pastoral guidance he was restored to the Lord, and went on to serve in Christian ministry in London, before being called to missionary service in India.[21]

Yet increasing success, and the urgency of the pastoral round, brought to Andrew Reed a sense that he was neglecting his personal walk with God. He strove for personal holiness: 'My paramount deficiency, is the want of a more devotional and heavenly temper. This would give a brightness to my character, a weight to my ministrations, and unction to my sermons, and a sweetness, serene and abiding to my disposition. But to this I cannot attain.'[22] To add to the pressures of a growing church and ever-increasing preaching engagements, another major dimension of Andrew Reed's ministry was beginning — that of philanthropist. It grew spontaneously out of the acute social needs he regularly encountered in his pastoral ministry.

4.
The cry of the children

The path of a nineteenth-century Christian philanthropist was never a smooth one. Starting a charity was work for the kind-hearted, but not for the faint-hearted.

4.
The cry of the children

Within a few months of his induction as the minister of the New Road Chapel, Andrew Reed was summoned to the bedside of a dying man. As the man poured out his heart to the young minister, he told of the death of his wife a few years before, and then spoke of the heavy burden that most troubled him now. He knew he too was dying and, when he had gone, who would care for his two children? Although Andrew Reed was a single man with no children of his own, he was deeply moved and promised to do what he could. On his arrival home, he shared the tragic story with his sister Martha. Together they agreed to take the children temporarily into their own home after the father had died. In the weeks after the funeral, Andrew began to look for a more adequate and more permanent solution for the children. He found a kindly widow who lived in Old Gravel Lane, who agreed to care for the children in her home if Andrew would pay all the expenses involved. As a young man, newly called to a church with a small congregation, his financial resources were limited. Feeding and clothing children is no easy matter, and it was a struggle to keep up the commitment, but Andrew firmly stuck to his promise.[1]

With this simple, spontaneous act of pastoral care began the philanthropic career of Andrew Reed. In many ways it is no surprise that Andrew and his sister should have taken the decision to help the dying man and his family. The tragic death of both of Mary Ann Reed's parents, and the cruelties she endured from her stepmother, made the family acutely aware of the sufferings of others. In response she opened her home to care for a number of orphans. It was natural that Andrew and Martha would decide to do the same. More surprising are the long-term consequences of their small act of kindness.

It was Andrew's hope that in time an orphanage could be found which would take the children whom he and his sister had temporarily fostered. Hearing of one in Wapping, he and Martha visited it, but to their horror they found that, although the orphans were offered board and lodging, little children as young as five years old were forced to work for between eleven and thirteen hours a day in the owner's spinning workshop. When they reached the age of twelve, he then bound the children as apprentices in his shoe factory on Tower Hill for a further seven years. For their work they were paid a pitifully small allowance. When the owner of this orphanage eagerly offered to relieve the Reeds of the burden of caring for the children, Andrew responded grimly that undoubtedly the man's work was 'good speculation; but it was not *charity*'.[2]

The plan to set up an orphanage

As he returned from the visit to Wapping, Andrew turned over in his mind what he had seen and heard. When he reached home he resolved to start a new orphanage for destitute children, learning from the painful lessons he had been taught. It should not just be for orphans who had lost both their parents, but should also be open to those who had lost their father, and whose mother could no longer support them. Although the children were to be given education, and taught skills that would help them to find a job in the future, the orphanage was not to be run like a business, or to be dependent on the work done by the children.

There were other orphanages in the London area at the time, such as the famous Foundling Hospital started by Thomas

Coram in 1739, which catered especially for illegitimate children, the Marine Society (1756) for 'destitute boys of good character' and the Orphan Working School (1758). However, the number of places available for needy children was pitifully few, and it was not until the 1860s that the number of orphanages reached a peak; by 1878 there were at least fifty in the London area.[3]

For such a scheme, Andrew Reed needed the support of those who could offer significant financial backing. At a meeting in his home on 24 June 1813, he shared his plans with a number of friends. Many were sceptical, believing that an orphanage could not be supported by charitable donations alone and would need to 'pay its way', but he was determined to ignore the solution of the doubters.

A second planning meeting was held two weeks later in the home of Andrew Burt, a solicitor who belonged to the New Road congregation. It proved an even more discouraging gathering. Of the twelve people who had been invited, only three arrived, and that included the host and Andrew Reed himself! However, Reed was a man of resolute purpose and vision; better three who were firmly committed to the task than twelve fair-weather friends. The trio pressed ahead with arranging a public meeting, drawing up an appeal to be issued and setting out the 'design' — the foundational principles upon which the charity was to be run. They decided that the children to be helped were to be the 'destitute and orphan'; they were to be supported practically with 'clothing and maintenance', and given education and training so that they could support themselves in adulthood. As a Christian minister, Andrew Reed insisted that the children be taught the 'principles of religion and virtue'.[4]

The 'Appeal'

Although a man of steadfast principle, Andrew Reed was not averse to some measure of compromise to ensure that a scheme got off the ground. To placate some who had wavered in their support, he initially allowed the orphanage to be called 'The East London Orphan Asylum and Working School'. Reed had fought hard to avoid the inclusion of the last three words, and in fact in future usage the term 'Working School' was speedily discarded, but at an early stage it was expedient to allow its usage.

The 'Appeal' on behalf of the charity was published, setting out how serious the problem of children left fatherless and destitute in the East End of London had become. In addition to living in increasingly crowded and unsanitary conditions, many men in the East End were employed in jobs where death was an all-too-common occupational hazard, as sailors, soldiers and dock workers. Britain was involved in a series of armed conflicts at the time: the Napoleonic Wars raged until 1815, and between 1812 and 1814 there was war with America. The sudden death of a father could instantly plunge a stable family into poverty, with little or no support for the children. Reed drew attention to this in the 'Appeal': 'Our manufacturies, our merchandise, and above all, the long continued wars in which we have been plunged, have stripped innumerable families of their head, and reduced them to a condition the most destitute and deplorable.'[5] Such families, through no fault of their own, could be forced into dependence on parish poor relief, or even into the workhouse. Some preferred to starve rather than lose their dignity by being labelled 'paupers'.[6]

Andrew Reed found mothers and children who had turned to crime, including prostitution, to feed their families. He was deeply moved that, through no fault of their own, the sudden death of one or more parents could reduce children to criminality, or to being stigmatized as paupers for the rest of their lives. It was his intention to offer caring but discerning charity. At a time when many refused to help the poor, accusing them of being the authors of their own misery through their laziness, immorality, improvidence or recklessness, Reed was anxious to strike a careful balance. He explained that the charity would stand for the needy in the face of 'any prejudices against the poor and dependent classes of society', but it would also foster skills for a future life of independency through 'honest industry'. The poor should not surrender their dignity in the face of poverty, nor forsake morality.[7]

The work of the charity was targeted at those who had no other means of support. The use of the word 'Asylum' in the title was significant — it was truly to be a sanctuary, a place of shelter and safety for the vulnerable. Wealthy families could provide for relatives who fell into need, and the very poorest already had the support of the local parish in the Poor Law system, which, if far from ideal, was not in 1813 the harsh and often inhuman system it was to become after its reform in 1834. Between these two extremes were huge numbers who had no effective means of support when family tragedy struck. Other orphan children fell through the net because it was not possible to prove which parish bore the responsibility of their care.[8]

Overcoming obstacles

On 27 July 1813, a meeting was held in the public rooms of the King's Arms, Wellclose Square, to launch the charity. For all Reed's convincing arguments set out in the Appeal, the result was again hugely disappointing. As Andrew Reed took the chair he looked out upon a gathering of no more than seventy people, most of whom he recognized as members of his own congregation who had come along to support him. Trying not to show his discouragement, he pressed on with the business in hand. A committee was chosen, Andrew Burt was elected treasurer and a collection was taken. It amounted to just £66.

In the aftermath of the meeting, Andrew Reed prayerfully reflected on what to do. Here was a moment of crisis for the young philanthropist. Should face be saved, and the project abandoned? Perhaps to the public it was just another well-intentioned scheme which would come to nothing. But Reed was made of sterner stuff; his strong religious faith deepened his resolve. Besides, there were already two children to be cared for. His mind went back to the scene when Jesus Christ hung upon the cross. His death had seemed to all the world defeat and shame, but was proved through the resurrection to be glory and victory. Here was a powerful counterbalance to the deep despondency he felt, and he wrote determinedly in his diary, 'What! Despond with the Cross before you?' Underneath he sketched a picture of the cross, drew a circle around it and added the words: 'Nil desperandum.' It became his guiding motto, and he later had it engraved upon his personal seal.[9]

Yet such personal resolution brought no sudden end to his troubles; indeed if anything they deepened. One of those who had attended the public meeting of the charity was none other than the owner of the working asylum whose practices had so appalled Andrew and Martha. He silently observed the proceedings, saw the difficulties his young rival was facing and, when the meeting was over, he quietly began to approach members of the committee of the new and struggling charity, offering to unite his existing work with the newly planned orphanage, which he would manage. To Andrew Reed's dismay, some of the committee were taken in by his scheming and supported this offer. Reed again stood firm: he would rather the project should fail than have it associated in any way with such an unscrupulous character. In protest wealthy supporters resigned, and the charity tottered on the brink of collapse. When it became clear that Reed would not allow him to join the work, his opponent changed tactics, and threatened to take the new orphanage project to court over breach of promises he claimed to have received.

These were desperately anxious times, as Reed fought for the future humane care and well-being of children in the East End of London. It took considerable skill and great personal resolve to ride out such a storm, but Reed had the vision to see that compromise now would corrupt the whole work. He also had the ability to see solutions to seemingly insurmountable problems, and he was developing the diplomatic skill to carry them through. Eventually, and at significant cost to the supporters of the new orphanage, a settlement was reached. The man withdrew his complaints, his spinning machinery was bought by way of compensation and he retired from the scene, having once more comfortably profited by his 'charity'.[10]

Co-operation between Nonconformists and Anglicans

As his career as a minister developed, there were to be many further points of crisis: the path of a nineteenth-century Christian philanthropist was never a smooth one. Starting a charity was work for the kind-hearted, but not for the faint-hearted. One crucial issue, which was to come back and trouble Andrew Reed, was the religious complexion of the orphanage. As a Nonconformist minister, he was part of a religious minority who faced significant discrimination. When the orphanage was founded in 1813, Dissenters were still unable to sit as Members of Parliament, or on local councils; marriages in Nonconformist chapels were not recognized as legal; Nonconformists could not be buried in an Anglican churchyard with a Nonconformist minister present; and they could not take degrees at Oxford or Cambridge Universities. In 1811 there was an unsuccessful attempt severely to restrict their itinerant preaching activities. Andrew Reed was to challenge this religious discrimination publicly in the 1830s, when he was much more widely known, but at the birth of the orphanage he was a young minister working in a fairly obscure church. He knew that if the charity was set up as a purely Nonconformist project, the amount of

support from Anglicans, who formed the majority of the population, would be hugely reduced, and this would limit the
number of children who could be helped.

The solution was to present a Christian, but not sectarian,
scheme. To accomplish this there would be two honorary
secretaries. One would be Andrew Reed; the other was to be an
Anglican clergyman. The person he approached was the Rev.
C. W. Le Bas, a Church of England minister who had supported the project from its early days. His acceptance of the
post of honorary secretary was a huge boost to the new charity
and helped bolster the confidence of Anglican benefactors.
Other religious societies, such as the British and Foreign Bible
Society and the Religious Tract Society, successfully operated
with committees comprising equal numbers of Anglicans and
Dissenters, and there seemed every prospect that the joint
secretaryship could work.

It was Andrew Reed's hope that decisions about the future
denominational allegiance of the children, whether they were to
be Anglicans or Nonconformists, could be delayed until after
they were fourteen, the age the children left school for work.
The key need was to give the orphans a sound religious education, rather than create adherents of a particular denomination. He believed that the majority of children would come
from families with some attachment to the Church of England,
and it was likely to be the wish of their parents that they be
brought up to respect the Anglican Church. Reed therefore
decided that the basis of the religious teaching and worship in
the orphanage should be broadly Anglican in form, but that
there should be facilities for children from Nonconformist
families to be taught after a Nonconformist pattern. It was a
deeply difficult decision for a committed Dissenter such as
Andrew Reed to take, but the overriding principle had to be that
of Christian compassion to desperately needy children, not
slavish adherence to denominational systems. This resolved the
matter for him: 'When the question was whether the poor
orphans were to be left to suffer in ignorance, want, and sin, or

whether they should be adopted and blessed in agreement with the principles of the Church of England, I felt I could not hesitate.'[11]

Working carefully through these policy issues took time. To some supporters the charity seemed all talk and no action, and their enthusiasm waned further, but Reed was right to see that, unless such fundamental issues were resolved at the outset, the project would sooner or later sink without trace. It was a great sadness that those who came onto the board of the charity in later years, when it was established and flourishing, lacked the breadth of spirit, tolerance and concern for the greater good of the children that marked the vision of the founder.

How the charity was to operate

It took nine months from the first public meeting to overcome the initial difficulties, get the foundational principles set in place and establish the way the charity was to operate. At last, on 4 April 1814, Andrew Reed and Andrew Burt signed an agreement to rent a house in Clarke's Terrace to serve as an orphanage, at a yearly rent of £40. A matron was chosen and furnishings were collected. Reed himself lent the charity £20 to cover food and initial bills and stripped his own house of much of its furniture, which he donated to the orphanage. The first two girls admitted were those Reed and his sister had now been personally supporting for nearly three years.[12]

With so many orphan children in desperate need in London, and so many potential candidates, the next key decision concerned the policy for selecting other children for places in the home. The method chosen seems strange to modern minds, and even somewhat unfeeling, but it was a system used by most other charities, including orphanages and hospitals, and was thought to work. Reed had appealed for help for the 'defenceless child, cast upon the wide world, deprived of the fostering hand of parental tenderness, and destitute of a friend to guide its steps, relieve its wants, and wipe away its tears'.[13] The orphanage was to be such a friend, but it was not to be a faceless institution. It was nurtured and supported by individuals who invested personal time and finance in its running. It was therefore decided that these were the people who should have a say in the type of child they supported, rather than giving the responsibility to a small, and perhaps less personally involved, committee. Every person who subscribed one guinea[14] became a member of the charity and was given a vote at the annual meetings; a subscription of two guineas gave two votes, and so on. A donation of fifty guineas brought life membership, and 100 guineas a life governorship of the charity. Ministers who preached sermons to raise money for the charity were also made life members.

If a family member, or friend, of an eligible child could raise 100 guineas, the orphanage undertook to accept the child and provide for his or her care until the age of fourteen. For most this was impossible, and they had to try to mobilize wider support. To do this, the wider family and friends of orphaned children approached members of the charity, explained the circumstances of the child and sought their sympathetic interest. Members of the charity then used their votes at twice-yearly meetings to 'elect' children to the available places in the orphanage. Family members, sometimes grandparents or aunts and uncles, together with friends of eligible children, often became supporters of the charity to help secure their election, and to have a say in the way the charity undertook their ongoing care. With this close personal interest in the running of the charity, supporters were likely to be far more committed to its success. If a child was unsuccessful in one election, votes could be carried forward to the next. The Board of Management also had discretion to allocate proxy and unused votes to the most needy cases; their role in the choice of the candidates was strong.

The system undoubtedly had its faults, especially as the asylum increased in size. Problems arose because demand for places exceeded supply, and many children were disappointed. Some 'voting' charities faced accusations of people trading in votes and, with young and vulnerable lives at stake, this was inhuman, although there is no evidence of this happening in Reed's charities. However, with other orphanages using similar schemes, Reed had few viable alternative models to follow in those early years of the nineteenth century. The voting system was believed to work, and the most needy orphan children usually found a place somewhere. These were also the years, it should be remembered, when families which had unexpectedly fallen on hard times through bereavement or the all-too-frequent collapses of banks and businesses often had to resort to placing adverts in papers containing heart-rending pleas for help, in the hope that some benevolent individual would read of their plight and be moved to help.

When the charity was small, and the number of children seeking help was limited, the system worked well. At the first election in July 1814, four were elected, and the highest number of votes received for a child was seventeen. By the twentieth century, the number of votes needed to secure election ran to several thousand.[15] Perhaps in different circumstances and in different days, Reed would have adopted another method of selecting the children. Two decades later, when George Müller began his orphanage in Bristol, run famously on 'faith' principles without overt appeals for finance, the founder took a dominant role in selecting candidates. When the Baptist pastor C. H. Spurgeon began an orphanage in 1866 with money given to him by Mrs Hillyard, an Anglican minister's widow, he declared that they 'would have nothing to do with the voting system'. Instead applications were dealt with by the managers, with no regard to their religious background, although a number were orphans of Baptist ministers. Admission was simply on the criterion that the orphans were in a state of 'utter destitution'.[16] Reed's scheme was a product of an earlier age, but it was certainly more democratic, and families and friends could in theory have a direct say in how the institution caring for their children was run.

Compassionate care

Although the beginning made by Reed was small, and shaped by the practice of other charities, his scheme was none the less thorough, and far ahead of many other orphanages in the compassionate care offered to the children. The daily management of the orphanage was wisely delegated into the hands of a Ladies' Committee. Key figures in this were Mrs Burt, wife of Andrew Burt, treasurer of the charity, and Andrew Reed's sister Martha. She sometimes chaired the meetings of the Ladies' Committee, and regularly visited the children.[17] They showed a deep practical and caring interest in the running of the home. When there were early allegations that a child had been disciplined incorrectly, the matter was investigated promptly. Although the matron was found to have acted properly, the Ladies' Committee saw to it that rules were drawn up to ensure that there was an appropriate response to different types of misbehaviour. When another child complained of being hungry, the committee again investigated the matter and ordered that the children be given 'as much as they could eat' at all mealtimes, and Andrew Reed delivered a report to the directors about the diet of the children.

The ladies also ensured that there was suitable reading material for the children, including books on natural history, as well as religious books for children. They arranged for each child to have a box under his or her bed in which to keep their personal possessions, and all possible steps were taken to further the health of the children. In 1815 Fanny Merryweather was sent to stay at the seaside for sea-bathing to help with a skin complaint she was suffering from.[18]

This was no grim and impersonal institution full of half-starved children, such as the workhouse regime later satirized by

Charles Dickens in his novel *Oliver Twist*. The values of practical, detailed concern for the needs of vulnerable children were inculcated from the top down. The vision of Andrew Reed was a key reason for the success of the orphanage: he aimed at creating a family atmosphere. Children were given personal care and attention and the education that was so vital for them to secure the prospect of employment when they were adults. This may help explain the popularity of the charity, with ever-increasing numbers seeking admission.

Royal patronage

Before long Reed was convinced that the orphanage should not be a local and limited venture, but should be presented to the public at large as a national institution. In February 1815, after a hard struggle, he convinced the charity to drop the word 'East' from its title, and it became 'The London Orphan Asylum'.[19] To be a national institution, the charity would need influential support. Andrew Reed decided that the way to do this was by securing royal patronage for the project.

Throughout his charitable career Andrew Reed believed in aiming for the top when presenting the claims of the lowest in society. Royal patronage would not only bring prestige to the work, but also give confidence to the subscribers. In what was still a very hierarchical society, where rank and deference were all-important, it is surprising that Andrew Reed, a young Nonconformist minister with little by way of social rank, prestige or reputation, should attempt to convince a series of members of the royal family to support the charity. Even more astonishing is the degree of success he achieved in persuading royalty, including ultimately Queen Victoria, to become patrons for his charities. It speaks highly of his personal courage and charisma, but also of the wisdom of his appeal, which was based simply upon the principles of Christian compassion and charity. Even though he was a Nonconformist, and the royal family deeply committed to the Church of England, this simple non-sectarian appeal to the great principle of Christian charity struck a chord in the minds, and pocketbooks, of many holding high rank in society.

In April 1815 a dinner was held in the City of London to mark the institution of the charity, and from Kensington Palace came news that His Royal Highness the Duke of Kent was willing to preside. As the third son of King George III, brother of the future kings George IV and William IV and father of the future Queen Victoria, the support of this senior member of the royal family was most important. The duke took a close interest in the new asylum and gladly agreed to become a patron of the new institution, the objects of which, he declared, were 'so replete with philanthropy and benevolence'. His impact on the infant and struggling charity cannot be overestimated. When he sadly died in 1820, Andrew Reed recorded in his journal: 'The Duke deserves our esteem the more, in that he did not despise us when we had few friends.' The Duke of Kent was instrumental in persuading his brother Augustus, the Duke of Sussex, to become a patron in 1819. A series of royal patrons were to follow, including King George IV in 1823, King William IV in 1833, Queen Victoria in 1837 and Prince Albert in 1843.[20] This granting of royal patronage gave the new charity enormous credibility in the eyes of the public.

At the suggestion of the Duke of Kent, the committee appointed gentlemen to concentrate their fund-raising efforts locally, by visiting extensively and promoting the work of the charity in the East End, from Bow to Bermondsey, from Spital-fields to Stepney. The work was extremely demanding, but Andrew Reed reported that 'The success was great. He jokingly commented, 'I scour London crying "Money, money, money".'[21]

The charity grows

The project was now well established. The first group of children admitted had all been girls, but in June 1815 Andrew Reed persuaded the committee to admit boys as well. At first there were no premises suitable for their accommodation, so they were fostered out to local families in Limehouse, before a house in Hackney Road was rented for the boys. In 1816 the girls were moved to a larger house in Bethnal Green.[22] Andrew Reed remained the dominant, but not all-controlling, figure. He was developing great administrative and businesslike abilities, skills that appealed to other businessmen. In the early years, and without cost to the charity, he undertook almost all of the administration, except handling the money, which he gladly left to others. An office in the City of London was taken, at No. 10, St Mary Axe, and in order to relieve some of the burden on Reed, busily running a growing church, a collector of subscriptions and a sub-secretary were appointed.

When a banker in Lombard Street hinted that the administration of the London Orphan Asylum was becoming extravagant, Reed hastily visited other asylums, collected figures as to their administrative costs, and proved how cheaply and efficiently the orphanage was being run. When he presented the figures to his accuser, the man was so impressed that he promptly gave an increased donation![23]

As the charity developed, Andrew Reed constantly examined himself and his motives. He grew to deeply love the cause, for all the efforts and anxieties it occasioned him; philanthropy gave him 'real and elevated pleasure'. He was also conscious of new powers and abilities developing within him, of which he had not been previously conscious. In all he wanted to glorify God; ultimately it was to the Lord that he was accountable. As he wrote in his journal, 'May He who is the judge of the widow and the fatherless prosper our cause and purify our motives.'[24]

5.
Joy, trial and sorrow

`This world never appeared so shadowy; heaven never appeared so near'
    (Andrew Reed on the death of his sister Martha).

5.
Joy, trial and sorrow

After five years as minister of the New Road Chapel, Andrew Reed was married to Elizabeth Holmes of Reading, eldest daughter of a merchant in the City of London. At first the match seemed unlikely, and when Andrew had sought permission from her father to marry Elizabeth he had been refused. Jasper Holmes, a wealthy, committed Anglican, was unimpressed by the offer from the none-too-well-paid minister of a fairly obscure East End Nonconformist chapel, and he clearly believed Elizabeth could secure a better marriage. However, over time her father came to appreciate Andrew Reed's seriousness and the improving prospects of the New Road Chapel. He had also periodically attended a chapel of the Countess of Huntingdon's Connexion, and shared Andrew Reed's evangelical convictions. Eventually he relented, and Andrew and Elizabeth were married. The couple were well matched and their marriage was extremely happy. Elizabeth was to prove another vital support in Andrew's ministry, alongside his sister Martha.

Family life

Marriage to Andrew brought significant sacrifices for Elizabeth, as she moved from Castle Hall in Reading, where she had lived with her parents, to a small but comfortable house on New Road, close to the chapel. A year after their marriage they rejoiced together in the birth of a son, called Andrew after both his father and grandfather. To one who loved children, the experience was thrilling, as Andrew wrote in his diary: 'I write this date with new sensations — those of a father! Blessed be God, how good thou art... With the name of father give me the providence, wisdom, and affection of a father, that I may train up my child for happiness in heaven.'[1] This prayer was more than answered: young Andrew Reed grew to love the Lord, and followed his father in becoming a minister of the gospel.

As was the experience of so many parents of the time, the joy of parenthood was often tinged with pain. Sadness came in 1818 with the death of an infant child of just a few weeks. The couple were heartbroken, but found great support from Andrew's sister Martha. In 1819 a second son, Charles, was born, and then in 1821 a daughter, named Elizabeth after her mother. Two further sons, Martin and Howard, were born to the Reeds, but they also had to face the tragedy of the death of two other children in infancy. Despite the dark moments, family life was a source of great happiness for the Reeds, although inevitably as the philanthropic work developed much of the burden of caring for the children devolved heavily on Elizabeth. None the less, the children became closely involved in church work and in visiting the orphanages with their father.

Mindful of the tragedies that had befallen his parents after the birth of their children, Andrew decided to move Elizabeth and the young children to a rented house at Cheshunt, a rural spot north of London, away from the unhealthy environment of the East End of London. The house on New Road had been convenient for church business, but its proximity to the chapel building encouraged a constant stream of calls at the door and interruptions to his time for study, prayer and preparation. Andrew maintained lodgings near the church, where he stayed for several days each week for meetings and pastoral visitation. The time he spent at Cheshunt gave him the opportunity to prepare sermons and to write, and also to devote more time to his young family.

Dark years

There was another pressing reason for the move to Cheshunt. Martha's health had begun to deteriorate alarmingly. She was unremitting in her labours in the Lord's work, and a brief spell to recover health in Broadstairs only brought a renewed determination to be more urgent with every action and to live with an approaching eternity in mind.[2] A little before Andrew's marriage she had moved back to live with her parents, who had sold the china shop and were now living in Bethnal Green. This still gave her plenty of opportunities to be involved in the work at New Road Chapel. However, the increasingly unhealthy living conditions in the East End of London, especially the poor air quality, were badly affecting Martha's health. Her parents decided to rent a cottage in Cheshunt, to bring some relief to their daughter's increasing sufferings. Here she continued to busy herself with tract distribution, teaching children, visiting the poor and sick and inviting those she met to cottage meetings where the gospel was preached. These visits from one who was herself struggling with illness and in frequent pain were warmly received; people were touched by her gentleness and kindness. Her motto was: 'Fear not, neither be discouraged, for I, the Lord thy God, am with thee in all places whither thou goest.'[3]

The peaceful retreat of Martha and her parents was suddenly and unpleasantly interrupted. Without notice, the businessman who had bought the china shop from Andrew's parents went bankrupt. He had been paying for the business in instalments, but the sum had been far from paid in full, and the elderly couple were left with little income. Already caring for a young family, and pressurized daily by the demands of a growing church and fund-raising efforts for the London Orphan Asylum, Andrew now found that his parents and sister were financially dependent upon him. He took on the responsibility of paying the rental of their cottage, but Martha's health was becoming increasingly precarious. In addition to the breathing difficulties from advanced tuberculosis, it became evident that she was also suffering from cancer. She found walking increasingly painful and was soon confined to a mattress on the floor, unable to leave the house or even to see the garden surrounding the cottage which she so loved. To comfort her, the children she had once taught to read now visited her, and she delighted to hear their simple prayers.

For Andrew, who loved Martha dearly, seeing her suffer such acute pain was almost unbearable. He had cared for others in their suffering, but this was so close and personal. He found questions running through his mind: if heaven was such a joyful place, why did God take people there by such a hard road? How could such a frail, broken and diseased body stand up to such relentless sufferings?

But Martha was resolute, determined to die in Christ. 'I have been so afraid of dishonouring him,' she whispered to Andrew. Her life wasted away before the helpless eyes of her family. And so, in December 1821, the end came gently and quietly; Martha was just twenty-eight years old. Andrew recalled the sense of standing on the verge of two worlds as she passed into the presence of her Saviour: 'This world never appeared so shadowy; heaven never appeared so near.' They laid her to rest in the Cheshunt churchyard. At the funeral Andrew looked to his side and saw his father's six-foot frame, bent with age and grief, trembling under the burden of emotion. As they turned from the open graveside for the last time his father let out a low groan. Andrew's faith was shaken; he was shocked to find himself thinking rebellious thoughts against God, which he quickly rebutted with the words of the funeral service: '... in sure and certain hope of the resurrection'.[4]

It took Andrew several years to recover from the blow occasioned by the death of Martha. The sadness was compounded by further events. The little daughter born to Elizabeth and Andrew soon after Martha's death, and named after the dearly loved sister, survived only two years, and died in 1824. The following year Andrew's father, then aged seventy-six, also died. He had never truly recovered from the loss of his daughter, but left behind rich memories of his humility and devout faith.

Through these long years of family sadness, which stretched from 1821 to 1826, Andrew made no entries in his personal journal; the act of reflection was simply too painful. Yet the memory of Martha's single-minded devotion to God sustained him; in 1814 she had written, 'A simple and active dependence on the Saviour is the great object of Christian experience. May my trials be sanctified to this end, and then I shall glory in tribulation.'[5] Only simple and active dependence on the Saviour saw Andrew and Elizabeth through those dark years. With sadness in 1825 they moved their reduced family back to East London, to a house which they had built at Cambridge Heath, Hackney, and which was to be their home for the rest of their married life.

No fiction and its aftermath

Continued prosperity in the church, and the progressing work of the London Orphan Asylum, offered some consolation in the midst of family sadness, but other events combined to cloud the skies. One particular difficulty arose from Andrew Reed's decision in 1818 to write a religious novel. It certainly was an unusual decision for that period, and it led to an unseemly controversy blowing up at the time when the family was grieving over the death of Martha.

The attitude of evangelical Christians to literature, particularly fiction, was at the time an uncertain one. Many novels were strongly anti-Christian, or included material that was clearly immoral. Some churches developed their own libraries, ensuring that the books on the shelves were especially theological, or concerning natural history, geography, or social history, but not fiction. Christians worried about the way that novels captured the imagination and stirred thoughts and emotions — was this acceptable to spiritual development?[6] However, evangelicals such as Hannah More, a close friend of William Wilberforce, made a determined effort to use imaginative fiction for religious purposes, in which they saw some success.

Clearly Andrew Reed struggled with this tension over using fiction in a religious novel, but bravely defended his decision. Why should the field of literature be left solely to the 'world'? Why should literature not be used to illustrate good habits, good opinions and good principles? If all imaginative and illustrative stories were to be rejected, what about *Pilgrim's Progress*, or even the biblical parables? If the imagination was not to be used, why had it been given by God? Reed argued that the field of literature should be won for the gospel: 'The mass of a nation will neither be moral nor religious, till its literature becomes so; and its literature can never be sanative or pious while scorned and abandoned by the friends of religion and piety.'[7] However, caught in the uncertainty over the use of imaginative literature for religious purposes, he named the novel *No Fiction: A Narrative Founded on Recent and Interesting Facts*.

Francis Barnett had been known to Andrew Reed since the time they had worked together as Sunday school teachers and fellow members of the Society of Contending Brethren. Barnett had for a period been a lodger with Reed's parents, living as part of the family, and had attended Samuel Lyndall's ministry at New Road with Andrew. However, he had shown symptoms of mental instability, with bouts of heightened excitement followed by periods of deep gloom. Eventually Barnett had abandoned his work, his friends, and apparently even his faith, and had wandered the countryside in a deranged state. He then enlisted in a regiment bound for Canada, and had not been heard of since. His friends sadly concluded that he was dead.[8] Andrew Reed was deeply upset by these events, and worried over the dangers of young people falling prey to the temptations of youth and turning their backs on the Christian faith. The importance of the subject grew in his mind: he dearly wanted to warn other young people against slipping down such a path. So Reed conceived a two-volume novel on the subject, based

loosely on Barnett's life, and designed to draw object lessons for
the benefit of young people. The work was written during 1818
and published anonymously the following year.

Reed was convinced that this was something God had laid
on his heart to do, and friends, including the venerable Matthew
Wilks, encouraged him in the project. He should have seen the
danger signs when, just before publication, Barnett was found
to be alive and returning to Britain. However, it was believed
that he had fully recovered from his previous instability, and
Reed pressed on with bringing the novel into print and dedicat-
ing it 'To Youth, As the Bloom of this Age, and the Promise of
the Future'. He added the prayer that the Saviour might deign
to smile upon it: 'Open for it avenues of usefulness! Let it be a
guide to the ignorant, a beacon to the careless, and a stay to the
unstable.'⁹ Perhaps he secretly hoped that Francis Barnett
would not read his friend's thinly disguised account of his life,
but when he did, events followed with a certain inevitability.

In the preface to the novel Andrew explained that he had
taken some liberties with the facts, and added the rider that this
was 'less frequent and more trivial, than the reader will be
disposed to imagine'. Yet he pressed on with the pretence at
fiction, and the cloak of anonymity, hoping readers would
consider 'rather *what* is said, than *who* says it'.¹⁰ The story was
largely a repetition of the events of Barnett's troubled life, but a
strong moral tone was added. In the book Barnett, renamed
Lefevre for the purpose of fiction, found his faults were exaggerated to make the moral point: a weakness for alcohol was
emphasized, and the commission of an act of fraud introduced
as the reason for his leaving his job. However, as a counterbalance to the failings of his character, a hopeful ending to the
novel was introduced, with Lefevre restored to his right mind,
happily settled in work, contented and busy in benevolent
activity. Perhaps Reed felt this placed him on a securer footing.
The other main character in the novel is Douglas, highly pious,
doing all he can to arrest Lefevre's decline and instrumental in
his restoration. He is clearly based on Andrew Reed's own role.

No Fiction is not a great work of literature, but the story rattles along at a good pace and the moral tone is consistent. It was initially well received both in the press and by private response. Reed sold the copyright of the first edition for £100, a modest sum — yet Jane Austen only received £110 for the copyright of *Pride and Prejudice* in 1812. The book began to sell well, but it was not long before friends recognized Andrew Reed as the author and Francis Barnett as the subject. At first it was thought that Barnett was flattered to feature in the novel, especially with its hopeful ending. But then things started to go badly wrong. Barnett applied for a job as assistant secretary with the London Orphan Asylum. Reed's influence secured him the post, but there were those who questioned his suitability, on account of the story of the fraud Lefevre was depicted as having committed in the novel. Reed protested that this was a fictional addition, but questions remained over Barnett's suitability for a position that involved handling money.

At first Barnett performed well in the post, but before long his mental instability returned, accompanied by a return to drink. When he was forced to resign, he turned on Reed venomously, accusing him of being the cause of his first bout of illness and of its recurrence. This, he claimed, had been caused by the publication of the novel and its aftermath. He wrote to Reed accusing him of 'fabrications, falsities, and calumnies, as it regarded myself': fictitious characters, conduct and depravity had been portrayed in the novel as if they were real. Barnett then published this letter and followed it up with his own *Memoirs*, giving his version of events. Reed pleaded with him not to pursue the matter in this way, but Barnett was relentless. *The Memoirs of Francis Barnett* are the product of a deeply embittered, rambling and unsettled mind. The work levels a series of serious charges against Reed and his family. Andrew Reed's parents are accused of treating the much-loved, and now deeply mourned, daughter Martha as a servant; Andrew Reed is accused of avarice in settling for the New Road pastorate and of marrying Elizabeth for her money. Barnett asserted that Andrew Reed had been left a substantial sum of money by a widow, together with, rather strangely, a 'wig'. To these he added charges against Reed of duplicity and falsity, and of his preaching being the cause of Barnett's own suicidal tendencies. A flurry of other pamphlets followed throughout 1822-23, just as the family were struggling to cope with the grief occasioned by the loss of Martha.[11] These were indeed dark days, when depression clouded his heart.

Francis Barnett was determined to turn the issue into a scandal and ruin Andrew Reed's ministry, as he believed the book had ruined him. For a while it appeared that he might succeed in this. The controversy seemed to gather ground and some ministers ceased to associate with Reed. The work at New Road Chapel also began to suffer. Whereas between 1811 and 1818 an average of around fifty new members joined the church each year, only sixteen joined in 1823 and 1826, and just fifteen in 1825. 1824 was a brighter year, with twenty-eight additions, but it was not until 1827 that the numbers of new members joining the church began consistently to rise. In the early 1820s the furore surrounding *No Fiction*, the challenges of caring for a very young and growing family, the grief and hurt to his faith occasioned by the loss of his sister Martha, and the demands of the flourishing London Orphan Asylum, all took their toll on Andrew Reed and the New Road Chapel.

No public response to the controversy was offered by Reed until 1823, after the *British Review* had used a review of the book to vilify not only its author, but Dissenters as a whole. It was the latter charge which provoked a rejoinder from Reed, who defended the use of fiction as a means of religious improvement and asserted that he bore no ill will to Barnett for his conduct.[12] Then he said no more, and resolutely waited for matters to run their course and blow over. Although discouraged by the loss of friends, he refused to be crushed by events. He never mentioned the controversy in the pulpit, although there were those within his church who called for his removal from the pastorate. His early mentors Matthew Wilks and

George Collison, who had encouraged the publication of the novel, stood by him and ensured his ostracism in ministerial circles was not complete.[13]

Sadly, time proved the reality of Barnett's mental instability. While he was flaying Reed's reputation in public, Barnett was also writing private letters to friends commending him and repenting of his actions. His erratic behaviour deepened into serious mental illness, until he had to be confined to a mental asylum. It took him many years to recover, but in 1831 Barnett wrote to Andrew Reed (a letter Reed never made public for fear he would be accused of vindicating himself), expressing repentance for his past actions and desirous to restore their friendship.

Thirty years later, as Andrew Reed retired from the ministry, the elderly Francis Barnett wrote to one of Reed's sons. In the letter he expressed his thanks for all Andrew Reed had done for him, and his continued concern for the retiring pastor's welfare. Barnett was troubled with a lingering sense of guilt for what he had done, but was deeply grateful for the continued assurances from Andrew Reed that he bore him no ill will, that all was forgiven and that he should rest assured of forgiveness from God for his past actions.[14]

The consolation Andrew Reed drew from these disturbing events was that the controversy only served to heighten awareness of the novel and increase its circulation, and thereby the good it accomplished. Over the years he heard by letter or in personal conversation from individuals who had been blessed by the book. Some wrote describing how they had been converted through the novel, and at least one person was inspired to go into Christian ministry. Others were encouraged to pray for family members who had veered from the faith. The book was remarkably popular: an American edition followed, as did translations into French, Dutch and German.[15] Sales of the novel continued throughout Andrew's life, and by 1862 it was in its eleventh edition.

Good therefore came out of a very salutary experience. It had been a mistake to mix biography and fiction, and reality had been too thinly disguised for it to stand the test of scrutiny. The subtitle, 'A Narrative Founded on Recent and Interesting Facts', invited the audience to enquire as to what the 'Interesting Facts' were. Reed should also have been more realistic about the likely reaction of Barnett, with a past track record of instability. Although he remained convinced that the project had been laid on his heart by God, when he published the book he was still haunted by a secret fear 'lest I should have taken a step I may repent'.[16] Pastoral concern for young people struggling with the temptations he and Francis Barnett had faced pushed him into action, but with hindsight he realized that more caution should have been exercised.

Meanwhile, Reed consoled himself with another writing project, of a far less controversial nature. This was a work of religious biography, setting out the life of his sister Martha. Published in 1823,[17] the book sets out to explore Martha's spiritual development and present her as an example for other Christian young women to aspire to. The style is somewhat florid, but was considered elegant in its day, and on the whole the book was well received, especially in America, where it sold better than in Britain. Again Reed was encouraged by letters from readers who had been helped by the book. From the tragedy of the death of his sister, some good had come.

The lives of Christians are not without periods of darkness and trial. There is a mystery in how these sometimes appear to come in concentrated periods, when one blow is swiftly followed by a series of others. This was Andrew Reed's experience in the six traumatic years from 1821 onwards. Some problems were of his own making, but most were not. He struggled with deep discouragement and periods of dark depression, his faith severely challenged. But by 1827 the worst was past. Additions to membership in the church began to increase more rapidly. He was invited to give the monthly lectures to the Congregational ministers of London in that year, an indication of his rehabilitation in ministerial circles. These addresses were subsequently published.[18] That same year he also resolved to embark on another philanthropic project for the benefit of infant children. It was a matter that had long lain on his heart, and one which, just before her death, Martha had urged him to do something about. Meanwhile, the years after 1821 were also highly eventful in the history of the London Orphan Asylum.

6.
A home for the helpless

'We might have made all the exertion we have, yet all might have failed... If the London Orphan Asylum exists, its maker and builder is God, to whom may all the glory be given'

(Andrew Reed).

6.
A home for the helpless

It was soon clear that the London Orphan Asylum could not continue for long in a series of rented buildings, and by 1818 Andrew Reed had resolved that a purpose-built orphanage should be erected. He also pledged that no start should be made on construction work until two thirds of the sum needed had been collected. The project required very large sums of money to be raised, and he began to direct his attention to the men who worked in the streets around the offices of the charity — the merchants, bankers and stockbrokers of the City of London. Reed especially concentrated his efforts on the Stock Exchange.

Fund-raising

The energy that Reed threw into the project to help the children was staggering. In the early years of the fund-raising campaign he devoted every Thursday to the task of visiting and selecting donations from businessmen, and much of three other days of the week was spent in deputation and committee work. His ability to raise funds from sources ranging from the royal family to ordinary chapel members was astonishing. On one morning alone 350 guineas were pledged. An indication of Reed's success in tapping for compassionate purposes the vast wealth of the City of London is revealed by the lists of subscribers published in each annual report. In 1820, of 2,742 subscribers 288 gave their address as 'The Stock Exchange', and many others also gave addresses in the City.[1] Support also came from a wide range of concerned Christians. Reed rejoiced that, in the early days, the leading supporters of the charity shared his theological perspective, including evangelical laymen such as Thomas Fowell Buxton, who was soon to take up William Wilberforce's mantle in the campaign against slavery, and the evangelical Daniel Wilson, of St John's Chapel, London (where Wilberforce also worshipped). Wilson later became the Bishop of Calcutta.[2]

In addition to raising the amount required for the building project, by 1818 the charity was in need of the enormous sum of £3,000 per year to support the children in its care. Reed believed that many of the merchants, bankers and stockbrokers who worked in the City of London were possessed of a humanitarian spirit, but were so busy in their occupations that they did not have time to respond to any charitable inclinations they had. Reed and his committee therefore offered themselves as an accessible channel through which such compassionate feelings could be readily directed, and the well-run charity that was developed inspired confidence in the business community that money would be used responsibly.

He believed that in all humanity, by virtue of God's common grace, there was an element of compassion. This humanitarian charitable impulse was from God, and could be successfully drawn out in support of a strongly Christian charity if people trusted its leadership and clearly understood what the funds raised would be used for. By confronting busy, and maybe hard-hearted, businessmen with the suffering of others, and igniting a spark of compassion for their fellow creatures, Reed believed he was doing the work of God. Awakening businessmen to the needs of others might soften hearts and be the first step towards opening their eyes to their own spiritual needs. On this basis he was able to win support from those who did not necessarily share his evangelicalism and, without being diverted from his fundamental aims, to raise far larger sums for needy children than would otherwise have been possible. It was a broad-minded approach that not all evangelical philanthropists later in the century would have taken.

When George Müller began his orphanage in Bristol two decades later on the 'faith' principle, he believed that an orphanage run in simple dependence upon God would be a powerful witness to God's goodness. He did not wish to rely upon regular subscriptions and, although he communicated his hopes and plans, he made no explicit appeals for money. It was also important to Müller that money be given from 'scriptural motives' and that donors should not later regret their generosity. This method pushed Müller's faith to the limit and there were periodic cash-flow crises, but he testified to how each need was met. Such an approach meant that long-term planning for the orphanage proved difficult, and there were a number of short-term financial shortfalls, as he recorded in his *Personal Narrative*. Certainly the simplicity of Müller's approach in the early days, with almost all giving channelled through him personally, is very different from Andrew Reed's approach. However, Müller was not simply passive in waiting for money for his charity: he made full use of opportunities of sharing news from the pulpit, placing information about the work in the evangelical press and publishing his own *Narrative* in order to publicize needs. What is less well known is that he received large-scale financial assistance from the Bristol sugar magnate Conrad Finzel, who became convinced that a major fire at his factory was the judgement of God for his lack of generosity to charity. He therefore decided to devote one third of his income to charity, of which Müller's orphanage was one of the principal beneficiaries.[3]

The Baptist preacher C. H. Spurgeon began his Stockwell Orphanage with a £20,000 gift for the purpose from Mrs Hillyard, an Anglican minister's widow. The sum was largely in the form of shares in railway companies. Spurgeon's scheme depended heavily on giving from churches in the Baptist denomination, and he hoped that they would endorse the orphanage as their own — even Mrs Hillyard became a Baptist. Spurgeon confessed he lacked Müller's 'courageous silence' and made frequent appeals for his orphanage, which also periodically faced serious financial pressures. Spurgeon was far more open than Müller as to the sources from which charitable aid could come, not restricting support solely to those who shared his evangelical and Baptist convictions. Grand bazaars were held to raise funds, and one of the houses at the Stockwell Orphanage was paid for by the workmen who were employed in constructing the orphanage.[4] Similarly, Spurgeon was happy to publish subscription lists in his magazine *The Sword and the Trowel,* giving names and the size of the donation where this information had been supplied.

Reed believed that more could be accomplished by appealing to a broader constituency on the basis of simple Christian charity. Those who supported the work were aware of its strong faith-basis, and none of them were opposed to its clear Christian tenets. The approach of Reed's charities was also followed by other strongly evangelical charities. There is no doubt that Reed, Müller and Spurgeon all acted from strong Christian conviction and with the highest integrity, and all were able to meet desperately urgent needs. Had people questioned the appropriateness of Reed's policy, his answer might well have echoed that of William Booth of the Salvation Army, later in the century. When offered £100 by the well-known agnostic the Marquis of Queensbury, Booth was counselled not to take the 'dirty money'. He replied, 'If the money is dirty, we will wash it in the tears of the widows and orphans.'[5]

Whoever Reed appealed to for help, whatever their status in society, everything was done in a spirit of absolute dependence on God. His text for the year 1819 was: 'With God all things are possible.' When it became clear that the building project for the London Orphan Asylum had sufficient funds to go ahead, Reed adopted what was to become a characteristic proceeding. He travelled the country visiting other orphanages and schools, taking measurements, jotting down plans. He was determined that the London Orphan Asylum should learn from best practice, although he observed that much of what he saw was not working well: 'I have received more suggestions from the defects than from the excellencies I have witnessed.' On his return home he carefully compiled the facts and figures into tabular form. He had a growing conviction that the charity was going to be 'one of the great and permanent institutions of the land'.

The pressure that such work placed on him, alongside his pastoral labours, became almost overwhelming. When he was advised by his doctor to rest, he acknowledged that the cost to his health could be great, but he refused to let up the pace, and wrote, 'My joy is, that amidst all my difficulties it prospers. May it bless thousands of poor orphans when I am no more.'[6]

Plans for the new building

As a temporary measure, the house in Hackney Road was extended so that the expanding family of both boys and girls, now numbering around 150, could be housed under the same roof, but what was needed was a new site and building. In early 1821, a site of eight acres in what were then fields between Clapton and Homerton was bought for 3,500 guineas, with the unanimous support of the committee. It was an area Reed knew well, near Hackney, where he had spent his student days.

Life quickly became a whirl of preparing instructions, arranging committee meetings and negotiating contracts. A competition was held and no less than thirteen architects submitted designs for what was clearly going to be a prestigious project. It was a painful process, for Andrew Reed found that some had become supporters of the charity only with the intention of securing work for themselves or their friends. When thwarted in their efforts they could become very uncooperative, especially if they were influential. Yet Reed again took courage from the knowledge of why he had undertaken such work: 'It is for the orphan and the widow; nay it is for Him who is the Father of the fatherless.'[7]

The design the committee resolved to accept was the most aesthetically pleasing of those submitted, but needed many emendations in order to make it suitable for the purpose of an orphanage. It was Reed who made the changes, and saw that they were implemented. He urged a simpler and more economical plan. He insisted on practical measures: to prevent falls, he wanted no steps on the ground floor for children to negotiate during their daytime activities; he wanted adequate accommodation arrangements for the supervisory staff, with the schoolmaster accommodated in one wing, the schoolmistress in another and the matron in the central section, each based in the midst of the duties for which they were responsible. He also ensured that there was scope for the enlargement of the accommodation. Rooms were planned to be proportionate in size, and with sufficient height to give plenty of air for the children; even the lights were to be at equal distances and heights.

The internal plan of the orphanage, therefore, was largely Andrew Reed's own work, although the impressive façade and outer shell were the work of the architects Messrs Goldring and Inman. The building, designed in classical style, with a boys' wing on one side and a girls' wing on the other, and an imposing porticoed chapel in the centre, joined to the wings by a colonnaded walkway, became a scene much painted by artists. Reed's simpler design was costed initially at between £12,000 and £15,000, although the final outlay was nearer £25,000. There is no doubt that had the grander scheme originally proposed been implemented, it would have sunk the charity. Reed's attention to detail was immense, heightened by a sense of responsibility that it was his plan that had been adopted.[8]

Raising such sums was a major undertaking in days when many workers lived on less than £50 per year. Reed mobilized the support of the press, and then approached the Governors of the Bank of England, the London Docks, the East India

Company and the Corporation of the City of London, where he was part of a deputation which stood at the bar of the Common Council to plead the cause of the orphan. James Capel, of the leading stockbroking firm, became an early supporter. The high point of these endeavours came when the patronage of the new king, George IV, was secured. By the time of the anniversary dinner of 1822, £10,000 had been raised and building work could begin.

The foundation stone is laid

The laying of the foundation stone on 5 May 1823 was planned as an occasion of great ceremony. A procession of forty carriages left the London Tavern and headed for the site at Clapton. The Duke of York, the brother of King George IV, was to lay the foundation stone, and other dignitaries included the Prince Leopold of Saxe Cobourg (widower of the much-lamented Princess Charlotte), the Lord Mayor of London and the Bishops of London and Gloucester. At the site a huge crowd of over 5,000 people gathered around a platform built for the occasion over part of the basement foundations, upon which the dignitaries sat. The proceedings began with a speech from the Lord Mayor and a dedication prayer from the Bishop of London. Then a group of orphan children made their way onto the platform in order to sing a hymn.

Suddenly, and without any warning, tragedy struck. The raised wooden platform collapsed, and many of the children were thrown down into the basement foundations, as were a number of the dignitaries. Fortunately, the rest were able to jump clear, but panic seized the watching crowd, which surged forward, towards the edge of the open foundations. The dignitaries promptly took command of the situation and calmed the crowd. The children were quickly pulled to safety, and the Duke of York resisted suggestions that the ceremony be abandoned; the rest of the programme was speedily completed and the crowd was soon dispersed. Amazingly, injuries to the children and participants were minimal, but a workman who had been standing under the platform was killed. Hopes of a large collection for the orphanage from such a huge crowd were also dashed. At the evening dinner which followed later, when nerves had settled, £2,800 was collected, although understandably the Duke of York felt unable to preside on that occasion, as he was still recovering from the shock of the tragic events of the afternoon.[9]

While the stone-laying ceremony was still in progress, Reed launched his own enquiry into what had happened, demanding a report from the clerk of works as to who had been killed and details as to how the platform had been constructed. It quickly became apparent that the supports for the platform had not been adequately driven into the ground and had not been properly fitted with plates to spread the load. For this the surveyor blamed the builder, the builder blamed the clerk of works and the clerk of works blamed the foreman. He in turn blamed the workman who had been killed. Wherever the blame lay, the sad fact remained that the ranks of orphan children, for whose benefit the charity had been started, were increased by four through the tragic events of the day; the victim also left a wife and a dependent mother. The charity paid the costs of the funeral, and a collection was held for the man's family.[10]

Because the accident had endangered members of the royal family it was reported extensively in the newspapers. The board sought to lessen the damage done to the name of the charity by inserting an advert in *The Times* lamenting the accident and assuring readers that a full investigation was under way. The tragic events, and the attempts of contractors to evade personal responsibility, also undermined Andrew Reed's confidence in the building trade, and he resolved to take a major role in directing and overseeing construction operations himself. He started to visit the building site each day, issuing clear directives. Through his hands-on approach he ensured that the main fabric of the building was roofed over before the winter of 1823 set in.

To his consternation, Reed found that the contracts had not been handled well and costs had escalated rapidly. As funds ran low, some suggested holding a special theatre performance to raise funds; others a grand ball. Remembering the temptations which he had faced as a youth, Andrew Reed set his face against such worldly expedients: 'It has not yet come to this, that we must dance for the charity.'[11] Through the steadfast efforts of its supporters the money was steadily raised, but the building project was fraught with difficulties, including the bankruptcy of the builder, leaving the charity to deal with the sub-contractors and the receivers.

At last, on 16 January 1825, a formal ceremony for the opening of the building was held. At a breakfast for 1,200 persons, the Duke of Cambridge presided with his son Prince George. On 27 July 1825, the twelfth anniversary of the foundation of the orphanage, the children moved into their spacious new home. The day began with a religious service in the chapel, and then the orphans and committee sat down to dinner together.[12]

A demanding schedule

So ended a hugely stressful, but none the less successful, phase of Andrew Reed's early philanthropic career. It came in the midst of the dark years surrounding the deaths of his sister Martha and then his father, and the controversy over the publication of *No Fiction*, which makes his achievement all the more remarkable. He could only sustain such work by highly disciplined habits. He rose early each day, and studied in preparation for his Sunday preaching ministry until noon. He did pastoral visitation in the afternoon, although much of the rest of his time was devoted to overseeing the work of the orphanage, to which he walked regularly. Evenings were often

The London Orphan Asylum

spent at the church or in committee work at the offices of the charity in the City of London. The strain of his absences upon family life, and the work of Wycliffe Chapel, was considerable, but he was sustained by his prayer: 'God bless and succour the defenceless.'[13]

The completion of the building did not end his personal efforts for the welfare of the orphans. Andrew Reed drew up a scheme for the education of the children, superintended putting up gymnastic equipment, oversaw the diet of the children in conjunction with the matron and directed the laying out of the ornamental grounds around the orphanage, donating many trees and shrubs. He also involved his young family in the project. On Saturdays he would take lunch with the children at one o'clock, accompanied by his two eldest sons. He was present to welcome newly arrived children, and to offer words of counsel and instruction to those leaving the orphanage to begin life as young adults. He visited the sick children in the infirmary and accompanied the orphans on their annual summer outing to Wanstead Forest, where he joined in with the games and fun that made up the day.

Andrew Reed subjected himself to an extremely demanding schedule. Philanthropic work was now taking up almost half his time: it drained his energy and his pocket; it was his thought by day and his dream by night. At times the pressures told on his health. With a growing church and a young family to support, he reproached himself with having given too much attention to the orphanage. Yet he discerned the unseen hand of God in all that had happened, as he wrote in his diary: 'The thing grew unexpectedly on our hands; and it seemed impossible to relax in effort without being unfaithful.'

So much could not have been achieved without the vital contribution of Andrew Reed's wife Elizabeth, overseeing the care of their own children in his all-too-frequent absences. She took on much of the work previously done by Andrew's sister Martha, involving herself in the Ladies' Committee, and steadily encouraging her husband to keep on with the work that had been entrusted to him by God. Still, he could not help feeling that he was losing the first love of his call to the ministry. His beloved charity, with the honours and prestige brought by associating with leading figures in society, from royalty to politicians, could easily have turned his head from his work as a Christian minister. He resolved to pray that he should never lose his sense of priority: 'May I remember that I am a minister of the New Testament! What is there equal to this? The pursuits of the philosopher, the patriot, the philanthropist, are nothing compared with the minister of Jesus Christ.'[14]

The two emphases in his life were held in creative tension. His calling to Christian ministry challenged him to follow the example of Christ, who preached the good news and went about doing good. Andrew Reed's good works were simply the practical outworking of his faith. Ever since his first offer to help the children of the dying man in 1812, compassion for the plight of orphans deeply moved him to practical action. The orphanage had grown, from that simple act of kindness, into an uncomplicated scheme to 'afford maintenance, instruction, and clothing to destitute orphans of both sexes, and to put them in situations where they have the prospect of an honest liveli-hood'.[15] He was thrilled with the evidence before his eyes every day that his compassionate vision, conceived when he was only twenty-six years old and just two years into his ministry, was being carried out.

The education and training received by the orphans

Although the London Orphan Asylum primarily provided shelter, it also played a vital educational role. This was essential if the children were to obtain employment in the future, and not fall back into dependence on the Poor Law. At the beginning of the nineteenth century just over half of the British population could sign their own names, but for many that was the limit of their academic abilities; by the 1830s matters had improved somewhat, and it has been suggested that three quarters of working-class people could read, but only 30% could write.[16] With the prevalence of such low standards, the education received by those in the orphanage was far in advance of that available to most other children. This gave them a huge advantage when it came to seeking future employment, and was at least some compensation for the tragedies they had suffered early in life.

Reading, writing and arithmetic formed the core of the curriculum, and in addition to this girls were taught to spin, knit and sew. Religious instruction was also fundamental to the education the children received, with Bible teaching every day, and the children taken to church each Sunday, where the matron helped them to follow the readings and sermon in the Bible.

In view of the tragic backgrounds from which the orphans came, the staff of the orphanage had a vital role to play: they were to offer the children the parental comfort and support that they had been so cruelly denied by family tragedy, to be 'a friend to guide [the orphan's] steps, relieve his wants and wipe away his tears'.[17] It was to be a 'home' in the richest sense of the word.

When the children were old enough, and of sufficient maturity — usually at the age of fourteen — they were given opportunities to serve apprenticeships in various trades, for terms of between five and seven years, and many girls were sent to work in domestic service. Thus established in a trade, they were fitted for a lifetime of future employment.[18] Over time, the emphasis on apprenticeship and domestic service lessened, and the children who had benefited from the high level of education available were increasingly placed in situations in the offices of City firms, or in positions as clerks, or in skilled trades.

Certainly the enlightened Christian compassion of Reed's London Orphan Asylum was in advance of the practice of the Foundling Hospital, which in the 1790s was sending children as young as six years old to work as apprentices in factories in the

Midlands and the North of England. While the intention was to train the children up to a trade, and they were regularly visited, the scheme could expose little ones to harsh conditions and long hours of work.[19] The factory apprenticeship scheme was continued by the Foundling Hospital into the middle of the nineteenth century, although by then the children sent out in this way were usually over the age of fourteen.[20] Most of the children who passed through George Müller's orphanage in Bristol were placed in positions as domestic servants, for which there was much demand, but which offered limited future prospects.[21]

The backgrounds from which the children came

The children who came to the London Orphan Asylum for help were in great need, and their families had experienced acute tragedies. Of those admitted in 1818, Eliza Evans was one of five destitute children; their father had died and their mother was terminally ill. Mary Smith had lost both her father and mother, and her elder sister was struggling to support her. John Aveling's mother had died in a fire, and six months later his heartbroken father had died, leaving three children. Jane and Amelia Evans were two of six children whose father collapsed and died of a heart attack while their mother was in labour with her sixth child. Little Samuel Oram's father had been confronted by sudden financial ruin and, in distress at his 'embarrassed circumstances', had taken his own life.[22]

The loss of one or more parents was the ultimate tragedy for a child, but through such terrible bereavement children were flung into abject poverty through no fault of their own.[23] Unless the orphanage was able to help them, they would face the great social stigma of requiring help from the Poor Law. Most of the families were already in a financially vulnerable state before tragedy struck: the first 100 children listed in the 1833 report came from families in which there were already on average five or more children to support; the death of one shoemaker left twelve children orphaned. Many families were already in need, with incomes of £100 or less per year, before the main wage-earner had died. Most of the fathers of the orphans had been occupied in trades typical of those who attended Reed's chapel, as artisans, tradesmen, shopkeepers, craftsmen and clerks; a significant number had been sailors and members of the armed forces. Children of labourers, or domestic servants, were less commonly admitted to the orphanage.[24]

A number of other orphanages that developed in the later nineteenth century were aimed specifically at the children of middle-class parents. The British Orphan Asylum, for example, sought to help 'children of middle-class parents ... who in their lifetime were in a position to provide a liberal education for their children'. So too with the Royal Asylum of the St Anne's Society, which was designed to help 'parents who have seen better days, and have moved in a superior station in life'.[25] In its earliest years, under Andrew Reed's guidance, the London Orphan Asylum was able to help children from lower social backgrounds than these other charities and provide assistance to some of the most needy children in the country. However, they did not seek to take children whose families were already being supported by the Poor Law; rather they sought to prevent orphans from dropping to that level. In this, it might be argued, Reed and his charitable committee were at fault. The very poorest could not raise money to obtain subscriptions; nor had they the resources to solicit the subscriptions of others on their behalf. Nevertheless, the committee was convinced that children of pauper parents were already receiving assistance from the Poor Law and the major gap in social provision was for parents just above this class. They received no assistance from the Poor Law, and had no personal financial resources to ride out any major family crisis. It was to these people Reed believed he had a mission. He spent many hours with widows in the distress of their bereavement, helping them to secure the election of their children to the orphanage, or assisting children who were leaving the asylum to find a place of employment.[26] In this way dozens were spared the trauma of seeking help from the Poor Law system. As the nineteenth century wore on, and Reed's founding influence on the charity waned, fewer of the children admitted appear to have come from the lower ranks of society. In 1838 Reed still longed to expand the work, and feared his fellow committee members were resting on what they had done, rather than pressing on. Year by year the numbers of those applying for admission far exceeded the total of places available — he hoped to be able to provide for 100 admissions a year, rather than the thirty possible: 'We have been doing too little, fearing to go on.' For all his impatience at the level of progress, through the prodigious labours of Reed and his committee, an enormous amount had been achieved. Yet he resisted taking the credit. What had been done had been accomplished only through the blessing of God: 'That the object is effected, I ascribe to the blessing of Divine Providence. We might have made all the exertion we have, yet all might have failed... I am indebted to God for the thought, energy, opportunity, and disposition... If the London Orphan Asylum exists, its maker and builder is God, to whom may all the glory be given.'[27]

7.
Wycliffe Chapel

'Great God and
Saviour, I am nothing
without Thee, and I know
Thou canst bring me to
nothing. Let me lean on
Thee, for I am weak,
and learn of Thee, for I
am sinful'
(Andrew Reed).

7.
Wycliffe Chapel

The years between 1821 and 1826 were ones of great difficulty and sadness for Andrew Reed. This was also a period in which New Road Chapel did not prosper as it had done in the first ten years of his ministry, when 302 new members had joined the church. Perhaps he had been distracted by the demands of the London Orphan Asylum, or the furore over the publication of *No Fiction*. The deaths of his sister Martha and his father certainly took a toll on him spiritually. However, in the late 1820s there was an increasing sense that the spiritual low point had passed. Reed felt a growing awareness of God's blessing on his pulpit and pastoral ministry, and he believed that his congregation were becoming more serious about spiritual matters than ever before. 1827 was the turning point, yet it was not a year in which he was any less busy with philanthropic work; indeed he was to start another major charitable work in that year.

During a communion service that year he urged his members to devote one hour a week on a set day to prayer for blessing on the ministry at New Road Chapel. There were a growing number of conversions among the young people of the church. In 1826 only sixteen new members had joined the church, but in 1827 the number increased to twenty-seven. Then the growth became more rapid: at a single church meeting in 1829 the number of candidates proposed for church membership totalled twenty-seven, and in all forty new members joined during the year. Attendance at services was always much greater than the number of church members, and by the late 1820s the chapel was frequently crowded. It was clear that the New Road building was becoming too small for the congregation.[1] So, at a time when he was still busy with many duties, including the London Orphan Asylum and other major charitable and educational projects that were just beginning, as well as regular church meetings, daily study, prayer and sermon preparation, Andrew Reed had added the task of leading his church into a major building programme.

A time for reflection

After the birth of the last of their children, Elizabeth Reed suffered from a prolonged period of ill health, and for part of 1829 their doctors ordered both her and her husband to take a lengthy period of rest from the daily strains of pastoral life. Andrew took Elizabeth and the children to stay with friends in Cheshunt and gave the period over to prayer, reflection and planning for how the church should move forward. He was convinced that God was at work in the congregation, but his longing was to see his church making a significant impact on the densely packed areas of housing developing in the East End. Included in his plans was a programme to train people for door-to-door visitation, whereby they would distribute the Scriptures and engage in religious conversation. He also prayed for an increased interest in worldwide missionary work.

One particular concern for Andrew Reed was the lack of time he had been able to devote to his own spiritual growth. He knew he needed additional time for prayer, reading and reflection, so that he might have more to offer his congregation: he did not want to see those who had been entrusted to his care running ahead of him and to find himself left behind in the spiritual race. He needed to rest solely on Jesus Christ, who alone could supply him with the moral and spiritual courage and power to fulfil his duties. Although he was busy in God's work, and there were now signs of fruit all around, he was deeply aware of his personal failings. His period of self-examination left him longing for a closer walk with Christ, and deeper holiness: 'I look still for better things; but sin is ever with me, darkening my mind, burdening my heart, paralysing my hand, and preventing my usefulness. When shall I be free?'[2] Despite the crowded congregation at New Road, he lamented his weakness as a preacher: 'I have never yet preached as I desire. It is my *passion*. I would fain offer some example of a good sermon before I die.' Yet he cautioned against a tendency to over-seriousness, and reminded himself: 'A smile costs nothing, and it may gain a great deal.' He lamented what he saw as a tendency to selfishness — there had been times, he readily admitted, when he preferred his own inclinations to the will of God. On occasion he struggled to pray as he should, but he knew the negative consequences of this: 'Everything is hard to me when prayer is hard.' What he longed for as he looked ahead into the early 1830s was some new and powerful dealing of God in his life.[3]

When he laid the fruits of his reflections before the principal officers in the church, the elected deacons, Andrew Reed found loyal support. For a large church, their number was kept fairly small — nine in 1839, and seven at the time of Reed's retirement in 1861.[4] They met each month, and became a staunch body of supporters for their minister's work. Every candidate for church membership was visited by two deacons and asked to give a profession of faith, or provide evidence of transfer from another church. Such harmonious and supportive relationships amongst the leadership were of vital importance in the steady expansion of the church. Reed's plan of regular visitation of the houses round the chapel brought an enthusiastic response, and in the project they took a key role.[5]

A new chapel

Plans for the new chapel moved forward in early 1830, and the congregation threw itself wholeheartedly into the scheme. A site near to the existing New Road Chapel was secured, just behind the London Hospital, and close to the busy Commercial Road and Mile End Road. The New Road building had seats for 800 people, but by 1829 the congregation frequently numbered 1,200, with many forced to stand. It was decided to build with potential for future growth, and the new building was designed to accommodate 2,000 people. Andrew Reed laid the foundation stone for the new chapel on 28 July 1830, and building work proceeded rapidly. A simple Doric design was adopted, with a high façade and two columns supporting the portico, under which were large doors at the top of a short flight of steps. Inside the building was a prominent central pulpit, with a gallery along both sides and across one end of the building.

As was his practice in the building of the orphanages, Reed frequently attended the site, checking that the work was being properly carried out and giving great attention to detail. The night after one visit he experienced an unusual dream in which someone came to his house and told him of an accident at the new chapel. Andrew Reed was not one to place great store on such experiences and dismissed the dream as owing to his preoccupation with the work going on. He set about his usual morning of study, but was unable to settle to his sermon preparation and could not forget what he had dreamt. Eventually he abandoned his books and went to the building site to check the works. As soon as he arrived, he realized that all was far from well. Heavy rain had fallen during the night, and some of the foundations and walls for the basement of the chapel had caved in. The workmen were busy trying to patch up the collapsed masonry before anybody noticed what had happened. Had they not been stopped, and the faults properly corrected, the foundations would have been greatly weakened; with a full

Wycliffe Chapel

church and packed gallery in the future, a catastrophe would have been waiting to happen. Under Reed's instruction, the fault was corrected and the rest of the work completed carefully.

On 21 June 1831 the new chapel was opened. George Collison offered prayer and Dr Joseph Fletcher of Stepney Old Meeting preached. The church was crowded and a collection of £400 was taken, although Andrew Reed later privately admitted he had put in £100 of this from his own funds, to encourage the flock, and he had added £100 from other friends. He had pledged the first £100 towards the building for the London Orphan Asylum, and was keen to repeat the gesture with the chapel project.[6]

The members of Andrew Reed's church responded to the building project with great enthusiasm, and by 1840 the debt had been repaid.[7] The former chapel building was sold to a clergyman who had left the Anglican Church, who reopened it under the name of the Reformed English Church.[8] For Reed there was great sadness in leaving the New Road premises, but the expense of the move was to be amply repaid.

The church soon settled back into its regular pattern, with services each Sunday morning and evening and on a Wednesday evening. The prayer meeting was held on a Friday evening, with communion celebrated once a month on a Sunday afternoon.[9] The cost of the site and building was £7,722, of which in total Reed gave £573 from his own resources, and other wealthy friends added a further amount close to £1,000 — including money from some of his key supporters in the orphanages: David French, Thomas Fry and William Monk. The bulk of the sum, however, came from the giving of the ordinary members of the congregation, many of whom were of very limited means.[10]

Sunday, 27 November 1831, five months after the opening of the new chapel, was Andrew Reed's forty-fourth birthday. As he was reading the words of Luke 22:32 in his devotions, the account of how Peter denied his Master before being restored to his service struck him with new force: 'I have prayed for thee, that thy faith fail not: and when thou art converted, strengthen thy brethren.' Reed felt this was applicable to his circumstances: busy with so many projects, he had drifted from Jesus Christ, but here was promise of restoration and of future usefulness. He prayed all the more earnestly for a deepening of his own spiritual life.

The cholera epidemic

In early 1832, cholera swept through London. Andrew Reed resolved to stay at his post to support his congregation, and minister the gospel of everlasting life to those facing the terrible epidemic. After preaching at a morning service in early January he himself was taken ill, and unable to preach in the evening or midweek. Fears that he had succumbed to the disease were soon allayed, and he had recovered by the following Sunday, but the sense of alarm created by the virulent spread of cholera in the area was growing. He announced that he would meet with any who were spiritually concerned on the following Wednesday, and many who were anxious about their state before God attended. He spent much time counselling and praying with those who came, and by the following church meeting, thirty-two people had professed conversion, and were admitted to communion.

The sense of God being at work in the midst of the tragedy unfolding all around them grew. Reed urged the congregation to 'walk humbly with a present God, and to remain in prayer for greater tokens of his mercy'. Special meetings were arranged for those employed as domestic servants, and then meetings for the young people of the congregation. Over two hundred young people crowded into the larger vestry, and from this meeting a further twenty-seven were believed to be 'subjects of a Divine change'. For three Sunday evenings after these meetings Reed preached exhortations rather than sermons. These were then printed, and a thousand copies of each were distributed in the area, with the titles 'To the Thoughtless', 'To the Thoughtful', 'To the Young Convert'. The tracts were widely read, and attracted further visitors to the services.[11]

Personal weakness and family grief

Then this sudden upturn in the work of the gospel in very difficult circumstances received a check. Perhaps as a result of his strenuous efforts, Reed fell ill, and was unable to preach for a period. He had not long returned to his regular pulpit ministry when an urgent message with grave news was received at his home. His mother, Mary Ann Reed, lay dangerously ill at Cheshunt. Andrew rushed to her bedside, but she was already unconscious. She never recovered, and died soon afterwards, on 17 September 1832.

Reed was stunned to be bereaved so suddenly of one to whom he owed so much in his personal and spiritual life. In the face of the shock, his own health faltered again, and at the age of forty-five he was left wondering whether he himself would live long. His yearning was that his life might not be useless or helpless, but that 'Christ may be magnified in me'. Fearing death, he sought forgiveness for his faults — from his family, his church and, above all, from God: 'Whether I live or die, I desire to throw myself, as a creature ready to perish, into the arms of boundless mercy, through the infinite atonement of Christ Jesus the Lord.'[12]

He was in fact to be spared for almost another thirty years of ministry, and by November 1832 he was back in full harness. The harvest of the first months of that year was being repeated at its close: in late November and early December he spent twelve out of fourteen nights at the chapel counselling enquirers concerning the faith. In all, 1832 saw eighty-six new members join the church, a huge increase on the thirty of the previous year, and over forty more were to follow in early 1833. Cholera had certainly created a sense of fear and uncertainty in many that had led them to spiritual searching, but this is not the sole explanation of these events, for in 1849, when cholera again swept through London, there were only thirty-three additions to church membership.[13]

In the midst of physical weakness and family grief, Andrew Reed found that his ministry had been used in ways he had not previously experienced. In his journal he gave all the glory to God: 'Great God and Saviour, I am nothing without Thee, and I know Thou canst bring me to nothing. Let me lean on Thee, for I am weak, and learn of Thee, for I am sinful.'

Great care was taken over the preparation of the converts for church membership, and Reed was heavily involved in this work, together with his usual preaching and pastoral duties. During this period he was frequently at the chapel five evenings each week, in addition to meetings associated with the charities. In many situations, when facing fierce opposition and criticism, Andrew Reed was able to exercise firm self-control, but as he heard what God had done in the lives of many, sometimes in tragic circumstances, he found himself reduced to tears. Sensing the spiritual urgency of the times, he threw himself into the work with all his energy. The work of God in their midst in 1832 was to him a sign of God's blessing on the new Wycliffe Chapel building.[14]

8.
Suffer the little children

`They are orphans, and want tomorrow's bread — four little ones, under six years of age; and your door is closed to them all . . . whither are they to go? What are they to do?´

(Martha Reed in a note to her brother).

8.
Suffer the little children

The London Orphan Asylum had been established to care for children aged from seven to fourteen, by which time, in the early nineteenth century, they were considered to be on the threshold of adulthood. However, Andrew Reed quickly became aware of a need to do something for children who were under the age of seven.

The need was impressed more firmly on his mind in 1821, not long before Martha's death, when he received a note from his sister, who was still deeply concerned for the pastoral care of others despite her rapidly deteriorating health. In it she gave details of a group of four orphan children, all of whom were under the age of six and entirely destitute. Andrew was away from London at the time, and when Martha communicated with the London Orphan Asylum to see if the children could be admitted, her request met with a sad refusal. None was over seven years old, and therefore none could be admitted. Martha urged Andrew to change the asylum's policy to help cases such as this: 'They are orphans, and want tomorrow's bread — four little ones, under six years of age; and your door is closed to them all ... whither are they to go? What are they to do? God will help you if you will help them.' She then added a note, which well expresses the reaction of Martha and her brother to cases of chronic need: 'The greater the necessity, the greater the charity: we must have a wing at Clapton for infants; and it shall be called our nursery.'[1] Andrew kept the note and treasured up these thoughts in his heart. Martha did not live to see the outcome.

Plans for a new orphanage

As each election of candidates passed, Andrew became more acutely aware that the London Orphan Asylum was doing vital work, but was not helping the most vulnerable children of all. Thinking about the proper care and education of infants was still little developed at the time. Early efforts in the education of infants began in the early 1820s, and Andrew Reed followed these developments with interest. In 1826 he proposed to the board of the London Orphan Asylum that they extend their activities to include children who were under the age of seven. The governors agreed that the need was real and approved of the idea, but concluded that, with the charity already refusing admission to so many children aged over seven because of lack of resources, it was inappropriate to extend their activities any further.[2] The finance required to care for infants, some mere babes in arms, was simply too great.

Andrew Reed deferred to the board in their desire not to stretch the resources of the London Orphan Asylum too far. He was also keen not to extend his own commitments further, feeling he had been neglectful towards his own congregation, the growth of which had suffered during the years after 1821. Over the next year he formulated in his mind a scheme for a separate institution and sought to gain the approval of friends who had helped him in the past. In 1827, with the London Orphan Asylum well established in its new building, signs of renewed growth in his chapel, and the dark and despairing moments of the early 1820s behind him, he felt himself free enough of other commitments to begin a new venture. He convened a small meeting at his house, attended only by Reed himself and two other friends, James Taylor and David French. He kept the board of the London Orphan Asylum closely

informed as to what was happening; Reed wanted the new
asylum to be a supplementary charity to the already established
work. It was initially intended that when the infant children
reached the age of seven, they could be eligible for the support
of the senior charity.[3]

When he issued a public address in favour of the new
asylum, Reed argued that it was the first orphanage designed to
help orphaned infants (the Foundling Hospital was for illegitimate children abandoned by their mothers). He stressed the
desperate need of those for whom the charity was intended.
Addressing the concern of the day that charitable relief robbed
the poor of their independence and rendered them permanently dependent on others, Reed pointed out that this charity
was aimed to help those in need which could neither have been
anticipated nor prevented. For such it was the duty of the
community to provide. A note on the title page was added,
'especially those who are respectably descended', to allay fears
that the charity was merely duplicating the work of the Poor
Law system. For those who had suddenly been plunged into
poverty, or who faced it through no fault of their own, the
shame and stigma attached to entering the workhouse was
enormous. Reed argued that to support a child bereaved of its
parents was doing an 'unquestionable, perhaps an incalculable,
good'.

The orphanage was for 'destitute Orphan Children under the
age of seven', and the first call on the charity was to be from
children who had lost both parents. However, children who had
suffered through the loss of their father, the family's principal
wage earner, leaving a mother struggling to support infants with
no state benefits or support, were also allowed to be admitted.
In a significant humanitarian addition, the charity also declared
that it was willing to accept motherless children whose father
was disabled from work. In the face of children with such need,
Reed declared, society was commanded by a 'voice more than
human' to step forward, and offer a 'parent's care and sympathy and protection'.[4]

The charity was instituted at a public meeting held on 3 July 1827. Once again Reed gathered around him prominent friends and supporters. President of the meeting was George Byng, MP, who had given wholehearted support to the London Orphan Asylum and who was quickly won over by Reed's appeal. To fill the position of secretary, Andrew Reed sought an Anglican clergyman and approached Dr James Rudge of Limehouse, who accepted the appointment. He was later succeeded by Dr Kenney of St Olave's, Southwark, and then in 1834 by Rev. Hunter Fell of Trinity Church, Islington, who was much more active in the position than either of his predecessors had been. Another important appointment was that of John Buckler as agent: he organized the office and oversaw the collection of donations and subscriptions. Reed sought to take a less prominent public position in the charity, and appears on its publicity only as sub-treasurer. However, there is no doubt that Andrew Reed remained the organizational and inspirational genius behind the project.

News about the charity spread fast, and the response showed how necessary it was. At its inauguration widows in desperate need of support for their children descended on the meeting place and filled the corridors, holding their infants in their arms.[5] The scheme proposed placed it at the forefront of educational thinking: the charity was not only to board, nurse and clothe the children, but also to educate them.[6] This all-encompassing support made the guardians and mothers of orphaned children all the more desperate to secure their admission. It would provide children whose lives had been marred by tragedy with a start in life that they could never have envisaged.

Small beginnings

In October 1827 the first election of children to the charity was held. The beginnings were still small, and Reed was disappointed that it could only accept four children. Sadly, the great cost of medical care meant that only those in reasonable health could be admitted, and there was great fear of admitting a child with an infectious disease which would spread rapidly amongst the other children in the orphanage.[7]

Most children were admitted by election, but, as with the London Orphan Asylum, it was possible for the relatives of orphaned children to undertake payment to enable the acceptance and support of an orphan. For such children placed 'on the establishment' a means-tested fee was set, dependent on the circumstances of the wider family or supporters. Families and friends with an income above £400 were considered to have sufficient resources to be able to arrange their own provision for orphans for whom they had responsibility.[8] The committee had the right in an emergency to place a child in the orphanage pending the next election, when he or she would be recommended for acceptance. In very special cases, even the need for a vote could be dispensed with.[9]

Until a suitable property was secured, Andrew and Elizabeth Reed opened their home to two of the first children elected into the orphanage, and the others were fostered by different families. Eventually a suitable property in Northampton Place, Hackney Road, was identified, previously used by the sister charity, the London Orphan Asylum. It was also very near Reed's own home in Cambridge Heath, Hackney, allowing him to visit the children regularly. A matron was appointed, and by December the first children were in the home and were reported to be 'comfortable and happy'.[10]

Keys to success

Fundamental to the success of the project was ensuring a sound financial basis for the future. Encouraged by the advice of the stockbroker John Capel, the initial subscriptions were invested in stock, to produce a lasting and steady return, rather than condemning the charity to a hand-to-mouth existence. Capel himself, along with Andrew Reed and two others, stood as one of the trustees for the amount.[11]

Another key to the project's success was obtaining royal patronage for the charity. By February 1828 the Duke of Gloucester, the brother of King George IV, had agreed to become a patron, but only after making careful enquiry as to certain aspects of the scheme. He was concerned that the charity appeared to exclude disabled children, and the committee had to reassure him that this only meant children with life-threatening handicaps, which the orphanage lacked the resources to cater for.[12] The London Orphan Asylum had been greatly helped by the support of the Duke of Kent and in March 1828 the new charity rejoiced in a gift of ten guineas from the Duchess of Kent, indicating her willingness to act as a patron.[13] This gift was to prove most significant, for with her support came that of her young daughter, Victoria. Unbeknown to them at the time, the latter was later to become queen. Her own early tragic life, with the death of her father, was to encourage her deep interest in the new charity aimed at orphans in far less fortunate circumstances than she had been.[14]

The Reeds' personal involvement

Despite all his concerns as to how the London Orphan Asylum had absorbed his time, taking him away from family and church, Andrew Reed felt constrained to invest great amounts of time and energy in the Infant Orphan Asylum. Committee meetings were at least monthly, but it was almost five years before he missed one. To ensure that some of the mistakes of the early years of the London Orphan Asylum were not repeated, every aspect of the orphanages fell under his scrutiny. In addition to the General Committee, Reed served on the House Committee, the Stewards' Committee that arranged the anniversary dinner and the Building Committee. Mrs Reed also served on the Ladies' Committee, which closely supervised the care of the children. From the appointment of a teacher to the colour of the uniforms that the children wore (according to the matron, dark colours showed the dirt less and needed washing less frequently) and even the quality of the bread, Andrew and Elizabeth Reed were involved in decisions that had to be made. By the end of its first year of existence, the Infant Orphan Asylum was catering for twenty-eight children. Andrew Reed frequently called at the house, discussing arrangements for the education of the children, their diet and clothing. He bought toys for the nursery and pictures for the walls. He was anxious above all for the happiness of the children who had faced such trauma in their early years. In contrast to many boarding schools of the time, where children were often left cold and half-starved, Reed insisted that nourishment should be 'fresh and abundant, having all the variety desirable for diversity of appetite and constitution'. He was a firm believer in the impor-tance of fresh air in the nursery, which should be 'warm and genial' in the winter and 'cool and refreshing' in the summer. He could not bear to hear little children crying, and insisted that staff should always seek out the cause — were they unwell, or unhappy? Reed wanted the garden to be filled with flowers and bird-life, which the children loved, and contact with a child's mother, brother, or sisters was strongly encouraged, with visits from other members of the family allowed once a week. Andrew Reed was convinced that in the nursery were children who had been made in the image of God. They were therefore 'the noblest of the Creator's works', and deserved the best: 'Let this training be worthy of such a being.'[15]

The search for a permanent home

In 1830 the house next door to the existing premises in North-ampton Place was leased, and the two properties knocked into one. Space remained a pressing problem. Not only did demand for places far exceed what the orphanage could offer, but also the presence of many children in closely confined spaces led to the rapid spread of disease. The infections of nineteenth-century childhood spread with great virulence amongst the children, placing them at great risk, with no immunization available and few adequate medicines to treat them. Measles was a major problem, and then in 1831 whooping cough, which claimed the life of one little boy.[16] The urgency of finding larger and more suitable premises increased. By the end of 1831 there were sixty-two children being cared for in the orphanage.

Making use of his close contacts with them, Andrew Reed urged the royal family to do all they could to make the Infant Orphan Asylum a national project. He also wrote to the former prime minister, and hero of the Napoleonic Wars, the Duke of Wellington, urging his help in creating for the orphaned infants a permanent home worthy of the nation.[17] What Andrew Reed had in mind was securing a grant of Crown land, on which an orphanage could be built as a national institution. Again, for a Dissenting minister without family connections to leading figures in government or royalty, the proposal was a remarkable one. The response he received is testimony to the high level of respect and trust he had built up over the years of his charitable work. The reply of the Duke of Wellington was positive: 'It is a good cause... I will back your application,' and he encouraged the application for Crown land.

Reed then wrote to the royal family and with typical bold-ness suggested one of the most prominent sites available — near Regent's Park, where land was then valued at £1,000 per acre. Almost inevitably, when the reply came in 1833, it was in the negative, but with the denial of the land came a gift of £50 from Queen Adelaide (wife of King William IV), who was to become a strong supporter of the charity. Reed knew this gift was worth hundreds of pounds in the prestige it brought to the charity, and on the strength of it he urged other figures in authority to follow suit. The Duke of Cambridge, another of the king's brothers, weighed in with a large donation. Andrew Reed did not stop there, and next begged money from leading figures in the Bank of England, arguing that the suffering of infant children was a debt the nation should do something about.[18] He never forgot the promises of support from the royal family concerning land for the charity — he hoped to redeem them at some time in the future.

Support from all sections of society

Within five years of its small beginnings, the Infant Orphan Asylum was attracting support from all levels of society. In addition to that of Queen Adelaide, a number of dukes and leading members of the clergy gave their support. Notable amongst them were the evangelical Sumner brothers, J. B. who was Bishop of Chester and later Archbishop of Canterbury, and his brother C. R., Bishop of Winchester. Other leading evangelical laypersons were supporters: the Truman and Hanbury families, famous for their brewing interests, Thomas Fowell Buxton and the merchant-trading Hankey family — Thomson Hankey rose to become Governor of the Bank of England between 1851 and 1853. At a very different level, the girls of the London Orphan Asylum clubbed together to make a small donation and gain a vote in the annual election.

The high point of each fund-raising year was the annual charity dinner, held in venues such as the Guildhall, or the Hall of Christ's Hospital in London. Some of the children from the orphanage attended, and were specially trained to sing to the guests. There was a short religious ceremony, and other orchestral musical items were offered: in 1843 entertainment was provided by the band of the Coldstream Guards. The president of the dinner was usually one of the aristocratic patrons — in the 1840s they included the Duke of Wellington and Prince Albert. Although tickets cost around a guinea per head (a large sum of money in those days), over two hundred people attended. The event was a focus for large and generous giving by those who attended and huge sums were collected for the charity on the night. In 1838 the annual dinner raised the sum of £1,850.[19]

Much good was also done by the preaching of sermons on behalf of the charity, at which collections were taken, and through the soliciting of regular subscriptions and collections. The ability of Andrew Reed, who was himself a generous subscriber, to attract funds from such a wide range of sources is notable. The support of prominent evangelicals, drawn to Andrew Reed's evangelicalism, was understandable, but his boldness and personal charm and integrity extended sources of funding much further. For those who were so busy in business and financial life that they neglected the need for consideration of higher matters, the Infant Orphan Asylum was an accessible outlet for charitable sympathy. Reed believed that doing good to the most needy was a duty incumbent on all in society, regardless of their religious views.

Staffing and running the orphanage

Employing suitable staff for the asylums was always a crucial concern for Reed. They had the most crucial contact with the children; ultimately it was on them that the happiness or unhappiness of the children depended. Their being of the right character was of great concern to the committee. It was repeatedly stressed that the women appointed should be 'motherly'.

The wages paid for their services were set at the going rate for that particular occupation. In 1835 a nurse received £15 per year and a junior nurse £12, but a nursemaid only £8. The cook was paid £14 and the housemaid £10. In addition to these modest amounts accommodation and clothing were provided. These were posts held by single women, and the maids would probably be young teenagers. The first matron was paid £30 per year, plus accommodation.[20] There was no shortage of applicants for the posts. It should also be noted that in the middle of the nineteenth century many Church of England curates were paid only £40 to £50 per annum, on which amount they often struggled to bring up families.

When a schoolmaster was appointed, the importance of giving the children a high-quality education was stressed. The first teacher appointed in 1828 received only £20 per annum, but that appointment did not prove satisfactory.[21] When a further appointment was made in 1833 a more generous remuneration package was agreed, and the proposed salary of £70 was increased to eighty guineas (£84).[22]

In the early years of the charity, much practical assistance was given by the Ladies' Committee, on which Elizabeth Reed served. They regularly visited the children, and kept the committee informed about the general state of the orphanage. When one member visited and found that a boy had been confined to bed for two days as punishment for a misdemeanour, her complaint that this was excessive was acted upon. Their maternal eyes were drawn to childhood illnesses, to baby Wyatt's distress during teething, or to Mrs Barrow's battles with the mountains of washing.[23]

The children who were admitted

The charity was formed to assist children who were in serious need. Periodically the orphanage gave details about the children it was helping which provide insight into the frequent tragedies that beset families in early-nineteenth-century cities. When Sarah Ann Marriott was only two years old, her father had died, leaving Sarah's mother suffering from a terminal illness and trying to bring up five children. Jemima Usher's father, a tallow chandler, had died, leaving a wife and three children. Jemima's mother had later died in a catastrophic fire in Fenchurch Street, along with the smallest of the children. Four-year-old Henry Crossman's father had been a journeyman tailor, but both his parents had died, leaving eight children whom an elderly relative was attempting to bring up. William Folkard, aged four, and his brother Charles, aged two, were from a family of eight children left wholly dependent on their mother by the death of their father, who had worked for the General Post Office. Four of the children in the Folkard family were mentally handicapped. After the death of nine-month-old Ellen Griffiths' father, who had been a seaman, her mother had been run over by a cart while carrying the little infant in her arms. Ellen had miraculously escaped, but her mother had been killed in the accident.[24] The charity, for all its struggles to develop and frustrations at having to turn away so many children, was providing vital relief to families devastated by terrible tragedy.

The occupations of the fathers of the orphans suggest that the charity was helping families from the artisan and upper working classes — plumbers, tailors, butchers, bricklayers, clerks, carpenters. A few came from the middle classes, being the children of schoolmasters or ministers of religion, but those from the higher classes were excluded. The charity was aimed at those who had no prospect of help.

The procedure for admitting the children to the charity was again the election system used by the London Orphan Asylum, and most other charities of the day. A donation of half a guinea per year allowed the donor to have one vote in the annual election of new candidates; a guinea gave two votes; five guineas in one year gave life membership and life entitlement to vote. This was believed to be the fairest method, allowing the families of those in need to present their case and the supporters of the charity to have a personal say in those it was caring for. There is no doubt that the cases of greatest need did secure admission — such as the Scanlan twins, born several months after the death of their father to a mother already caring for four other children.

Sadly, demand for places always exceeded supply. At the first election there were twenty-eight candidates for only four places, and a minimum of 316 votes was required to secure

Polling for an election to the Infant Orphan Asylum

From the painting by George Hicks, 'An Infant Orphan Election at the London Tavern' © The Museum of London

admission. Those who were unsuccessful could apply again, carrying forward votes they had previously received. Amelia Sheriff received just fifty-two votes in the first election in 1827 and 302 votes six months later, but was successfully elected in October 1828 with 1,353 votes. By 1842, when twenty-five places were available every six months, the top candidate received 24,414 votes, and the twenty-fifth was elected with 4,073 votes. The charity was by then a very major institution, and less personal than when it started in 1827, yet the size of the votes indicates the huge interest and investment in it by its donors. Persistence and proof of real needs generally secured a child admission — in 1842, a total of eleven out of twenty-five places were taken up by children being presented in the election for the second time.[25] Urgent need was not ignored. In 1838 the orphanage was asked to assist an infant of just two months old, whose parents had married just twelve months previously. The father had died within two months of the marriage, and the mother two weeks after the birth of the baby, who was left without any family or relatives to support her. The prompt acceptance of the child thrilled Andrew Reed, who wrote in his journal, 'This is the triumph of charity; I thanked God afresh for the Asylum.'[26]

The need to turn away so many candidates troubled Reed. The sadness of those who were disappointed spurred him to do more, to press the claims of the charity harder, to urge its supporters to greater efforts. He believed that, if they attempted to do more, God would honour this and supply more. He could not rest easy until the orphanage had accommodation for 500 children.

Prominent supporters

By the 1830s the range of support was extensive. The patronage of Queen Victoria came with her accession to the throne in 1837. Of sixteen presidents, nine were peers of the realm and four were bishops. Their role was largely by way of endorsing the work of the charity and encouraging wider support; the running of the charity was vested in the committee.

Other famous families were by then prominent supporters: the Barclay family, also evangelicals, made famous for their brewing and banking interests; the Quaker Fry family, famous also for banking and chocolate manufacturing; the Gurneys (also Quakers) and the Rothschilds. The decision to locate the office for the charity on Threadneedle Street helped tap another significant source of funding. Financial and commercial interests were generous benefactors — the Governor of the Bank of England and eight others working at the bank were prominent subscribers. In 1836, of 2,850 subscribers, 169 gave their address as 'the Stock Exchange', and in 1838 the British Gas Light Company made a donation. Notable was the number of families who subscribed to the charity — husband, wife and, often, their children. The prominent evangelical Lord Ashley, later to become Lord Shaftesbury, and his wife were both donors.[27]

It was probably a good thing that the plans for a grant of Crown land and a building for the Infant Orphan Asylum did not come to fruition in 1833, for in the following year Andrew Reed was urged to temporarily set aside his church and charitable commitments and be part of a delegation from the Congregational churches to the United States of America. Willing volunteers stepped forward to fill his place in the charities during his absence, although they longed for his speedy return. Mr Byng grasped his hand on their farewell: 'God bless you, my dear sir, and send you safely back to us! For the poor orphans will miss you.'[28] Little was Andrew Reed to know that within two weeks of his departure for America, the Infant Orphan Asylum would be plunged into crisis.

9.
Delegate to America

In Richmond he noticed
an advertisement for a
sale of household goods,
with slaves listed for sale
alongside six feather
beds, as if there were no
difference between them.
Reed was appalled...

9.
Delegate to America

Andrew Reed's parents had long been committed to churches with an Independent form of church government, and he held firmly to their principles. He believed that the head of the church was Jesus Christ, and no human rank or bureaucracy should interfere with that divine order. Reed was involved in a number of societies and agencies operated by the Independents, and later by the Congregational Union.

In 1829 he was elected to serve as a member of the committee of the Home Missionary Society, established by Independent churches to encourage evangelism especially in rural parts of England.[1] When in 1830 a 'Provisional Committee' was appointed to consider the 'desirableness and practicability of a General Union of Congregational Ministers and Churches', Reed was invited, along with other laymen and principal ministers of the London churches, to serve as a member. This led to a meeting in May 1831 to establish a Union of Congregational Churches, to promote evangelical religion among Independent churches, together with brotherly affection and co-operation, fraternal correspondence, collection of statistical information and financial assistance with erecting places of worship. Such co-operation amongst like-minded Congregational churches was something Reed was keen to promote.[2]

Although convinced of the rightness of Congregationalism as a system of church order, Reed never became a narrow denominationalist. He appealed for unity amongst Christians based on oneness in the gospel and urged, 'Our pulpit must be open to all who preach Christ.'[3] When delivering the anniversary sermon for the London Missionary Society in 1831, Reed declared his belief that evangelical unity was essential to the evangelization of the world. While the church remained divided into parties, 'The worldly will remain scandalised or indifferent. They will justify themselves in postponing an inquiry after the truth, till its professors shall have agreed on what it is.'[4] Such views led Reed to encourage efforts to promote wider unity amongst evangelical Christians. In 1839, and again in 1845, he met with other evangelical leaders to discuss the formation of an 'evangelical union'. He was deeply disappointed that the outcome of these discussions was merely the Evangelical Alliance of 1846. If evangelicals were united in the fundamentals of the gospel, then Reed believed what was needed was not merely an alliance, but an evangelical union of churches. He argued that oneness in the truths evangelicals held dear was to be the sole criterion for membership; differences on secondary issues were not to be a bar to membership.[5]

Delegate to the American churches

One of the desires of Andrew Reed was to develop fellowship internationally between like-minded bodies of churches in different nations. In 1833, he was given an opportunity to give tangible expression to such hopes when he was asked to be part of a delegation to the Congregational and Presbyterian churches of America and Canada on behalf of the Congregational Union. It was a matter he needed to think and pray about very deeply. He talked matters over at length with Elizabeth, from whom he would be away for several months, but she encouraged him to look positively on the request. He was concerned about the prolonged absence from his children and from the orphanages, particularly the Infant Orphan Asylum. There was also an increasing sense that God was at work in Wycliffe Chapel, and he worried over being absent from the church at such a time. The deacons of the chapel proposed an evening of prayer over the matter and if at the end of this it appeared to Reed to be the will of God, he would go. The congregation was reluctant to let the pastor, through whom God had done so much, set off on a lengthy and possibly perilous voyage, but at last agreed that he should go. Reed was much moved by their affection and concern for him, and by their willingness to submit to the greater cause of Christ. He was justifiably somewhat fearful for his own safety on the trip, and placed his financial affairs in a settled state and rewrote his will before setting out. None the less he concluded that 'If God has bidden me go, He will attend me.'[6] In his absence, Reed's friend and mentor George Collison agreed to preside over the church meetings of Wycliffe Chapel and to oversee the deacons and church officers. Reed's companion on the trip was Rev. James Matheson of Durham.

In the early nineteenth century, a 'special relationship' between Britain and America should not be assumed — indeed, there remained significant tension between the two nations. The American Declaration of Independence had come in 1776, in the midst of growing conflict and then a bitter war, which drew in France, Spain and Holland against the British. The war, which ended formally in 1783, resulted in humiliating defeat for the British. Discontent was to simmer between the countries through parts of the nineteenth century, and the two nations were at war again briefly between 1812 and 1814. There were repeated tensions over issues such as the settlement of the American-Canadian border, the Oregon territories and the Civil War of the 1860s. One hope of Andrew Reed was that by Christians working together in fraternal relationship, 'peace, intercourse and union' might develop between the nations. Instead of wasting their energies in conflict, Britain and America should use their influence, singularly given by Providence, to work together to promote the welfare of other nations and the extension of the gospel.[7] The visit served to confirm him in such views.

On 16 March 1834, Reed and Matheson set sail from Liverpool on a trip which was to last eight months. An account of the visit was later published, largely written by Andrew Reed. It is probably the best-written of his works, a mixture of travelogue, personal reflection and spiritual commentary. Reed describes the natural beauty of the still largely undeveloped land he visited and the spiritual and social character of the people he encountered. By the 1830s he had travelled widely in Britain and Europe, and was determined to take the opportunity to see as many of the renowned sights as possible in the then little-known 'New World'. His *Narrative of the Visit to the American Churches* captures the mixture of excitement and personal deprivation he experienced, particularly when travelling in the underdeveloped states away from the eastern seaboard. The book also conveys the shock and repulsion at some of the things he encountered, especially through witnessing the suffering of the slaves, for slavery was still legal in America.

Reed and Matheson's Atlantic crossing took twenty-four days and included some very rough weather. Although suffering badly from seasickness in the worst of the conditions, Reed did all he could to be out of his 'coffin-like' cabin, and even tied himself on the deck during one storm to observe and experience its violence. Every aspect of nature was in a heightened state, full of raw power. Awed by the knowledge that the merest snapping of a rope or the shifting of a plank would bring disaster to the wooden sailing ship, his being was thrilled with 'an unutterable conception of Nature and of Omnipotence'.[8]

The British delegates were welcomed to New York by the Presbyterian Assembly then in session, before they moved on to Washington. Here they were introduced to the president, General Jackson, then sixty-eight years old but still 'soldier-like and gentlemanly'. Reed preached in the Presbyterian church before the president and fifty or sixty members of the Congress, whom he found very attentive.

Impressions of travel in America

The travellers also took the opportunity to visit George Washington's house and tomb and the scene where William Penn signed his treaty with the Native American Indians in 1682. Reed was particularly moved by Plymouth Rock, the first landfall for so many pilgrims escaping religious persecution in Europe, with the simple graves nearby of those who had perished in the endeavour. He was moved to call it the most sacred spot on earth, 'except the one spot where the Holy One suffered'.[9]

The natural phenomenon that most powerfully affected Reed, as so many other visitors, was the Niagara Falls, already an established tourist sight by this time, but still comparatively undeveloped. Although he was disappointed by the shabby buildings erected nearby, he found almost overwhelming the force of the torrent, which made the rocks beneath and around him tremble: 'The power, the sublimity, the bliss of that spot — it cannot be told.' Such natural beauty drew his thoughts nearer to the Creator: 'It raises the mind a step higher in conceptions of the power and eternity of Him whom "to know is life eternal".'[10]

At Niagara the delegates parted company, Matheson moving on into Canada, and Reed exploring the less well-developed mid-western and southern American states. He noticed a deterioration not only in living, but also in social and spiritual, conditions, with increased evidence of the problem of alcohol abuse.

Where possible, Reed travelled by boat, along the eastern seaboard and on major inland lakes and rivers. When this was not feasible, he found travel by coach was a tortuous experience, jolting along barely existent tracks, often wallowing in mud. One coach advertised as 'splendid', and equal to 'any in the States', took twenty-eight hours to do 110 miles on the journey from Cleveland to Columbus, Ohio. Good fenced land was for sale at $8 per acre, amidst boundless, pristine forest, where log cabins abounded.

Deep in the magnificent forest Reed found himself drawn near to God. A thunderstorm in the depths of the forest was thrilling: 'O, it was grand! God's own voice in God's own temple.' He encountered some of the early Mormons resolutely making their way to the Far West.[11]

As he moved on towards Cincinnati, Reed was troubled by the lack of manners and low moral standards amongst those he met: travellers frequently had their baggage stolen or rifled through, and he was never comfortable sleeping in a room without a lock on the door. At one inn he complained on behalf of a lady traveller over the lack of such a device: he was simply handed a nail and told the lady could use it to nail her door shut overnight! Reed was also uncomfortable about sharing bedrooms with strangers, who were often rough and uncouth. It was not uncommon for a traveller to go to sleep in a single bed and wake up in the morning to find that someone else had climbed in beside him during the night. At one overnight stop Reed insisted on a room to himself, and was assured that no one would be allowed through the door during the night. He woke in the morning to find that, although the innkeeper had been true to his word, and the door was secure, someone else was sleeping on the floor, having climbed in through the window!

At Cincinnati he visited Harriet Beecher Stowe, author of the powerful anti-slavery work *Uncle Tom's Cabin*. Here he also witnessed the Fourth of July Independence Day celebrations, and was left feeling very uneasy at the sentiments of hatred and vindictiveness still being displayed against England fifty years after the end of the War of Independence. Despite the coarse lifestyle of many of those with whom he shared his journey, Reed found great strength and vigour in the local churches of the town.

From Cincinnati he moved to Louisville on the Ohio River, where cholera had raged and temperatures soared to 100 degrees. Wearied by the physical demands of travelling, often surviving on only three or four hours of sleep per night, and

required to rise at 3 a.m. to meet coach-company schedules,
Reed began to fall ill. The heat was utterly debilitating, and
mosquitoes and flies tormented him. He found that Lexington
in Kentucky had been devastated by the cholera epidemic and
500 lives had been lost. Yet, in the midst of such suffering,
many had turned to God, and churches were well filled. One
church had seen 500 professions of faith after four days of
mission services.[12]

From Kentucky Andrew Reed travelled into Virginia, crossing
the Alleghany, Appalachian and Blue Ridge mountains of
Virginia. He rode on the outside of the coach to enjoy all he
could of the natural spectacle, and where possible made detours
to see sights such as Hawk's Nest and the Kenawa Falls —
where he found his spirits soaring in praise to God as the waters
lifted up their voice 'from the deeps beneath, to Him who holds
the waters in the hollow of His hand'.[13]

The contrast between the awesome natural beauty of the
region and the behaviour of many constantly struck Reed.
Although from the artisan class himself, he had by now become
a gentle-mannered English Nonconformist pastor and he was
amused at the way American men in the rougher parts always
found it necessary to put their feet up when sitting. Whether it
was on fender, stove, desk, or mantelpiece, they were 'never
satisfied till their heels are on a level with their head'. The
practice of chewing tobacco, and then spitting out the juice, he
found almost universal and utterly revolting. The noise made by
people spitting while sitting in meetings, even religious ones,
was like the sound of rain falling on a roof and, disconcertingly,
spitters took pride in how close to an object they could spit out
their juice, without actually hitting it. Reed once sat in a meeting
just in front of a man who spat constantly onto a pile of sawdust
on the floor close beside his feet. He found it almost impossible
to concentrate on the meeting, constantly fearful that his
neighbour would fail in his aim and splatter his coat. He was
relieved that the man managed to miss him every time. Even

people who were ill in bed were provided with a mound of sand on the floor onto which they could spit.[14]

Slavery

Far more troubling to Andrew Reed was what he saw in states where slavery was practised. He was distressed when he encountered children who were slaves in the inns where he stayed being ordered by their masters to perform the most menial of tasks for him. In Richmond he noticed an advertisement for a sale of household goods, with slaves listed for sale alongside six feather beds, as if there were no difference between them.[15] Reed was appalled by the slave system. Seeing human beings created in the image of God treated in this way was to him 'pure despotism'; between slave and white there was a 'monstrous inequality of law'. Field slaves were treated worst of all: they were 'bought and sold as cattle: they do the work of cattle; they are provided for as cattle'.[16]

Despite their suffering, Reed found among the black slaves a deep spirituality. Many attended the white churches, but they were segregated and forced to sit in the gallery. Reed made a point of visiting a number of black churches, although he found that in Virginia it was illegal for them to meet without a white man present. Few of the slaves could read, and there were no books, but he found amongst them a love of music. He was moved to hear Isaac Watts' hymns being sung by a black congregation, who gently swayed together in time with the music, and also strong gospel preaching. He judged the black expressions of spirituality he witnessed to be superior to what he found amongst the white churches. While his heart was heavy with the oppression endured by the slaves, he rejoiced in the spiritual hope that many held dear. Walking in the fields near Philadelphia, Reed passed a cottage where an old black man happened to be reading aloud a passage from the fourteenth chapter of John's Gospel: 'Show us the Father, and it sufficeth us.' To Reed the scene encapsulated the plight of the man's oppressed race, in the midst of all the wrongs against them, longing for the highest matters of all.[17]

The rejection of slavery by churches in the northern states was warmly applauded by Andrew Reed. Here he found that all who were religious were 'prepared to admit and deplore the evil of slavery in itself'.[18] This was not the case further south, where strongly committed Christians were prepared to justify the ownership of slaves. As he reflected on the issue he was shocked by the inconsistency of this stance: 'The vilest despotism in the presence of boasted equality? — The deepest oppression of man, where the rights of man are professedly most honoured! No, this cannot continue. Slavery and liberty cannot exist together; either slavery must die, or liberty must die. Even now, the existence of slavery is a violation of the Constitution of America.' His appeal was passionately strong: 'Yes, the slave must go free.'[19] It was to take a terrible civil war to bring such an outcome, a war that was still being waged when Andrew Reed died in 1862.

The suffering of the indigenous peoples of America also did not go unnoticed by Andrew Reed. Of the 500,000 Native American Indians, Reed observed, 'No people have suffered more.' It was time they were allowed to live in peace and security, 'in the inviolable possession of their lands, their laws, their liberty'. He called upon the United States to be true to its profession of being a land of liberty 'by preserving the Indian, and Emancipating the African'.[20]

Although he had been troubled by the abuse of alcohol as he travelled in the less well-developed areas, Reed applauded the positive influence the temperance movement was having. Many areas where the temperance cause was strong witnessed a very positive improvement in social and moral conditions. The United States Temperance Society had been founded in 1826 and by 1835 claimed to have 1,250,000 supporters and to have reclaimed 10,000 drunkards. Reed was thrilled by their achievements: 'They have laboured and prayed ... and the plague is stayed.'[21]

Revivals and revivalism

From Philadelphia, where he met up with James Matheson again, Reed travelled back through New York into New England. Here Reed had a number of engagements to fulfil: visits to some of the famous colleges, a meeting with William Sprague and an invitation to preach in Northampton, Massachusetts, made famous in the previous century by the ministry of Jonathan Edwards.

William Sprague

The meeting with Sprague was an important one, and Reed was invited to preach at his church at Albany, New York State. Sprague was a leading thinker on the subject of revival, and Reed was anxious to discuss the subject with him. Throughout his travels Reed had noted — sometimes with interest, at others with great concern — the new revivalist methods that were gaining ground in the churches.

In 1835, the year following Reed's transatlantic visit, the American Charles Finney was to publish his *Lectures on Revivals,* an account of such methods, based on his wide experience of using them. Finney did much to popularize the techniques, which focused on a series of well-advertised and carefully planned meetings, at which earnest preaching was offered, with a strong appeal at the end of the sermon directed at the emotions and the will of the hearers. Those seeking further counsel were invited to come to the front of the meeting and sit on the front pew, known as the 'anxious seat'. Enquirers were dealt with personally in an after-meeting. Reed had seen these techniques in action and had great concerns about them. He felt the preaching and exhortations were often over-emotional and could create a sense of hysteria in a congre-gation; he observed in certain gatherings endlessly repetitive singing of parts of hymns and songs, which wore some people out and overexcited others. Reed did not like the practice of the preacher walking amongst the congregation as he made his appeal, although he was convinced that preaching should be urgent and directed at the heart. Yet, as will be seen, he had attended one revivalist camp-meeting deep in the forests, at which he had been prevailed upon to preach, and had found great blessing.[22] Reed did not accept the rightness of using the techniques of revivalism, but was interested to see what could be learned from the movement.

He found that Sprague agreed with him that Calvinists had things to learn from what had been happening. In his own *Lectures on Revival*, published in 1832, Sprague had offered a cautious Calvinistic antidote to the views of the revivalists, arguing that not all conversions were sudden, that excitement did not necessarily constitute a revival, but that direct preaching was essential in evangelical gospel ministry.[23] Reed began to see that revival was sovereignly sent by God but, in the mystery of his providence, there were times when people had longed for it and prayed for it and prepared for it, and revival had come.

Wherever he travelled, Reed carefully questioned ministers in America about their experiences of revival, and how it had come about. Although at New Road, and subsequently at Wycliffe Chapel, they had seen periods of blessing, he began to long that in his own church he might see a touch of genuine revival.

Of great importance in his thinking was a visit to Northampton, Massachusetts. Although he was disappointed to find that the house where Jonathan Edwards had lived had been demolished, he saw that his legacy remained strong eighty years after his departure from the town: 'The pious persons have much gravity and steadiness of character.' This lasting legacy was important to Reed, for he believed that the opposition to Jonathan Edwards in the years after the revivals under his ministry, and his subsequent dismissal by his congregation, had weakened confidence in the fruits of those awakenings. He was invited to preach in Edwards' pulpit, for which he felt deeply honoured. As he prayed and meditated before preaching he walked through the burial ground and spent a little time beside the grave of the saintly young missionary to the Indians, David Brainerd, who had been cared for by the Edwards family in the last months before his death. Reed hoped in the 'recollection of him to find an improved state of mind for my own duties'.[24]

David Brainerd's tomb

He was encouraged to discover that there had been a number of revivals in Northampton in the decades subsequent to Edwards' departure, and those in 1819, 1826 and 1831 had been particularly powerful. Although the church rebuilt in Edwards' day could accommodate 1,600 people, it had become overcrowded, and in 1810 a second Congregational church had been built to supplement it. The population of the town was 3,600, four fifths of whom were Congregationalists, indicating the strength and vigour of the continuing work of the gospel. A further revival had occurred in 1833, in which preaching was 'simple, powerful, calculated not so much to produce excitement of feeling, as deep and strong convictions of truth and duty'. Some 250 local people had been converted in a period of six weeks, and about fifty outsiders, and their ages ranged from the elderly to young people. The younger converts, many of whom were teenagers from the Sunday school, were given a longer period of preparation before being admitted to church membership. In the year between the revival and Reed's visit in 1834, none of the converts were known to have gone back on their profession of faith.[25]

Memorable visits and lasting benefits

A number of American colleges were visited by Andrew Reed, including Princeton, where he saw the grave of Jonathan Edwards. At Amherst, he learned of a revival amongst the students in 1827, which had begun with a sermon by the president of the college and had seen half of those considered irreligious being converted. Reed attended the graduation ceremonies at Amherst and at Andover College, where the spirit of devotion impressed him. On their visit to Yale on the 8th September, Reed and James Matheson had the degrees of Doctor of Divinity conferred on them in recognition of their efforts to promote unity and fellowship between the churches.[26] Reed had also been given the honour of being elected an honorary member of the American Board of Commissioners for Foreign Missions in Boston.

As well as the moving visit to Northampton, Massachusetts, Reed also went to Newbury Port, where George Whitefield had preached his last sermon just before his death. In England Reed had preached from pulpits in which Whitefield himself had stood, seen his books and sat on his chairs, but none of this was to prepare him for just how close to Whitefield he was to find himself in America. His party was led down into the vault in which Whitefield was buried, where stood three coffins, that of Whitefield in the middle. His host, as was the custom of the time, then slid back the lid and there before his eyes was the skeleton of George Whitefield himself, Reed's great hero of his youth. He had hardly recovered from his surprise at this sight when his host leant into the coffin, lifted out Whitefield's skull, and handed it to Andrew Reed as the honoured guest! With characteristic understatement Reed recorded his shock: 'I could say nothing; but thought and feeling were busy!' He later expressed his hope that, in the future, more care would be taken with these precious exhibits.[27]

His time in New England also allowed opportunity to meet other leading figures in evangelicalism, including Dr Gardiner Spring and the controversial Dr Lyman Beecher. His benevolent interests were also not forgotten, and Reed attended a meeting held on behalf of the newly opened Female Orphan Asylum at Portland, Maine, where he was pressed to add a few words in support of the institution. In the midst of the 'little fatherless family' he was at once transported back to his work amongst the children of the London Orphan and Infant Orphan Asylums; here he felt at home more than almost anywhere else in America.

Building on his conviction, formulated in his charitable work in England, that amongst wealthy businessmen, industrialists and merchants, there was a huge store of benevolence that was waiting to be educated and mobilized, he took the opportunity to speak to a specially convened meeting in New York. He urged the merchants there assembled to apply their efforts to 'contribute to the higher interests of religion and virtue'.[28] His hope was that benevolent projects, such as he had inspired in London, would develop as fruits of the gospel in America.

A valedictory service was held in New York on the 30th September, at which the thanks of the Presbyterian Church in the United States and the Congregational churches of New England were expressed to Reed and Matheson. It was believed they had drawn like-minded churches on both sides of the Atlantic into closer fellowship through their visit.

Their return sailing took just seventeen days, and was accomplished in good weather. On their arrival they were amazed to find that the English coast had been devastated by three days of severe gales, which had wrecked nearly fifty sailing vessels, and left four ships stranded in the approach to Liverpool harbour, while the one on which they were travelling had been spared any such traumas. The success of the mission, the preservation from the closeness of cholera and from the Atlantic storm, Andrew Reed attributed to the 'fervent prayers of churches on both sides of the Atlantic'.[29]

As a result of the visit, Reed was convinced of the strength of the ties that united Britain and America — ties of language, literature, religion, even great similarities in their political systems (he believed the presidency was like an elected and limited monarchy). Common blood and common origin united the nations. He optimistically believed that closer links between the religious communities in both countries would make warfare between America and Britain impossible, and that if they were at peace, then peace throughout the world might follow.[30] In 1835 Reed was able to welcome American delegates on a return visit to the churches of Britain, a token that his hopes for fraternal union were being fulfilled.

Reed himself was personally deepened and matured by the experience of his visit to America, more hardened to physical adversity, more self-reliant and perhaps less prone to depressive moments. His world vision was broadened, and he was now prepared to travel anywhere in the world to serve as a missionary, if so called. He was approaching the zenith of his ministry, but, as before, his desire remained above all to be able to be useful for God. This hope was to be remarkably fulfilled in Wycliffe Chapel a few years after his voyage across the Atlantic.

10.
A house by the forest

'To do what we had to do, seemed impossible; but we all felt that it was for the orphans, and God succours such as succour them'

(Andrew Reed).

10.
A house by the forest

Less than a fortnight after Andrew Reed's departure on his trip to the churches of America, tragedy struck the Infant Orphan Asylum. While his ship was being battered by storms in the middle of the Atlantic, measles swept through the children's cramped accommodation in Hackney Road. The medical officer desperately pointed to the 'extreme inadequacy' of the existing arrangements, and several members of the committee out of their own resources rented another house to bring some relief, but it was too late. Many children suffered distressingly, and tragically three of them died in the epidemic.[1] Action was unavoidable now; something had to be done about the inadequate living accommodation, or further tragedy would strike.

The move to Dalston

At the darkest hour hope appeared. A large mansion at Dalston, near Clapton, became available in 1834, owned by the Hankey family, who were well-known evangelical benefactors. Unable to consult Andrew Reed, the committee decided to act swiftly, and a lease was purchased for £2,750. It was a bold move, but the annual dinner the following April raised £1,335 towards the cost. Expansion continued apace and an extension costing £1,404 was decided on in the October of the following year after Reed's return.[2]

The move to Dalston was only temporary, but it provided some relief in the midst of serious difficulties. At last the charity was attaining the size and prominence for which Andrew Reed had hoped, and the children were being housed in more appropriate premises. Yet to him, as with all the charities he set up, the children and those who cared for them were not nameless members of an institution. He always referred to them as 'the family'.

The cause of the infants, and children in the London Orphan and Infant Orphan Asylums, had never been forgotten by Andrew Reed on his visit to America. Deep in that land, far from home and feeling ill, with cholera spreading rapidly around, death seemed a very real and present danger. He wrote in his pocket book, 'Thousands of miles from home, missed by the orphans. My God, be near to them and to me!'[3] When he returned, the orphans were quick to greet him by his new title, Dr Reed.

The search for a site for a new building was not abandoned after the move of the children to Dalston House, which it was soon realized could only be a temporary measure. In 1837 the Infant Orphan Asylum had 103 children under its care, with a further eighty seeking admission. Many of the parents of the children were themselves in poor health, and their orphan children were highly susceptible to illness. The problem of the rapid spread of infectious diseases was not fully solved by relocation to Dalston — that year saw fifty-seven cases of whooping cough, eighteen of measles and six of scarlet fever. Sadly, during the year five children had died. Reed's hope was to build up accommodation to provide places for 300 children, with fifteen nurses and twelve domestic servants. This could never be accomplished at Dalston, even with extensions. He therefore boldly proposed that twenty of the leading supporters of the charity should pledge to lay £100 on the foundation stone of a new building, and 100 ladies £5. If this were done he confidently asserted that building work would commence at the end of 1841.[4] It was a prediction which was to prove remarkably true.

The site at Snaresbrook

When faced with a specific project or urgent need, Andrew Reed was always prepared to make available prodigious amounts of time to seeing its successful completion. In May 1840, a building committee was formed, with Reed in a leading position. A range of sites were considered, from North London to Surrey, but the one that particularly attracted him was one of ten acres at Snaresbrook, well situated on the edge of Wanstead Forest, six and a half miles from the centre of London. Whereas land at Streatham was selling for £600 per acre, this was available for £100 per acre.

Deeply concerned at the problem of illness amongst the children, Reed carefully canvassed medical opinion, which declared that the rural setting was highly salubrious and was ideal for the needs of little children. Some complained that the distance from London was too great, but he responded with a characteristic mixture of perception and careful research. He foresaw that London would soon spread into the Lea Bridge area, and he had reason to believe that there would be a railway station at Forest Gate.[5] He had also not forgotten the promise of Crown assistance in purchasing a site in the future, and this part of Wanstead Forest was Crown land.

Prince Albert lays the foundation stone

The purchase of the land was secured in May 1841, and on the 10th June the first turf was cut by Andrew Reed himself. He then found himself summoned to a meeting with Queen Victoria and Prince Albert at Windsor Castle, during which the prince offered to lay the foundation stone on the 27th

Prince Albert

June. The committee put in train plans for this prestigious event, which was widely publicized, and looked forward to with great expectancy.

And then, with only a matter of days to go before the ceremony, their plans suddenly began to fall apart and the charity faced great embarrassment. At a late stage in the negotiations it was discovered that Crown rights extended only to parcels of land of no more than five acres, and the chosen site was of ten acres. Speedy negotiations ensued to get round this problem, which had only just been resolved when the charity was presented with a protest from some local residents about the loss of their historic rights relating to the forest as a consequence of the sale of the land. Reed once again rushed to visit Windsor Castle to deal with this matter, and then obtained a reversed legal opinion from a law lord before the matter was resolved.

Barely had Reed recovered from dealing with these unforeseen crises, when a message arrived from Prince Albert indicating that he was suddenly required to perform another official function with Queen Victoria on the 27th June, and the only available alternative date was three days earlier — the 24th June. The timetable was rushed forward to have everything ready for that day instead. By an enormous effort of will, and with great persistence, skill and diplomacy, Reed negotiated his way round this series of problems, as he recorded in his journal: 'Never more heavy work... To do what we had to do, seemed impossible; but we all felt that it was for the orphans, and God succours such as succour them.'[6]

The day turned out perfectly. Although the period of notice given was short, thousands attended the stone-laying ceremony. The prince's cavalcade arrived on time in beautiful weather and, as the carriage drew to a halt, the orphan children sang a song composed by Andrew Reed especially for the occasion: 'Hail to the Prince whose noble hand erects the orphan's home.' Those standing nearby could not help noticing the tears in the prince's eyes as the little children sang, and Andrew Reed was glad to see the human touch in the consort of Queen Victoria.

The stone was tapped into place with a mallet carved from oak from the Royal Exchange, with an inscription to the prince. At the end of the service he returned it saying, 'This, Dr Reed, by all right, belongs to you, and I beg you to accept of it.' That evening Andrew Reed laid it on his desk at home, and wrote in his journal, 'Thank God, the deed is done: now for action.'

Three days later, at the inaugural banquet, attended by the happy and healthy children from the orphanage, it was announced that £7,000 had already been subscribed for the new building. Reed recorded his relief: 'Blessed be God, we shall now get a home for the homeless and helpless.' The sight of such a magnificent gathering in the interests of little orphan children left in many cases without a friend in the world moved him deeply. His prayer that night was that God would 'defend and provide for the fatherless children and widows, and all that be desolate and oppressed'.[7]

Plans for the building take shape

The choice of architects for the project was notable. Gilbert Scott was the principal architect, but much of the work was done by his associate William Moffatt. Scott was later to achieve fame for his work on St Pancras Station in London and the Albert

Memorial. Both Moffatt and Scott were up-and-coming architects who had been involved in designing a number of churches,
but were not household names at the time, and it was an act of
great foresight to award them the contract. They had, however,
both served apprenticeships in the office of the architect James
Edmeston, a personal friend of Andrew Reed who had been on
the first committee of the Infant Orphan Asylum. Edmeston
achieved lasting fame through composing a hymn which was
originally dedicated to the 'children of the London Orphan
Asylum', the sister charity of the Infant Orphan Asylum:

> Lead us, Heavenly Father, lead us,
> Oe'r the world's tempestuous sea;
> Guard us, guide us, keep us, feed us,
> For we have no help but Thee;
> Yet possessing every blessing,
> If our God our Father be.[8]

Andrew Reed, who was now experienced in the handling of
building projects after his involvement with those for the London Orphan Asylum and Wycliffe Chapel, took a strong hand in
shaping the plans for the new asylum. The work of Scott and
Moffatt was 'generally revised' by the building committee under
the direction of Reed.

Although the main construction was to be of brick, in a
mixture of Tudor and Stuart styles, it was decided to provide a
limestone facing. Andrew Reed led extensive investigations into
which stone material was most suitable, visiting quarries in
Whitby, Bath and Devon to inspect stone. Eventually it was
decided to face the walls with stone from the quarries of
Sneaton near Whitby, but to use a mixture of more expensive
Caen, Bath and Whitby stone for the windows, plinths and
cornices.

Reed, horrified by the ravages of infectious disease in the
previous buildings, was convinced of the virtue of plentiful
supplies of fresh air for the healthy development of little

The Infant Orphan Asylum, Wanstead

children. He insisted that the bedrooms and nurseries should be high and well ventilated — which created challenges for heating them in the winter. He inspected schoolrooms and dormitories in Edinburgh and Dublin, taking copious notes, and ensured that his ideas were incorporated in the plans. One wing was given over to schoolrooms, dining rooms and dormitories for the older children, and the other to nurseries and a chapel. There were also offices, laundry rooms and a kitchen. In the basement a steam engine pumped the water supply, and drove the washing and wringing machines.[9]

Frustrating times

The builder appointed to the contract for the Infant Orphan Asylum was William Jay, who had recently completed the Greenwich Workhouse. Doubts were expressed at the start of the project as to his firm's competence, but Jay promised to supervise all construction activities personally. The fears of the committee were soon realized, and Andrew Reed took to constantly visiting the site to inspect operations. On one occasion he had to intervene to stop the builder using a large quantity of poor-quality bricks, and several months later rejected a load of timber that was inferior. He was unhappy that walls under construction were not properly protected from the weather, with the result that they had been damaged by the frost and required reconstruction.

Concerns deepened as Reed found the clerk of works was often absent when he visited the site, and when in October 1842 work was almost at a standstill, the frustrations of the committee intensified. The children desperately needed more healthy accommodation than that at Dalston, and an opening date of 1843 had been projected.

The inevitable happened the following month when Jay's building company went bankrupt. He had badly miscalculated in his tender of £25,000 for the works. The orphanage was in fact to cost £30,000. To the consternation of the asylum's building committee, Jay's unpaid creditors began to move onto the site to claim building materials in payment of debts he had not met. The orphanage had to go to court to get the materials returned.[10]

In desperation the committee turned to another builder, but a further £5,000 had to be speedily raised in order to complete the work. The board took out a loan for the amount, and Reed stood as guarantor for £1,000 of it. A charity dinner was quickly arranged and Andrew Reed badgered the elderly Duke of Wellington to preside. The duke pleaded that his days of public duty were over, and that he was too aged and infirm, but Reed would not be denied. The duke duly arrived, and did his best to introduce the different contributions, even though he fell asleep in his chair between the toasts and Reed had to gently waken him before the ceremonials could continue. None the less, the desired effect was achieved and a further £1,400 raised.[11]

The Infant Orphan Asylum was born out of Andrew Reed's deep Christian concern for little children who had suffered the trauma of the loss of one or both parents. In his busy pastoral and philanthropic life he had given prodigious amounts of time to the conception and running of the orphanage, to fund-raising for it and to the planning and construction of a suitable building. All was ready for the culmination of his investment of love and energy in the celebrations for the opening of the orphanage on the edge of Wanstead Forest — a fitting home for children whose lives might otherwise have been hopeless. And then something almost inconceivable happened. At the crowning moment, when the prestigious building was opened a few months later in 1843, the name of Andrew Reed was absent from the list of honoured guests. Indeed, he was not even present at the ceremony.

11.
Politics

'We go about the world with a label on our backs, on which nothing more is written than the word "Fool"'

(Edward Miall, speaking on behalf of nineteenth-century Nonconformists).

11.
Politics

In an age of religious tolerance and diversity it is hard to understand the breadth and openness a Nonconformist like Andrew Reed had shown in being willing to work together with Anglicans, and those of other religious denominations, in his charitable ventures. At the time, to be a Dissenter was to hold the position of a second-class citizen in England. Although willing to work co-operatively with a higher philanthropic purpose in mind, he could not avoid the reality of the religious and civil discrimination of his day, the price of which he had already paid in declining the offer of studying at Cambridge University.

Reed's attitude to politics

Politics was by no means a dominant concern in the ministry of Andrew Reed and, compared with many other ministers of his time, his political engagement was limited. However, as a Nonconformist minister charged with the pastoral care of people who, like himself, faced much discrimination for their religious views, there were matters of public policy upon which he felt he had no alternative but to comment. His philanthropic ventures brought him into contact with many leading politicians, and close personal acquaintance with some of them gave him an inside knowledge of political operations and issues.

At his ordination, on the threshold of his public ministry, Reed was advised by George Collison, his tutor at Hackney College, to avoid 'mingling *worldly politics*' with religious instruction, on the grounds that it would 'pollute your own mind; it will introduce a worldly spirit into your ministry, and make you much more like a political demagogue than a wise, prudent, and holy minister of the gospel'.[1] He was well aware that any appearance of overt political involvement could prejudice both his church and philanthropic work, and he sought to ensure that the primary focus of his ministry remained spiritual. However, there were times when the pressures of the political situation in which Nonconformists sought to win their rights created great tensions for Andrew Reed.

The royal family

He was a strong supporter of the royal family, and this was to prove of great assistance in his philanthropic work, as they became willing to offer their patronage to the charities he founded.

When the much-loved Princess Charlotte, the only child of the Prince Regent, died suddenly in 1817, the nation was thrown into mourning. Andrew Reed preached a sermon on the occasion, later to be published, containing expressions of 'respectful condolence' on the loss of 'the hope of our nation, the heiress of our throne'. He described her as 'a flower … of unusual promise', and he applauded her deep concern for the welfare of the poor.[2]

The nation was again plunged into mourning in 1820 with the death of the Duke of Kent, who had been a strong supporter of Reed's charities, followed six days later by that of King George III, ending his remarkable sixty-year reign. Once more the occasion was marked by a sermon from Andrew Reed, which was also published. He offered it as a public tribute from the Dissenters to the memory of a king who, it was believed, had done much to support their rights. The king's gifts to those in distress and his royal proclamation to promote religion and suppress vice were remembered by Reed, who had met the king and on one occasion had attended the private morning devotions conducted for him. He took the opportunity to reassert the national allegiance of unjustly suspected Dissenters, so long as the state required nothing 'inconsistent with freedom and religion'.

The nation passed into a more uncertain religious and moral climate with the accession of the former Prince Regent to the throne as George IV. Somewhat notorious for his earlier flamboyant and colourful lifestyle, Reed ventured the hope that as king he would prove a 'real and eminent Christian'.[3]

Discrimination against Dissenters

It was the real discrimination against Nonconformists in the country that exercised Reed the most in the political sphere. In 1811, in what was seen as a repressive measure against them, Lord Sidmouth attempted to restrict the activity of itinerant preachers, demanding that they be required to obtain an official licence for their work. Extensively used during the Evangelical Revival of the eighteenth century by John and Charles Wesley, George Whitefield and a host of other ordained and lay preachers, itinerant preaching had been a key method of promoting the gospel.

Matthew Wilks, with his roots firmly in the Evangelical Revival, took a leading role in the protest against the proposed measure, and his active involvement in the campaign encouraged his young protégé Andrew Reed to add his own voice to the protests of Dissenters. Through this firm but vociferous campaign, which led to hundreds of petitions against the bill being sent to Parliament, and through the pressure of evangelical Anglicans in Parliament, many of whom had found great

spiritual blessing through the Evangelical Revival, the measure
was dropped.

Reed also supported the campaign that led to the repeal of
the Test and Corporation Acts in 1828, finally allowing Dissenters to stand for local and national government, to vote in
elections and to hold office in areas of national life previously
denied to them.[4] These were the beginnings of change that had
to come, and did come, but only slowly through the nineteenth
century. Ground was only given very grudgingly, and Nonconformists were viewed by many in the Establishment as second-
class citizens, and they knew it only too well. As the campaigner Edward Miall wrote, 'We go about the world with a
label on our backs, on which nothing more is written than the
word "Fool".'[5]

In 1833 Andrew Reed made his most significant contribution
to the growing demands to end the remaining legal discrimin-
ations faced by Nonconformists when he wrote *The Case of the
Dissenters*. Initially published anonymously so that it was not
connected with any name or party, it took the form of a letter to
the Lord Chancellor, Lord Brougham. The 'deep practical
grievance' of the Dissenters led to rightful demands, which were
set out firmly but moderately, in the following terms:

> *Equality of citizens.* They do not ask to be placed above
> the Churchman; they cannot submit to be placed beneath
> him. They claim, that no man shall be the worse, either in
> *purse, reputation, or privilege*, on the account of his reli-
> gious opinions... WITH THIS ALONE CAN THEY BE
> SATISFIED.

Reed stressed that he held no antipathy towards Anglicans,
but he argued that the existence of the Church of England as an
established church led to Dissenters being treated with 'scorn,
contumely and hate'. With its strong hierarchy, by its very
nature the Anglican Church had a natural and necessary
antipathy to democratic principles: 'To be consistent, the

Churchman *must* be, in the strictest sense of the term, a Tory, as the Dissenter *must* be a Whig.' Religious dissent was tolerated, but that was not the same as equality or even freedom — toleration of religious activity meant that permission was required to undertake some activities, and such permission could be withheld. Dissenters constantly lived under the shadow of having their religious liberty denied. Reed therefore stressed that the decision to raise the issue was not a political act, but was rather a religious one. In speaking out on a matter that involved basic human freedoms, he issued a call for 'the emancipation of religion, of whatever form, from the corruption of state influence and worldly patronage'.[6]

The Times called the pamphlet 'a temperate, but decided and unflinching work', and the *Evangelical Magazine* declared, 'In the present age no wiser defence of the Dissenters has made its appearance.'[7] Other reviews were mixed, and a flurry of responses from some notable quarters were published, which gave Reed an element of notoriety as a Dissenter.[8]

This conscientious stand as a Nonconformist was rooted in clear theological convictions, particularly his understanding of what the Bible taught about the church. Reed was convinced that any union between church and state was inimical to the kingdom of God, which was 'not of this world'; Anglican rites and clerical distinctions were opposed to the 'simplicity' of the gospel, and the denial to congregations of the right to choose their own ministers was a 'gross violation of the rights of conscience'.[9]

Although firm in his convictions, Reed drew back from the vehement tone of others. Three years after the publication of *The Case of the Dissenters*, Thomas Binney, the distinguished minister of the Congregational King's Weigh House Chapel in London, went so far as to declare that the Church of England 'is a great national evil; that it is an obstacle to the progress of truth and godliness in the land; that it destroys more souls than it saves, and that therefore its end is devoutly to be wished by every lover of God and Man'.[10] For all his reservations about

Anglicanism, Reed would not have uttered such sentiments, and was still prepared to work in ventures of Christian compassion with Anglicans who maintained the essentials of the gospel. However, the outbursts of Binney and others made such co-operation increasingly difficult. At least one Anglican clergyman was rebuked by the Bishop of London, Charles Blomfield, for working with Dissenters in Reed's charities.[11]

A further aspect of the legal discrimination against Nonconformists was the requirement that they pay rates to support the upkeep of the local Anglican parish church, even if they never attended it and gave generously to support their own church. There was a growing sense of outrage against this anomaly, especially when some Anglican vicars took Nonconformists to court for refusing to pay the rate. In 1836 Reed joined with others in speaking out on the issue, and called for Parliament to be petitioned on the matter. The campaign culminated in petitions containing a million names being delivered to Parliament, and the House of Commons voted in favour of the abolition of the church rates by a small majority. However it was not until 1868, six years after Andrew Reed's death, that the compulsory church rate was abolished.[12]

The campaign to abolish slavery

Another issue of moral and religious significance upon which Reed spoke out was that of slavery. To Andrew Reed, the ownership by one human being of another human being as a slave was utterly abhorrent. Through his charitable work he came to know leaders of the campaign to abolish slavery, such as Thomas Clarkson, William Wilberforce and Thomas Fowell Buxton. The owning of slaves in Britain had been made illegal in 1787, and the slave trade in British ships abolished in 1807. A major campaign was waged to end the ownership of slaves in the British dominions in the early 1830s. When in 1833 Parliament finally voted to emancipate the slaves, Reed called it 'the highest moral act our country ever performed'.[13] Sadly, in other parts of the world slavery continued to exist. Reed had observed the continuing practice of slave-holding on his trip to America in 1834, and he had come to the decided opinion that it was 'the vilest despotism' and the 'deepest oppression'. He was shocked that in the land of liberty such a cruel system should be allowed to prevail; one was bound to destroy the other, as he argued: 'Slavery and liberty cannot exist together; either slavery must die, or liberty must die.' He believed slavery to be utterly dehumanizing: the system practised in America was 'accursed, and only accursed... If it finds man benevolent it makes him cruel ... it is ordained, *that he who deals in man, shall become less than man.*'[14]

Education

In many ways the political concerns and involvement of Andrew Reed were fairly limited and uncontroversial, being typical of many Nonconformist ministers of the time and largely confined to matters with significant religious implications. However, it was in his concern over developments in the field of education, a central part of his work with the orphanages and a matter with strong religious implications, that he suddenly found the tensions of being a tolerated Dissenter working with Anglicans coming into full focus. Reed's recurring fear was that the Church of England, as the Established Church, would use its influence and privileges to dominate any government proposals in the field of education.

While he was a supporter of the appeal for free education for the poorest in the land, his fear of Anglican domination led to his opposition to schemes proposed in 1816 and 1820 for education under the control of a state department, and also to the plan for the appointment of a Committee of the Privy Council on Education in 1839. And it was over the proper education of the children in the orphanages for whom he cared so much that a storm was to break. These concerns reached a head with the announcement in 1843 of Sir James Graham's Factories Bill, which included significant proposals relating to education.

12.
Educational matters

'We want schools for all,
without offending the
consciences of any.
We ... will not trust the
interests of religion with
any particular
denomination...'

(Andrew Reed).

12.
Educational matters

In the mind of Andrew Reed, the educational and the religious needs of children were crucially linked together. The orphanages he established sought to provide care and education that would not just involve shelter through childhood years, but would prepare children for life. A vital part of such preparation was that they should learn about the Christian faith. Teaching the skills of literacy gave children the ability to read the Bible and have opportunities to explore the Christian faith. This concern for the spiritual and educational needs of children also featured high in the regular work of Reed's church, not only on a Sunday, but throughout the week.

Sunday schools

In the light of Reed's early experience as a Sunday school teacher, it was perhaps inevitable that this work would feature strongly in his ministry in the East End of London.

In the early nineteenth century Sunday schools were not aimed at the children of those who already attended church, but at those who had little or no connection with organized Christianity. They offered training in basic literacy on a Sunday for children who were unable to attend school during the week. Although from the early days there had been some religious component, as the century wore on, the emphasis on teaching about the Christian faith became stronger. Sunday schools were very popular with working-class children and their parents, and by the second half of the nineteenth century most children in British cities had attended Sunday school at some point in their lives. They were to prove the most likely point of contact churches had with those who did not attend their regular services. Until 1870, when the government introduced provisions for state education, Sunday schools were the only source of education for many poor children. They were a vital measure for the time, combining social and educational support with the hope that the children would learn about the Christian faith, and come to embrace it.

Robert Raikes was the person mainly responsible for popularizing Sunday school work, after he began his school in Gloucester in 1780. Just ten years later, a Sunday school was started in connection with the New Road Chapel, and this work was greatly expanded after Reed became minister in 1811. One of his earliest decisions was to establish a day school for the benefit of children from both the church and the neighbourhood, to extend the educational and religious teaching throughout the week.[1] Reed was highly optimistic about the Sunday school as an agency of evangelism, and he also believed that by teaching Christian standards of behaviour these schools would be a 'great preventative of moral deterioration in our land'.[2] Throughout the fifty years of Andrew Reed's ministry in Stepney, hundreds of children passed through the Sunday schools, where they were encouraged to 'look to Jesus as the only Saviour for sinners'.[3]

The New Road Sunday School was separated into boys', girls' and infants' sections. In 1829 the 180 children attending the Sunday school were being taught by a total of twenty-two teachers, but such was the rate of growth in the work that in 1833 a new building was required to accommodate the extra numbers.

Another Sunday school was also run in a very poor area of Bethnal Green by one of the deacons of the Wycliffe Chapel, with the assistance of twenty teachers from the church. This popular provision, which was soon attracting 400 children, was begun as the first step towards planting a new church in the area, particularly for the local people.[4]

The work of the Sunday school at Wycliffe Chapel became a family affair for the Reeds. Andrew was president of the boys' and girls' schools, and his wife Elizabeth ran a Bible Class attended by between seventy and eighty young ladies, many of whom subsequently joined the church. Between 1844 and 1846, his son Charles (who was later to become a leading national figure in the Sunday School Union) was Sunday school superintendent,[5] and Andrew Reed's daughter ran the infants' department.

As the congregation of Wycliffe Chapel increased rapidly in size during Reed's ministry, so too did attendance at the main Sunday school. It became a very important aspect of the work of the church. The 180 children of 1829 had become 450 in 1839. This numerical growth continued, with an attendance of 665 children in 1859. Caring for such numbers required high levels of resources, particularly of staff — in 1861 there were forty-three teachers.[6] The girls' was the largest of the departments in the school: in 1850 there were twenty classes, with 188 on the roll, and this had increased to 368 by December 1860, with twenty-eight teachers.[7]

Having started a day school connected to the chapel, Andrew Reed hoped that the Sunday school would be able to focus especially on religious teaching, but over time it was found that many of the poorest children who attended could not read, and special attention had to be given to their basic educational needs. The great investment of time and resources in the children of the Sunday school was rewarded with a steady stream of children making professions of faith and becoming church members. Of thirty-five teenagers in the Bible Class in 1853, twenty had become church members.[8] Reed saw that the children in their teenage years were at a vital developmental stage, making decisions that would affect the future course of their lives. He stressed the importance of making direct, personal appeals to the older and more attentive in the classes about the need to embrace the Christian faith. He also made himself readily available to meet with any who were spiritually concerned.[9]

The work of the Sunday school was not confined to helping children. An 'elementary class' for young people and older adults who were also unable to read was formed in 1854 and was held during weekday evenings. Although many who attended were adults, it was noted that, sadly, most were 'deplorably ignorant of religious truths'. None the less, they were keen to learn and possessed an 'evident disposition to receive instruction'.

The adult class was supplemented in 1857 with a weeknight class to teach reading and writing to children too young to attend the adult night school, and who could not afford to pay even a few pennies a week to attend the day schools.[10]

Through its Sunday school work Wycliffe Chapel was reaching some of the most needy children and adults in the East End of London. Lack of education was a chronic social need, which Reed's church was able to help meet. Although it took great investment of time and resources, his faithful workers saw clear educational and spiritual success in their work.

Day schools

Like many other evangelicals, Andrew Reed was willing to invest much practical energy in schemes for the weekday education of children. The responsibility for such schemes lay largely with churches, charities and private schools until the Education Act of 1870 allowed for the provision of schools run by elected local School Boards and funded by the levying of a local rate.

The day schools started by Reed soon after his ordination at the New Road Chapel were for both boys and girls. The venture

was in part intended to relieve the Sunday school of the pressure of teaching basic literacy and to allow its teachers to
concentrate on Scripture teaching. The schools proved a
success, and by 1839 the boys' day school had 280 on its roll,
the girls' day school was attended by 130 girls and the 'infant
school' had 120 pupils. Aimed at the children of the poor, these
schools provided a basic education, with a significant moral and
spiritual component. Although they were subsidized by subscriptions and collections from church members, attendance
was not entirely free — the children paid a modest fee of a few
pence each week.[11]

The impact the church had in offering children the chance of
education that would not otherwise be available was considerable. In total the day and Sunday schools at Stepney supported
some 1,100 children — 1,500 if the schools in Bethnal Green
were included.

A grammar school for Hackney

Where possible, Andrew Reed sought to co-operate with like-
minded evangelicals in other denominations, and this extended
to the educational field. One example was his decision in 1828
to put together a scheme to start a grammar school for the
district of Hackney in which he lived. This was run as a charity,
charging modest fees and providing education of a standard up
to a level where children could enter university. Religious
education was to be central to the project. Each day began with
prayer, Bible reading and a short exposition of Scripture, but a
firm principle was that religious instruction was to show no
denominational bias, to ensure that parents were not required
to surrender their children 'to the influence of doctrines they
disapprove of'. Discipline was to be firm, but in the initial years
Reed argued that the cane should not be used as a method of
punishment. It was later introduced against his wishes.[12]

The project won the support of many local evangelical Anglicans and Nonconformists, including the Hankey and Hanbury families. However, the staunch High Church Anglican rector of South Hackney, H. H. Norris, did all he could to oppose the scheme. He was indignant that any from the Church of England should operate with Nonconformists in this way, and he maliciously suggested that it was a non-religious school. When his opposition failed, he proceeded to establish a rival Church of England School.

None the less, the grammar school opened in 1829, with a strong curriculum and high-quality staff: two classics masters, from the universities of Oxford and Cambridge, were appointed. Demand for places was high, and Andrew Reed's son Charles attended the school.

With the grammar school established and prospering, and with other urgently pressing projects in his church and charities, Reed passed on responsibility for the school to others. Sadly, without a leader of Reed's skills to hold the project together, division amongst the supporters of the school crept in and it closed in 1844.[13]

Education as a political issue

In mid-nineteenth-century Britain, education was hotly debated in the political realm. The issue had strong religious implications, and Reed followed developments closely. He supported free education for the poorest of children, and his own church ran a ragged school in John's Place, Bedford Square, with their needs in mind. This was one of the most deprived areas in the neighbourhood, and services on Sunday evening were held at the ragged school, with a Sunday school in the afternoon and free instruction for children on weekdays. So many attended that there was often not enough room to accommodate all who sought to gain admission.[14]

A ragged school

Reproduced by courtesy of Professor Donald Lewis

Despite his concern over the inability of the poorest of children to attend day schools, Reed believed it was right to resist schemes to bring education under state control, and he used friends and contacts made through his church and charitable work to express his concerns.[15] He was convinced that the churches should wake up to their duty to provide effective education for all children, with a strong moral and religious component. When in 1843 Sir James Graham's Factory Bill, which included educational clauses, was announced, Reed feared that the government was about to intervene in education in a way that would prove immensely harmful to Nonconformists. The educational provision proposed by the bill was to be dominated by Anglicans, and this reinforced Reed's convictions that Nonconformists were again being discriminated against. These concerns drew him into a prominent role in the politics of education.

The influence of Edward Baines, Junior, on his thinking was significant. The connections with the Baines family were to strengthen with the marriage of Reed's son Charles to Edward Baines' daughter Margaret in 1844. From his position as editor of the family-owned *Leeds Mercury*, Baines launched a stinging attack on the bill, which he believed threatened the religious liberties of Nonconformists by placing the education of their children in the hands of Anglicans. Baines urged that the political power of the Dissenters be mobilized to resist the measure: 'I conceive that no friend of Religious Liberty could hereafter vote for a Member who had supported such an outrage on Religious Liberty and Religious Truth.'[16]

Reed had always been very careful to ensure that his political activities did not in any way harm the charities, and generally confined his political interventions to moderate protests against the lack of civil liberties enjoyed by Nonconformists. However, on this occasion he took a more public stance. He invited local ministers to a meeting at Wycliffe Chapel, where a committee to oppose the measure was formed. His efforts in the cause were characteristically impressive, emphasizing the urgency of the matter and urging co-operation as far as possible. The fact that bodies ranging from the Wesleyan Methodists to the Quakers supported the campaign is a tribute to his success. He hurried back and forth across London in a cab for three days rallying support, and securing delegates from seventeen religious and educational bodies to serve on a 'united committee' formed to oppose the government plan.[17] Reed chaired the London committee, with his son as secretary, and he toured the country speaking at protest meetings.

Reed did not regard the movement as a political campaign, but as a fight for religious rights and liberties. Although it went against his instincts, action was a matter of 'unquestionable duty' and pressingly urgent: 'We must pause no more.' He declared: 'We have no pleasure in agitation; we must now show that we are not averse to it, when the negligence of Government to our prayer, and the vital interests at stake, make it an unquestionable duty.' In more measured tones than Edward Baines, he distanced himself from any ideas that this was a purely political campaign — he expected little support from political parties or the national daily press. This was instead a movement of concerned individuals earnestly and respectfully pressing their case: 'Every one of us must act as if the fate of the Bill depended solely on himself.' He feared that, just as there was an Anglican state religion, if the 1843 proposals succeeded there would be Anglican state education. In this instance, the battle for religious freedom must be fought voluntarily, on principle, by religious men, from religious motives. In this campaign for religious liberties, a high spiritual tone was to be preserved: the influence of the victory would be greater 'in proportion to it being the result of a deep, calm, and earnest determination to preserve our religious liberties inviolate'.[18]

The resources of Wycliffe Chapel were mobilized in the cause. The teachers of the Sunday school drew up a petition opposing the education clauses, and a meeting of the parents of Sunday school children was called to share information about the campaign, and to encourage their support. 1,000 copies of a pamphlet written by Edward Baines were distributed.[19] In public speeches and in the press Baines and others maintained a fervent campaign; as it gathered momentum he wrote an open letter to his father-in-law Andrew Reed, as chairman of the London Committee, in which he went so far as to call the bill the 'most insidious and most deadly blow ever aimed at Religious Liberty since the accession of the House of Hanover'.[20]

Nonconformists placed much hope in Lord John Russell to intervene on their side in the matter. He was at the time leader of the opposition Whig party, and was to become prime minister three years later, in 1846. When Russell's own 'Resolutions' were produced, Reed found them totally unsatisfactory. This matter was an issue of freedom of religious conscience, and he believed that the provisions Russell set out still gave too much influence over the hearts and minds of Nonconformist children to the Church of England.

When Russell presided at a crowded meeting of the British and Foreign School Society in the Exeter Hall, London, Reed, who was one of the speakers, dramatically called on him to help the Nonconformists on the issue. He denounced the imposition of Anglican forms of worship on children as being 'tyrannical and degrading in the extreme'. Sir James Graham's bill, he believed, was one of many injustices Nonconformists had to face as a consequence of their religious opinions, adding his view that 'We will not trust the interests of religion with any denomination.' He implored Russell, as being himself a father, not to let the government dictate to him how he should bring up his children, declaring: 'Sooner than submit to it I would die.' Building to his conclusion, Reed denounced the bill as 'unequal, unjust, and therefore iniquitous'. It was, he claimed, contrary to the principles of British justice:

> We ask your Lordship to say, that we want schools for all, without offending the consciences of any. We want your Lordship to say, in reference to religion ... that we will not trust the interests of religion with any particular

denomination... We ask, in short, that we shall be free: in
labour, free; in trade, free; in action, free; in thought, free;
in speech, free; in religion, free — perfectly free.

As he sat down, Reed's speech was greeted with rapturous
applause from the large audience.[21]

Christians and church bodies deluged the government with
over 13,000 petitions containing just under two million signa-
tures. Faced with the weight of such opposition, the government
realized that they had no alternative but to withdraw the bill.

Reed rejoiced in the national victory he had helped to win,
but was not satisfied merely with success in blocking the measure. He now urged those who had opposed the bill to practise
what they preached, and do all in their power to 'promote an
education based upon sound and religious principles, free from
State help and Government control'. His own church contributed £500 to building Congregational schools, and he worked
to encourage the development of Homerton College as a
training institution for teachers.[22] Sadly, other churches were less
responsive, and the combined efforts of the Nonconformist
churches were not sufficient to tackle the rising tide of ignorance
through the nineteenth century, and only delayed the inevitable
introduction of state provisions for education until 1870.

State funding of education meant to Andrew Reed state
control of education, and the government dictating the form of
religious education that children should receive. He was
alarmed as to the potential consequences of this. He had great
admiration for the system he had witnessed in America in the
1830s, where local parents took the initiative in building a
school, and only when the project was well advanced did the
legislature offer assistance, allowing the local citizens to levy a
local tax, from which teachers could be supported. The American system had led to one in four of the population being in
education in New York State, as opposed to just one in twelve
in England. He attributed this success to local parental initiative,
and a lack of religious sectarianism in education. In America,

the absence of civil and class distinctions made schools accessible to all, whether rich or poor, which Reed applauded. So too
was the education of girls: 'Why should not our daughters,
equally with our sons, possess the advantages which these
institutions, when well conducted, so readily supply?' He
considered as iniquitous, however, the denial of education to
two million slaves in America.[23]

Education, to Andrew Reed, was part of the wider mission of
the churches. By dealing with the social disadvantage that was
produced by ignorance, and by taking opportunities to shape
minds that would be receptive to the Christian faith, vital
preparatory work for the spread of the Christian message was
being done. The victory in 1843 over a system designed to
favour the Anglican Church was a triumph of his anti-sectarian
views and helped in the struggle to secure recognition of the
religious rights of Nonconformists, by restricting some of the
forms of discrimination that helped create social inequalities.

However, his decision to step into the public arena as a
leading proponent of Nonconformist demands for fair and
equal treatment did not pass unnoticed by some Anglicans who
were supporters of the work in the Infant Orphan Asylum and
the London Orphan Asylum. For decades the charities had
flourished on the basis of happy co-operation between Anglicans and Dissenters, for the greater good of Christian compassion to the most vulnerable and defenceless children of all.
Reed had not joined the 1843 campaign with the intention of
creating a politically mobilized Dissent, and he drew back from
those who built on the protest to demand the disestablishment
of the Church of England. Sadly, his opponents could not see
such distinctions, and the decision to defend the religious rights
of Nonconformist parents was to be turned against Reed in his
work for orphans who had been bereaved of one or both
parents.

13.
Parting from friends

'The children's affections, like tendrils, have twined round my heart, only to be broken. I have visited them and their home twice a week, and now I must never cross the threshold. It is hard — very hard...'

(Andrew Reed).

13.
Parting from friends

When the London Orphan Asylum was started in 1813, Andrew Reed realized that the majority of the children that it would care for, and those who supported the charity, would come from Anglican backgrounds. Interdenominational ventures stood or fell on whether members of the Church of England would support them. Great success had been enjoyed by the British and Foreign Bible Society and the Religious Tract Society because they were able to involve Anglicans working alongside Dissenters. Considering his strong principles as a Nonconformist, Andrew Reed took the bold step to do all he could to accommodate the wishes of Anglican supporters. When it came to deciding what form the religious observance of the children should take, Reed magnanimously agreed that, so long as what was taught came from soundly scriptural principles, the Anglican Prayer Book should be used as a basis for the religious services. This policy appeared to work well, and became the unwritten understanding on which the Infant Orphan Asylum was founded.

This working agreement produced no difficulties until 1839, when a malicious rumour began to circulate that the charity was run by Unitarians, or even by atheists. Reed therefore proposed to the committee that the rules of the charity be amended with the addition of the clause that 'the education of the children be in accordance with the principles of the Church of England'.[1] This was agreed and seemed to resolve the matter.

The catechism for infants?

However, the issue resurfaced with the appointment of two secretaries to the board of the Infant Orphan Asylum. The Rev. Hunter Fell was appointed in 1839 and he was joined in 1842 by Rev. Thomas Stanton, another Anglican clergyman. New to the charity, they were both strong Anglicans and cared little for the previous consensual policy. Instead, they began to assert that the 1839 policy statement proved that the charity was Anglican in nature, blithely ignoring the fact that its founder and a key figure on the board was a Dissenter. They claimed the sole right, together with the Anglican chaplain, of choosing the books the children were to use in the orphanage. Previously Andrew Reed had been given an important say in this.

What the secretaries and board particularly insisted on was using the catechism of the Church of England with the little children, which they would have to learn by rote. When Reed realized what was happening, he immediately objected. Although he conceded that this had been allowed in the London Orphan Asylum, where the children were much older, it was inappropriate with very little children. This had been the uncontested policy of the asylum, allowing Anglicans and Dissenters to work harmoniously together for the previous sixteen years. Reed produced the opinions of Dr Rudge, the first honorary secretary of the charity, and the Bishop of London, whom he had consulted in 1827, who both agreed that the use of the catechism was inappropriate for infants.[2]

To Andrew Reed, teaching the children the Ten Commandments, the Lord's Prayer and the Creed and using the Anglican liturgy was sufficient. Alarmed at government proposals in the early 1840s to give the Anglican Church a controlling influence over religious education, Reed now saw the same thing happening in his charities, which would lead to orphans from Dissenting families having the catechism imposed on them. For older children there were other orphanages where Dissenting children could be sent, but none existed for infants.

Reed therefore sought to argue that the broader interpretation of the policy of 'according to the principles of the Church of England' was appropriate for little children until they reached the age of seven. After that age, if friends or supporters of the children conscientiously objected to the use of Anglican forms, there were alternative orphanages to which they could be moved. It was a step of considerable grace to admit this, especially as privately he was most unhappy that the catechism appeared to teach baptismal regeneration — a subject on which there was much disagreement within the Church of England, and a teaching which evangelicals especially rejected. Reed chose not to bring this issue into the public debate, but he wanted to avoid this contentious teaching being imposed on those without the ability to discern concerning such matters.[3]

The two new Anglican secretaries were utterly unmoved by these arguments. The ongoing superhuman endeavours of Reed to raise money for the charity and see their magnificent new building through to completion counted for little with them in their zeal for ensuring that the correct forms of liturgy were used. They insisted to the committee that this was the only way to educate the infants and guarantee the support of Anglican donors. Perhaps having little understanding of the foundational role of Reed in the charity, a majority were won round to their views. Rebuffed by his co-workers of so many years, Reed was heartbroken. His well-tried policy was set aside in the heat of the wider religious controversies of 1843.

A painful farewell

Reed spent a night in prayer seeking God's direction as to how he should respond. He could have fought his case, proved his point as to the original policy and sought to oust his opponents, yet his prayerful conclusion was that nothing should be done to endanger the support and happiness of the children. To fight on would create division and disruption just when the charity needed stability and continuity as the building project was completed.

On the 23rd February he travelled with one of his sons to the site of the new building at Wanstead, and climbed to the highest point of the scaffolding, from where he cast his eye over the nearly finished building. He stood quietly for a while, taking in the scene, and his son was surprised to see tears running down his father's cheeks, a very rare occurrence in public. The boy, not knowing the struggles going on in his father's heart, anxiously enquired whether he was unwell. His father looked down and smiled: 'No, it is only the pain of parting. The work is nearly done: I had hoped to see it finished; but that is not to be. I am looking upon it for the last time. This is my farewell visit.' As he climbed down from the scaffolding he plucked a flower from the garden he had helped to plant, which he carefully pressed and preserved.

Turning his back on sixteen years of devoted labour, he took up his pen and wrote a letter to the committee resigning from the charity. The letter was peaceable and gracious: 'Bitter as it will be to me, I will still think with pleasure on the happy hours we have spent together in the service of the charity ... though for a time I must feel as one who is bereaved of his children, my prayer will be, that the charity may be a national refuge, age after age, to the fatherless and motherless in their affliction.'[4]

Little understanding how important the issue was to a Nonconformist like Reed, who deeply felt the inequalities of the day, the committee reacted to his decision with surprise and shock. They feared how harmful adverse publicity would prove at this crucial stage of the charity's existence. They anxiously urged him to reconsider his decision, but then tactlessly only passed on their message through one of the sub-secretaries, rather than by a senior figure on the committee. A compromise was hastily suggested, that the new educational policy only be introduced after the move to the new premises at Wanstead, but Reed was now fixed on the course he should take. He

agreed to remain a trustee of the monies invested, but he took
no further public role in the work of the charity. The board
reluctantly accepted his decision, and sent a cordial letter
acknowledging 'his unwearied labours in the cause of this
charity from the period of its formation'.[5]

It was a devastating blow to Andrew Reed, as he wrote in his
journal: 'The children's affections, like tendrils, have twined
round my heart, only to be broken. I have visited them and
their home twice a week, and now I must never cross the
threshold. It is hard — very hard; but not too hard, if I have His
help to bear it.' For the sake of his religious convictions, he
knew it was a cost he had to pay. Some uttered recriminations,
arguing that the breach was his fault because he had made too
many concessions at the start. His reply was that, like the true
mother in the story of Solomon's wisdom, he could not bear
seeing the child he loved divided.[6]

The new building of the Infant Orphan Asylum was officially
opened on 27 June 1843 by the King of the Belgians. As dawn
broke that day Andrew Reed was out of his house and heading
for Wanstead. Before any others reached the scene, he took a
last look at the completed building and then walked deep into
the forest to spend the day alone with God.

The next day he received a message from a surprising
quarter. It was one of sympathy and understanding from Prince
Albert, who had read the reports in the paper of the opening of
the orphanage, and had noted that the founder of the institution
was conspicuous by his absence. Messages of sympathy and
support followed, many of them from those the charity had
done most to help, widows and orphaned children. Some were
almost too moving for Reed to bear: 'Alas for me! Kindness and
unkindness alike break my heart!' Poignantly in his notebook he
recorded the inscription designed for above the main doorway
of the asylum: 'A Structure of Hope, Built on the Foundation of
Faith, By the Hand of Charity.'[7]

Parting from the London Orphan Asylum

With a heavy heart, Andrew Reed pondered the implications of his decision with respect to his other charitable work. He realized that to be consistent he needed to resign from the London Orphan Asylum, which was also using the Anglican liturgy. Although there had been no opposition to him and his broad-minded policy such as he had encountered at the Infant Orphan Asylum, Reed was increasingly committed to the non-sectarian approach, and felt growing discomfort at the Anglican dominance of the London Orphan Asylum.

When in 1844 the committee sought to obtain an Act of Incorporation for the charity, Reed took the opportunity to tender his resignation so as not to have to oppose the measure publicly. The act formalized the requirement to train the children according to the 'formularies of the Church of England' and, with an Anglican chaplain who was also the headmaster, the orphanage was to be clearly tied to the Church of England.

The London Orphan Asylum committee did all it could to maintain his support. Friends visited Reed to urge him to reconsider, and the separation when it came was amicable, but none the less sad. Reed was parting from a charity for which he had worked for thirty years, and from friends with whom he had worked for much of that time. He recorded in his journal: 'There goes, then, another tie of life, and life itself quivers under the separation. I could hardly believe it: and the Thursday especially, which I had so long given to Clapton, seemed struck out of the week now that my occupation was gone. I must not only do the work of charity, but get the spirit of charity; and this is mostly derived through suffering.'[8]

His commitment to the high ideal of non-sectarianism was tested. Many Anglicans refused to work with him at all; nevertheless he still co-operated with others in the work of the local Bible Society auxiliary, and subscribed to the Anglican Church Missionary Society. He longed for closer union, but believed that the severance from the Infant Orphan Asylum and the

London Orphan Asylum was proof that it was all but impracticable in those days. In those testing times he believed that most Anglicans would not make concessions on even the smallest of matters.[9]

His picture remained on the wall in the boardroom of the London Orphan Asylum, and he allowed himself to be named as one of the vice-presidents — a gesture of kindness he could not resist. He kept a close interest in the charity's progress over the years, and constantly ascribed its success to God's hand: 'It has grown, but Thou, Lord, hast nourished it.'[10] A huge amount had been achieved by 1844. Through his efforts, hundreds of children had been cared for, and half a million pounds had been raised. The charities had spawned many imitators, and over the thirty years the benevolent spirit of the nation had grown appreciably. He never forgot the children of the London Orphan Asylum. Over ten years after he tendered his resignation, as he concluded the entries for his journal in 1855 he noted: 'The London Orphan Asylum reports 410 in the house, and 2,228 as having been provided for. Thank God!'[11]

None the less, the events of 1843 and 1844 almost broke Reed's heart. The enforced separation from the orphanages, in which he had invested so much love and care over so many years, was devastating. His spirits broken and his health uncertain, he turned from the committee rooms of the charities to his study and church vestry, where in silence he mourned 'as a parent for his lost children'.[12] It appeared to the outside world that the philanthropic work of the orphan's friend was over. He was fifty-five years old, and his energy levels were not what they had once been. Perhaps he should concentrate on his preaching work, and prepare for an honourable retirement. But Andrew Reed was still impelled by the threefold motivation that lay behind his vision for the Infant Orphan Asylum — faith, hope and charity. His Christian compassion was not exhausted: the story was not to end in 1843.

14.
Pastoral labours

The minister was never to lose sight of the eternal dimension of his calling: the work ... of the minister was `superior to earth, greater than time, and expanding into eternity. It relates to the soul...´

14.
Pastoral labours

His visit to America left Andrew Reed more convinced than ever of the importance of faithfulness in the ordinary business of church life, such as regular evangelistic visitation of an area, a well-run Sunday school and Bible class, maintenance of the prayer meeting and, especially, clear, decisive preaching. The regular Sunday ministry was resumed on 2 November 1834, and the congregation rejoiced at the safe return of their pastor. At the communion service on that day Reed reminded his church members of his frequent request that they set apart an hour in the week for special prayer. The deacons always set a strong example by the earnestness of their intercessions, and Reed rejoiced that he was 'strong in the prayers of my people'.[1]

The pastor and his flock

For several months, his spare energies were taken up with producing reports of the visit to America, and preparing the *Narrative* of his visit for publication. Then, in late 1835, he began to spend more time with the deacons of the church, seeking to foster their spiritual development, meeting them more regularly for prayer, to which meetings their wives were on occasion invited. He also sought to identify 120 members of the congregation who showed signs of spiritual maturity, and began to encourage them in prayer and personal spiritual growth, and to give them opportunities to exercise their gifts further. He was convinced that to advance the spirituality of the church there needed to be an increase in the spirituality of the leadership. Ultimately, as the minister, Reed was convinced that he was the person from whom this was most required.

He was deeply frustrated when, after dealing with this subject in his presidential address at the Board of Congregational Ministers in 1836, he found that the meeting degenerated into a discussion of the problems with Sunday schools, Bible classes and whether Nonconformist clergy were superior in spirituality to their Anglican counterparts. It was one of a number of occasions on which Reed was disappointed in his clerical brethren, although he characteristically blamed himself for the way in which the meeting had turned out, believing he had not spoken well enough on the subject.[2]

He deeply felt his ongoing need for personal holiness: if he were only dead to self and alive to God, he would be much more useful in God's service and much more of a blessing to his church, his family and the world at large: 'The sense of pleasing Him, is the most delicious and invigorating sense. And when a man's ways please Him, he "maketh even his enemies to be at peace with him".'[3]

A much more encouraging response to his challenge to increased devotion and seeking after holiness came from the people of Wycliffe Chapel. He began to direct his ministry at particular groups in the congregation. In 1836 he held special meetings for the new members of the church, and also for mothers. Then a prayer meeting for the fathers of children in the church was held, and Reed arranged to meet specifically with the older children, and urged them to commit themselves to Christ. He preached a sermon especially for young men, challenging the backslidden to return to God, and then a sermon to the unconverted, urging them to go home that evening and spend time before God about the state of their souls. He preached to them again on the Wednesday evening, and Reed then met with any serious enquirers in his vestry on the Friday evening.[4] His messages on all these occasions were simple, urgent and direct. Evangelism remained a constant priority throughout Reed's ministry, but he tended to give it an added emphasis in a concentrated period of outreach most years.

There was regular fruit from his efforts. One such instance was that of a hackney-carriage driver, invited to the church by one of the tract distributors. He came, bringing four friends with him, all of whom were deeply affected by hearing the gospel preached. All five were converted and became church members.[5] Another individual had moved into the area to be in close proximity to the local theatres and billiard halls, where he spent every night. He had not attended church for nearly thirty years, but came one Sunday to Wycliffe Chapel, where he was converted. As he was being accepted for church membership, he gave his testimony that the things he once loved, he now hated.[6] In 1840 Reed rejoiced that four captains of merchant sailing vessels came to faith in Christ and became members of Wycliffe Chapel.[7]

Andrew Reed maintained an important balance between the need for Christians to labour hard in the work of the gospel and relying absolutely on God, conscious that any success depends on him. The balance was crucially worked out in his church in a commitment to 'united and earnest prayer'.[8]

The pastoral pressures on the minister of a Nonconformist church of the size that Wycliffe Chapel had become were very great indeed. A steady stream of callers arrived at his home, and he received frequent requests to sit on committees and attend functions. Reed reminded a colleague that, although it was flattering to be in such demand and to be able to 'shed on a hundred different councils the glancing benefit of our presence and patronage', without prioritization really important pastoral matters, and time for study and prayer, were in danger of being neglected: 'We may proffer our help everywhere, and give it effectually nowhere.' He warned of the danger of when 'Earth eclipses heaven; Time overshadows a distant eternity'.[9]

The minister was never to lose sight of the eternal dimension of his calling: the work of the medical doctor was merely temporal and transitory; that of the minister was 'superior to earth, greater than time, and expanding into eternity. It relates to the soul; and relates to her in her immortal interests.' It was essential to press on, 'esteeming nothing done while so much remains to do'. Convinced of the awesome reality of heaven and hell, Reed stressed the urgency of the work of the gospel: 'Multitudes are continually passing the boundaries of life ... and are shuddering to find themselves naked and alone, ruined at the feet of the Great Eternal One. O continue — lest in the instant you forbear, your brother perish! Continue — lest in the hour you cease, the Judge come! Continue — it is more necessary to labour than to live!'[10]

The fruits of Reed's ministry brought with them much further labour. In 1833, a year when he often found himself feeling unwell, his church admitted 128 persons into its membership. There was a great deal of work to be done in preparing them for membership, in addition to preparations for his pulpit ministry and visiting those who were ill — he jokingly commented that he had 'a sick-list, like that of a medical man'. Other meetings and pastoral appointments kept him at the chapel up to five nights each week. He was deeply conscious of his physical and spiritual frailty — as he cried out, 'Great God and Saviour, I am nothing without Thee... Let me lean on Thee, for I am weak, and learn of Thee, for I am sinful ... correct my opinions, my tempers, my principles, my habits, and render me meet, who am most unmeet, for Thy service.'[11]

Within the running of a local church, Reed believed that the office of the minister was of great importance: 'The cure of souls and the honour of the Redeemer are his charge.'[12] It was to this high office Reed had been called and he sought to discharge it with great responsibility. The deacons of Wycliffe Chapel frequently pressed him to accept the services of an assistant minister. This was not usual practice for Nonconformist preachers of large churches and, later in the century, even the

Baptist preacher C. H. Spurgeon, when ministering to a congregation of over 5,000, for many years resisted the appointment of an assistant before allowing his brother to work part-
time to shoulder some of the ministerial burden. For all the size
and demands of his church, Reed felt this was not appropriate,
and prayed that from within the church membership there
might come sufficient resources to assist in the work. In this
hope he was rewarded when Samuel Plumbe moved to London from Tiverton. He was appointed a deacon, gave much
time to assisting Andrew Reed in his pastoral work and undertook some preaching. Plumbe's work in the church coincided
with the period of its most rapid advance and only came to an
end with his untimely death in 1840.[13]

Personal evangelism

One reason for Andrew Reed's resistance to the idea of accepting pastoral assistance was a fear that this might lead ordinary
church members to abdicate their duty and rely on the paid
'professional' to do the work. Their responsibility in the work of
the gospel was frequently explained, especially through challenges to prayer and engaging in personal evangelism. So often
the lack of blessing on the church was owing to a lack of prayer
and a lack of repentance: 'Our means are perfect; the promise is
perfect. The defect is with ourselves, and with ourselves alone!'
He urged that prayer be 'fervent, united, universal ... nothing
great has ever been accomplished without prayer'.[14]

     Personal evangelism was so important to Reed that in 1842
he produced a manual for ordinary Christians entitled *Personal
Effort for the Salvation of Men*, which grew out of a series of
lectures he delivered. He stressed the importance of communicating the Christian faith. It was an authenticating sign of the
true believer: 'Not to desire to impart it to others, is the evidence
that we have it not; and the degree in which we are blessed in it
is the degree in which we shall labour to bestow it.' Seeking the

conversion of people to Christ was the duty of Christians — this should be the ultimate aim in dealings with people: 'Nothing is done for a sinner till he is *converted*.' The answer to the need of the church was not ultimately new buildings, or endowments, but simply that 'the person who has known Christ should make him known'. Opportunities to share the faith should be prayerfully watched for: 'Those who watch for them seldom want them.'

Sharing the faith personally was not a matter of special techniques or methods, but rather of presenting the truth: 'Settle it in your heart that the truth is your only legitimate instrument, that all feeling not produced by it is spurious and dangerous; that it alone can convert and sanctify the sinner, and that if you honour it, the Spirit, its author, will honour you.' At the heart of the Christian message was the atonement: 'The cross of Christ was adequate and all-sufficient, so that God can be just, and yet justify the sinner.'

The sense of urgency that pervaded Reed's preaching also featured strongly in his instructions for personal evangelism; dealing with those enquiring into the Christian faith, he stressed, 'Urge him to a present act of faith, in the name and grace of Christ. Let him know that he is invited, that he is commanded to this.' The person should be convinced that 'if he is lost, he destroys himself; that if he is saved, he is saved by the might and mercy of Christ'. Yet Reed also discouraged pressurizing people emotionally into a response that might not be genuine; hearers should be allowed time to retire and consider the subject: 'Salvation is impossible without consideration.' Urgent prayer should follow a serious conversation with an enquirer, and nothing should be done to dissipate the serious impressions created: 'I have seen the most promising effects withered at once by three minutes' light or ill-timed conversation.'

In answer to those who felt unequal to the task of evangelism, Reed was of the opinion that if people could talk about their children, or their trade, they could talk about Christ. He gave examples of adults and children being used by God in this task, from a child of fourteen who brought nine people to a special service to a deaf lady who brought seven people, or a child of seven who was 'the instrument of converting one parent, and of bringing both under the means of grace'.

The work of evangelism, Reed believed, was not just a means of blessing to the unconverted, but also to the one sharing the gospel: 'If you would prove that you have spiritual life, do it by action. If you would improve the evidence and power of that life, still do it by action … if you would dissipate your doubts and anxieties, plunge not into subtle questions, but be up and active at your Saviour's bidding, and you shall know your love to God and to your brother also … while you linger, hesitate, and do no good to others, no good comes to you.'[15] Convinced of this, Reed undoubtedly made every effort to redeem the time and did all he could to encourage others to avoid wasting theirs. He urged the members of his congregation, and those of other churches, to live together in unity, and not to descend into factionalism, or opposition to the work of the church leaders or the minister. He had seen the witness of too many churches destroyed by such behaviour.[16]

Steady growth

For all the undoubted assistance Andrew Reed received from the members and deacons of his church, the pastoral round remained demanding. Yet his labours, and those of his faithful members, were richly blessed by God. He had arrived in 1811 to minister to a church of just sixty members meeting in a building capable of seating 800 people. By 1822 those sixty had become 362. The next ten years saw steady but unspectacular growth with 245 members being added to the church. Then the two decades after 1832 brought phenomenal growth, with 913 members added to the church between 1832 and 1841, and a further 622 between 1842 and 1851. The final decade, when Reed was increasingly affected by ill health and weakening of powers as he moved into his seventies, were years of more steady growth, with 318 new members between 1852 and 1861. In all during the ministry of Andrew Reed, there were 2,460 additions to the membership of the church.[17] In 1846 the membership of the chapel stood at 1,100, but congregations were always much larger. Wycliffe Chapel, capable of seating congregations of 2,000, was regularly crowded after the mid-1830s.[18]

Many of these new members were personally counselled and led to faith by Reed himself. In the first few months of 1846, 170 people came to see Reed 'under concern for their salvation', and most showed signs that a deep work of God had taken place in their lives. Some conversions were very unusual. One man who rarely attended church, and had never been to a Nonconformist chapel, had a strange dream about attending a chapel and hearing a remarkable preacher. He set out to find the chapel, and when he entered Wycliffe Chapel he said at once to himself, 'The very place!' When he looked up at the pulpit and saw Andrew Reed at once he again said, 'The very man!' He was utterly amazed, and heard the sermon with an open heart, as if the message were from God for him, and through faith in Christ he became a new creature. Reed was utterly humbled when he heard the man's story, for such occurrences were far from usual. It drove him, and his church, to deeper prayer: 'We must take hold of the arm of God. He will not forsake us, if we cleave to Him. Oh! May my people have a heart to test His faithfulness and His power!' And the call for prayer at such a time was vital — for in these very months of blessing there were growing difficulties for Andrew Reed as he faced opposition to his attempts to bring about changes to the running of the London Missionary Society from the directors of that organization.[19]

Outreach into the wider area

As Wycliffe Chapel rapidly grew, its size was not jealously guarded. During the course of Andrew Reed's ministry a series of daughter churches was started in the East End, including many members from Wycliffe Chapel. The sixth of these was opened on Hackney Road in January 1836.[20] There were also in 1842 six 'preaching stations', served by three local missionaries, in areas of great need where there were few other places of worship. Here services were well attended, and took pressure off the Wycliffe Chapel building, which was crowded with congregations of up to 2,000 people.

Some young men from the chapel were called as preachers, and trained in local colleges, before moving into pastoral situations. Other members were actively involved in a wide range of outreach work as the chapel put into practice Reed's emphasis on the involvement of ordinary church members.

Opportunities for Christian service for members of Wycliffe Chapel were numerous. Many Bible Classes and Sunday school classes were run both in the chapel or the 'preaching stations' and here, or in meetings in homes, there were frequent opportunities to lead services and preach. The area round the chapel was regularly visited through the work of the Christian Instruction Society, which employed a paid agent, but was also supported by seventy volunteer visitors from the congregation.

It was not just adults involved in the outreach work of the chapel: two 'juvenile societies' also gave young people the opportunity to engage in the work of spreading the gospel locally.[21] Wycliffe Chapel was not simply a very large congregation; it was also an assemblage of actively engaged workers.

Women in the church

Much of the work undertaken in the chapel was done by women ministering to other women and children. Andrew's sister Martha, and then his wife Elizabeth, had led the way in this. Of the nearly 2,400 additions to the membership of the church during Reed's ministry, 67% were women, a figure which is very close to the average found amongst free churches in the first half of the nineteenth century.[22] Many Nonconformist churches attracted a very large number of adherents in this period. There were frequently over four adherents for every member, and these were often men, who were less willing than women to make the commitment to membership. The activities run by women for women in the church were numerous, and very successful — from the Bible Class for Young Women, run by Miss Jolly, to the Mother and Infants' Friend Society, which gave relief to poor married women, including a visit to the mother with a parcel of clothes and necessary items for her and her newborn baby. The Dorcas Society (named after Dorcas in Acts 9:36, a woman renowned for a life filled with good deeds) raised money and sewed clothes for poor residents unable to afford clothing, while the Bethesda Society sent members to visit those who were unwell, and provided practical and nursing comfort and spiritual support to those in need. The Young Ladies' Christian Association combined Bible study and wider reading to encourage the spiritual life with preparing articles to be sent to foreign mission stations to help in the extension of the gospel overseas.[23]

Practical help for the poor

The congregation drawn to Wycliffe Chapel and its regular activities through the efforts of Andrew Reed and the members of the church reflected the populace of the East End of London in which it was situated. The area began to suffer from increasing poverty during and after the 1840s and, with a strongly local congregation, this began to be reflected in the decline in the annual income of the church, which reached a peak of £1,139 in 1850, and thereafter slowly declined to just £703 in 1861.

The congregation was never wealthy, and the income received from the regular way of supporting the ministry practised by most churches at the time — that of renting sittings in the pews to regular attenders — never exceeded £600 during the fifty years of Reed's ministry. The total from this source amounted to just £300 in 1853.[24] The evidence available suggests that those who attended the church were overwhelmingly of the working class — 89% of the fathers of children baptized in the church were from the skilled artisan group and below. They included many mariners, blacksmiths, carpenters, sailmakers, clerks and labourers. For such occupations wages ranged from one pound six shillings a week down to eleven shillings a week, and many were earning less than £50 per year.[25] Living on the margins of poverty, they had little surplus income to give to the church.

Many recognized that poverty was caused both by economic factors beyond the control of local people, such as trade depressions or the consequences of war, and also by some aspects of personal behaviour, such as poor management of financial resources and heavy expenditure on alcohol. One project designed to encourage financial prudence and forward planning was the East London Savings Bank, which Reed helped establish in 1837. Using the skills he employed in philanthropic endeavour, Reed obtained the patronage of leading mercantile and shipping firms in the area, and created a board of management which drew together individuals from different denominations and political parties. Most of the administrative work was undertaken by two well-qualified members of Wycliffe Chapel, who gave their services voluntarily. Reed was convinced that much poverty could be averted or lessened by planning and forethought; inscribed on each deposit book were encouraging mottos: 'A penny saved is a penny earned,' and 'What maintains one vice, would support two children.' Many members of the church were connected with the seafaring life, and to assist them the provisions of the bank were extended to include facilities for depositing wills and deeds and for supervising annuities.

Reed was anxious to show that such an institution could be run properly and charitably by Christian people, on business principles, at a fraction of the cost of other savings banks and schemes. A number of savings schemes established for the benefit of the poor suffered from financial mismanagement themselves and collapsed, taking with them the hard-earned savings of the needy people they were designed to help. With Reed's scheme, financial integrity was central and the absolute security of the deposits was ensured. Reed stood as one of the bank's guarantors and to prove the security of the scheme he and his children opened accounts in it. The bank's funds were deposited in the Bank of England.

From small beginnings, with just 791 accounts in 1839, the project became a great success, with 3,679 accounts in 1862, in which were invested a total of £622,478. There were no charges or deductions on the savings accounts, and interest was paid. A similar scheme, the Pence Bank, was started for the children of the church in 1845, with the intention of encouraging 'habits of carefulness and providence' amongst the young. This was run by John Fraser, one of the deacons of the church, and was again free of charge to the depositors.[26] Here were extremely practical and useful demonstrations of organized Christian philanthropy, providing financial guidance, stability and security for poor people and small-scale investors from the chapel and surrounding area. Pastoral care was to include an eminently practical component.

The congregation drawn to Reed's gospel ministry at Wycliffe Chapel was also overwhelmingly local: 73% of members lived in Stepney, and a further 20% came from other parts of the East End of London.[27] Many lived in areas of poor-quality housing in the neighbouring streets. Evidence of the poor social and environmental conditions comes from the Burial Register of the Wycliffe Chapel. Between June and December 1849 there were 479 burials. Of these, an astonishing 47% were of children, 19% being those of children under the age of one. It shows the appalling cost in infant mortality brought by the dreadful urban living conditions endured by many of those living in the immediate vicinity of the church. As a result of the problems of poor housing and poor diet, the local people were susceptible to frequent problems of illness and infectious disease.

Those months in 1849 were also ones in which cholera once again ravaged London. By the end of the outbreak some 15,000 people had died. The East End of London was affected badly and a number of Reed's congregation died. In September 1849 the cholera reached its peak: the weather was oppressively hot and sultry and 432 people died on one day. Out of concern for the congregation, Reed kept meetings at the church short, to avoid people spending prolonged periods in crowded places. It was a sad, discouraging time, with much pastoral anxiety, and without the spiritual upturn there had been in the cholera outbreak of 1832. Reed felt his responsibility greatly: 'The care of the body is mine, as well as of the soul.' The disease struck so rapidly, without distinction, that Reed confessed the people felt as if they were hemmed in, waiting to be shot down indiscriminately by an invisible hand. When the epidemic abated, a day of thanksgiving was held and was observed with deep gratitude by the congregation.[28]

Pressing social needs were matters of which Reed was acutely aware. To these he always responded with urgent pastoral and philanthropic activity, determined to use his energies, and those of his church, to provide a compassionate and constructive response to local needs. These endeavours ensured that people did not feel ostracized from the church by virtue of their poverty. Through offering a challenging and relevant preaching and teaching ministry, forming an actively engaged and supportive Christian community, and making available a network of supportive care — not just for adults, but also for local children — Reed and his congregation ensured that people, from the poorest to the successful, found at Wycliffe Chapel a welcoming spiritual home.

15.
Revival

In the midst of a camp meeting, in which revivalist techniques had been tried and had failed, through direct and plain preaching God had worked. Reed had experienced a touch of revival on his ministry.

15.
Revival

Ever since reading the life story of George Whitefield, who had played such a prominent role in the religious awakenings of the eighteenth century, Andrew Reed had been actively reading about the subject of revival, and had been longing for it in his personal life and in his church. As an evangelical Calvinist he emphasized the sovereignty of God in periods of blessing and, alongside the practice of George Whitefield, he looked to the thinking of Jonathan Edwards for a framework through which to understand seasons of spiritual awakening, or the 'surprising work of God'.

Andrew Reed described revival as being when, 'within a limited or comparatively short period, a church is greatly renovated in pious feeling, and a considerable accession is made to it from the classes of the formal and ungodly. Usually there is a previous state of spiritual depression amongst the religious people; and of irreligion and increasing wickedness in the neighbourhood.' His visit to America gave him the opportunity to witness both genuine revival and other attempts to encourage religious experience, often referred to as 'revivalism'. He found that the experience of genuine revival encouraged others to long and thirst for it; many American believers owed their conversion to times of revival, and churches that had not experienced revival were the exception.[1]

Observations based on his American visit

Reed carefully recorded accounts of local revivals given to him by ministers in America whom he visited. He found that some of the techniques popularized by revivalists such as Charles Finney had been attempted by various churches, including successive meetings on several days each week, visitation of an area during concerted periods of evangelism and after-meetings for enquirers. While he conceded that there had been some fruit from such efforts, Reed did not attribute revival to the application of certain methods.

Genuine revivals were quite different: in them the primary motive force was prayer and preaching, and they were marked by 'deep stillness and solemnity'.[2] Revival was a truly transformative experience: 'Life pervades everything. The people are raised above the ordinary level of existence.'[3] Everyday Christian life took on a depth, a richness and an intensity not previously known: 'They have found mercy, and they thirst to bestow it: they have dishonoured God, and they thirst to glorify him. They become missionaries for the time; and they move about in their families and their connections, warning, teaching, and entreating with tears, that they would be reconciled and saved.' The sense of reality and solemnity which pervades everything in the church becomes 'in itself a means of conversion'.[4]

Attractive as the means popularized by Charles Finney might appear, it was Reed's personal observation that 'In proportion to the diligent and wise use of scriptural methods, is the blessing.' A revival in the Geneva Presbytery of the state of New York had, Reed believed, seen the most desirable results where 'there has been the least departure from the ordinary means'. Biblical preaching, consistent prayer, faithful pastoral work and godly living lay behind true revival.[5] In times of awakening God chose in his sovereignty to use ordinary means in an extraordinary way.

On the basis of his extensive reading, and personal observation during his visit to the American churches, in his *Narrative of the Visit to the American Churches* Andrew Reed provided a thorough analysis of the approach of Charles Finney and other revivalists. Finney argued that the prayerful and systematic application of certain methods could create a 'revival'.[6] Reed observed occasions where some good had come through such techniques, but on the whole he retained an unfavourable impression of revivalism. He believed that the 'anxious seat', a place designed for people to go and sit to profess their anxiety for salvation, was a 'measure of action unwise and unsafe'. It was too inviting to the 'ignorant, the vain, and the self-conceited', whereas it was 'repulsive and difficult to the timid, the modest, and reflective'. To claim that those moving forward to sit on the 'anxious seat' were 'converts' created 'premature and unscriptural hope, and, therefore, dangerous and destructive delusion'. Reed observed that using such methods resulted in only somewhere between a fifth and a tenth of the 'converts' maintaining their profession for a long period, and many brought into the church gave 'painful evidence of the want of renewed character and conversation'.

Reed was also unhappy at those drawn into preaching, often without training, by such methods: 'Rash measures attract rash men,' some of whom had taken it upon themselves to denounce pastors and unsettle churches. Reliance on irregular methods reduced confidence in the ordinary means of grace.[7]

Rather than resorting to artificial measures to manufacture religious awakening, Reed believed that what was needed for families, churches and nations was genuine revival. It would 'heal our divisions; humble our spirits; and convert us from the insignificant and perishable, to the unseen and eternal'. It was demanded by the 'urgency of the times'.[8]

A camp meeting in the forest

On his visit to America Andrew Reed made a special excursion down the Rappahannock to visit a camp meeting at a remote location at Northern Neck, the northernmost peninsula on Virginia's bay shore, where revivalist techniques were much in evidence. It was an enchanting location, the tall trees standing like the pillars of a cathedral with their tops joining to create a natural roof, through which dappled sunlight fell. To Reed the main meetings were a disappointment and, although the preachers pressed long and hard for a response, few made their way forward to sit on the 'anxious seat'. After three days of meetings, the leading preachers were clearly frustrated by the lack of response to their exhortations from such large congregations.

All through each day smaller meetings were held in surrounding tents and Reed, a great lover of singing and a composer of hymns, was disappointed to find himself wearied by the incessant and repetitious singing of hymns or parts of hymns. The night-time services were highly atmospheric, with the lanterns of the congregation shining out amidst the trees in the dark forest. Exhortation and appeal followed from preacher after preacher, with little by way of response. The preachers then left the platform and started moving amongst the congregation pleading for a response, which Reed felt was placing them under too much emotional pressure. The singing became endless, with favourite couplets taken up and repeated over and over again. Reed commented that 'The effect was various, but it was not good.' Some became overexcited by the proceedings; Reed thought that one woman in particular was quite hysterical. Others were wearied by the repetition.

While all this had been going on, news that Reed was a minister of religion had reached the organizers of the camp meeting, and he was urgently pressed to preach a sermon. This placed him in a difficult position, for he could not consent to be involved in most of what was going on. He finally agreed to preach, but only in the morning service, and made it clear that he would do everything he could to dissociate himself from anything that smacked of excess. After what he had witnessed over the previous few days, the result of his sermon was surprising.

Reed preached to a congregation of about 1,500 people. As he began his message, he felt great earnestness and freedom, although he did all he could to quieten any noisy exclamations. A growing stillness fell over the congregation as he drew towards a close, and people were perceptibly leaning forward so as not to miss a word. Some rose up from their seats, gripped by the message; others began to sink to their knees; some began to weep, but the profound stillness was unbroken. Tears fell more freely as Reed drew his message to a close, and he felt tremendous power upon his preaching; every statement and challenge he made seemed to come out with an unusual authority, and he was able to apply it closely to the conscience and heart of the congregation. As he drew his sermon to a close, the silence was overpowering, broken only by the sound of quiet sobbing. And then suddenly the sound of almost universal weeping swept over the assembled people, and they all fell on their knees. As Reed looked round he saw the other ministers on the platform were on their knees, their faces bathed in tears. He too was overcome, and unable even to close the service in prayer.

The minister who had led the service urged him to pray, and to make an appeal; another minister begged him to try to reap a harvest in the moment: 'I fear many of my charge will be found at the left hand of the Judge! Oh, pray, brother, pray for us!' Even if Reed had felt it was right to do as they had asked, he could not have done so; he was speechless. But no human voice was needed, as he recalled: 'All, in that hour, were intercessors with God, with tears and cries, and groans unutterable.' He did not want to interfere with what God was so evidently doing.

After a long period of time Reed was able to utter sufficient words to close the service, but the people did not want to leave the hallowed spot and return to the mundane things of life. Another minister stood to pray, the congregation fell to its knees and prayer for blessing was offered, before Reed intervened to stop any further exhortation or appeal. He believed people should be left to their own thoughts and prayers. Reed had never witnessed such a remarkable service before, and had never known such power in the preaching of God's Word. Yet he knew it had been God's blessing on the ordinary means of grace, nothing else. The people who had been so affected slowly joined up again with their families, but there was nothing of the exuberance and excitement of the previous days — rather a gentleness and desire to serve one another, coupled together with universal joy.

Many were spiritually awakened through this meeting, including an official of the local state government, who had long resisted the gospel message, but who now appeared to have been soundly converted. Reed spoke briefly with those who sought counsel, and then referred them to the care of the ministers with whom they had come. He was asked to preach again at a later meeting, but he declined the invitation. God had been there; the place was holy ground, and he did not want to spoil what had been achieved that day. A witness at the scene later reported that there had been between sixty and seventy conversions through the service. In the midst of a camp meeting, in which revivalist techniques had been tried and had failed, through direct and plain preaching God had worked. Reed had experienced a touch of revival on his ministry.[9]

A longing to see the power of God

Such an experience was bound to have an effect on Andrew Reed's preaching. Before he went to America his ministry was always well prepared, and often built to a searching, challenging peroration, charged with suppressed emotion. On his return there seemed a new power and vigour and confidence in what God could do through faithful preaching of the Word.

In 1837 Reed reached his fiftieth birthday, aware that his physical prime was passing, yet he longed that 'as the outward man fails, the inward man should show its superiority, by becoming brighter and brighter. I need to wrap my Saviour's righteousness closer round me, to make His name my refuge and dwelling-place, and to rest my weakness and weariness on His might. I have need, with new power of faith and new elasticity of hope, to rise above all the accidents of life, and, rejoicing in its spirituality and immortality, to say, "God is the strength of my heart, and my portion for ever."' He made a number of key resolutions, conscious of the approach of the winter of life: to redeem the time, which was now short; to read only the most important books, and pursue the most important subjects; to continue to wrestle and labour for holiness to his dying breath; to give all the money he could for the glory of God; to strive not to allow the pressures of duty to make him depressed; to limit any speaking on public platforms over and above his regular preaching ministry in order to prevent his voice and health breaking down. His longing was to see 'the power of God in His sanctuary, and to feel it on my own spirit'.[10]

In late 1838 he had a renewed awareness that the spiritual life of the church was again quickening as it had in the early 1830s. Coupled with this, he found himself longing once more for a new work of God in his heart. Without this he would not be ready for what God might choose to do, and he set apart further time for reading and prayer. Yet he was again frustrated by the frailties of the body, with an annoyingly persistent throat problem of the type that dogged preachers in the days before the electronic amplification of sound. He received a warning from his medical adviser that he was in danger of completely losing his voice if he did not rest it completely. Disregarding his doctor, he pressed on with most of his engagements. Inwardly he was convinced that God was urging him to 'Go forward', yet he felt far from equal to the physical and spiritual demands.

Then, on 16 October 1838, God met with Andrew Reed in a powerful way. As he prepared for the services of the next day, he was overwhelmed with a sense of his 'exceeding sinfulness, ingratitude, and unprofitableness, — a sense of the forbearance, pity, and goodness of God, were present to me.' He was surprised to find himself weeping: 'A state of perception and feeling which had not been mine for months and years, had come over me... I seemed on the verge of a better state of life and action.' He quickly bolted the door, to prevent any distractions, and threw himself on his knees, sobbing out to God his deep sense of sinfulness and unworthiness. He begged for a purifying work of the Holy Spirit, and found himself being reassured by the words of Scripture: 'Is anything too hard for the Lord?' He knew God drawing very near; the words of the Bible spoke to him with fresh power. When he preached the next day his congregation was conscious of a difference in him.[11]

Revival comes to Wycliffe Chapel

Sensing that God was at work, the leaders of the church planned a week of special services for the first week of 1839. They felt that this would be a time when people would be most likely to be reflecting on the coming year. Reed and the deacons prepared for this by visiting all the families in the church, concentrating on spiritual matters and urging them to do all they could to attend the forthcoming meetings and to be earnest in prayer. In his ministry through late 1838, Reed preached on the themes of penitence and humility. He was gratified to see a more prayerful spirit amongst the congregation, and was thrilled that extra prayer meetings began to be spontaneously arranged.[12]

The week of special services began on New Year's Eve, a Monday, with a message in which Reed urged his congregation to reflect on the lessons of the previous year. New Year's Day was set apart as one of humiliation and prayer, with prayer meetings held throughout the day. During the week, Reed preached sermons aimed at specific groups in the church, such as professing Christians, and then for young people. Reed was surprised to find a delegation from the fathers of the young people asking if they could hold a prayer meeting while the service was going on, and he readily agreed. At the end of the service Reed offered to meet any who were interested in hearing further of the Christian message, and arrived to find the room was packed with some 200 people, many of whom were in tears. The next day was spent in meetings for the mothers and their children, and again large numbers were present, many of whom had little connection with the church.[13]

On the Sunday Reed took as his theme the command 'to repent'. Although this was to be the formal end of the week of special services, there was such a strong sense of God at work that he announced further services on the Monday and Tuesday evenings, directed at the unconverted. A number of students from local theological colleges who regularly attended the church took it upon themselves to visit the houses around the area, handing out tracts and holding open-air services. The teachers in the day school reported that some of the older children had spontaneously arranged an early-morning prayer meeting.[14]

In the next weeks, fearful that what was happening might become too organized, Reed decided to avoid perpetuating the special meetings, and held only occasional additional services. He sought to channel his efforts into the regular Sunday services, when he addressed the unconverted and unfolded God's plan of salvation. Day after day he made himself available at the church building to counsel those who had come under conviction of sin and were concerned about their spiritual state. Rather than bringing in speakers and helpers from outside the congregation, Reed involved his church officers and other lay leaders as much as possible. His oldest son Andrew, then a student aged twenty-one and who was later himself to go into Christian ministry, was also called on to take a service.[15]

Amongst the Sunday school children there were signs that God was at work. The teachers asked him to give a short exhortation and offer prayer at a meeting for thirty-six children who were considered to be especially concerned about religious matters. The following Monday a special meeting was arranged for those who had come under conviction of sin; it went on late into the evening as Reed and his deacons counselled and prayed with the many who came. Soon he and the deacons of Wycliffe Chapel were at the church almost every weekday evening, from 5 p.m. until 10 p.m., dealing with those enquiring after the way of salvation and those needing spiritual nurture after making a profession of faith. The Christian Instruction Society's regular visitation of the area, which had previously borne little fruit, suddenly began to yield a response. A special service was held for those who did not attend any church, and admission was by ticket only. Around 400 attended, and listened earnestly.[16]

The most intense point of the spiritual awakening came during the funeral service for Margaret Keith, a young woman who had been a missionary candidate for China, and was soon to be married. Emotions were running high over her tragic loss, and during the service many were weeping and some fell prostrate to the floor. From others there were emotional outbursts and a few were affected hysterically. Reed believed that such emotions were signs of 'human infirmity', a product of deep sorrow rather than indications of a work of God. Lest they might spoil the remarkable spiritual work going on in the church, he immediately cancelled the prayer meeting that was due to follow the service. When they were not encouraged, Reed found that such emotional outbursts disappeared from the services.[17]

The strain on Reed and his church leaders was enormous, but they were unwilling to slacken their efforts while it appeared that God was blessing the work. Although Reed fell ill for ten days in June, his labours were renewed through the rest of the month, and continued to the end of July, when a final enquiry service was held, with 200 attending. The heightened sense of spiritual awareness in the congregation had begun to lessen, and Reed realized that physically he and the church leaders needed a break from the work. He had personally counselled in depth over 300 people, preferring to see them individually rather than adopting the means of holding an enquiry meeting. He had not drawn in other ministers to assist with the meetings, believing that he and the church leaders knew the congregation best and could counsel them more appropriately than could comparative strangers.[18]

The period of religious awakening in the church went on for nearly six months. Many who had been converted during the early meetings began to apply for admission to church membership, but Reed and his church officers proceeded cautiously, carefully ascertaining whether any profession of faith was genuine and showed real fruit. On the 1st February, nineteen individuals were proposed for membership, but most were already known to the church as earlier converts, rather than the fruit of recent events. Reed did not want to bring discredit on the work by bringing into the church any whose spiritual change had not been fully tested. Soon after Easter a further seventy-one were proposed for membership, but twenty were asked to wait and apply later. In all, 1839 saw 168 new members (one of whom was Reed's third son) admitted to Wycliffe Chapel, compared to just seventy the previous year. The highest total of new members joining the church had previously been the 109 who joined in 1835 in the period of blessing in the church after Reed's return from America.

The results of those months of awakening in early 1839 continued to be felt in the following years: a further 105 new members joined in 1840, 110 in 1841 and ninety-four in 1842, numbers well above the average per year across the span of Andrew Reed's ministry. Conversions continued in the following years as the ripples of the spiritual awakening spread out, suggesting that the new converts were in turn bringing others to the services. Some of the new believers needed many months of nurture and spiritual growth before Reed felt they had reached the point where they were ready for membership.

Who were the converts?

The new members were overwhelmingly local people: 80% came from Stepney itself. None was believed to have come from a neighbouring church; almost all the converts had either been attached to Wycliffe Chapel in some way, or were non-churchgoers.[19] This remarkable time from January to June 1839 was not a highly publicized or worked-up sensation, which drew in crowds from elsewhere as spectators, but very much a local-church-based phenomenon. Much of what happened was spontaneous, growing out of the ordinary meetings of the church, without resort to special methods or techniques. Andrew Reed stressed that faithful preaching (emphasizing the sovereign righteousness of God, the reality of sin and the rich spontaneous grace of God) and a readiness to spend much time with people personally were the only means that were used in what took place. As he reviewed what had happened and saw its lasting results, he became convinced that he had seen what he had so much longed for — a time of revival in his church.

Some have levelled the criticism at revival that it attracts and affects those who are emotionally susceptible, particularly, it is claimed, women. In the awakening at Wycliffe Chapel, this charge is not borne out. Throughout the course of Andrew Reed's ministry, 33.1% of those who became members in the church were males, a fairly average figure for English Nonconformity in the period. However, during the years after the awakening, the percentage of new male members rose to 37.1% in 1840, 38.2% in 1841 and 41.5% in 1842. It seems clear that the revival was influential in the conversion of a very large number of men, some of whom had lived long on the fringes of chapel life but had never come to make a definitive Christian commitment. Religious awakening in the church brought them to the point where this could no longer be avoided. Others who joined had little or no previous church connection.[20]

Andrew Reed kept a careful record of individuals who were converted. They ranged from a child of seven to the elderly. Backsliders were restored, and assurance was found by those who had laboured long without it. Thirty additions came from the schools in Bethnal Green, and most of them were over sixteen. One woman aged seventy-two, who had only been visiting the area for three days, came to the meetings. Hearing a sermon on repentance, she was deeply affected. Reed recorded: 'I never witnessed a deeper sense of sin, nor more brokenness of heart on its account.' He called her a 'brand plucked from the fire'. A man who had enjoyed great financial success, but whose business had collapsed, came to the church seeking spiritual solace. He and his wife were converted and became steadfast church members. Another person who was helped was a minister who had fallen into sin, and had left his church to escape a scandal, moving to London in the hope of not being recognized. After attending the services he came to seek counsel from Reed, openly acknowledging what he had done. In tears he confessed: 'The thought of it drives me to the verge of madness; it makes life intolerable and hope almost impossible.' Andrew Reed showed him the way to find pardon and peace through true penitence. The man was finally restored to Christian communion.[21]

Reed's account of the revival

In the style of Jonathan Edwards' *Narrative of Surprising Conversions*, Andrew Reed produced an account of what had happened at Wycliffe Chapel, hoping that it would encourage others to pray for similar things to happen in their churches. In *The Revival of Religion* he stressed the genuine fruit that had come to Wycliffe Chapel and his belief that the converts would stand the test of time. A small number had wept and been humbled for a while, but such impressions had not been sustained and, sadly, they remained 'without hope in Christ'. Others had been alarmed and terrified, but Reed stressed that such emotions had not been sought by him, and these effects were produced only by the 'ordinary means' of preaching, prayer and visitation, rather than the application of special techniques. Specialist revivalists had not been brought in; only the pastor, his church officers and ordinary church members were involved in this work. No resort was made to the 'anxious seat', prolonged weeks of protracted meetings, or sensational preaching.

Above all, Reed believed, the work was God's. The granting of such a revival lay with God, but God worked through means: 'Revival is life, life improved or imparted; but life, and all the resources of life, are with God... The means were used because they were commanded; and they were used in faith and hope; but the means are from God, — the disposition and power are from God, — and the attendant blessing is from God.'[22]

Although revival was different from the ordinary life and work of the church, it was a difference of degree rather than of kind. In revival the influence of the Holy Spirit was more widespread, feelings more intense — normal Christianity was heightened to a degree far above that usually experienced. Human action could not bring about revival, but the church had to be faithful in the preaching of the gospel and in earnest prayer if it was to happen. Reed's thinking was very close to that of Jonathan Edwards, in whose pulpit he had been privileged to stand a few years before: revival was a remarkable communication of the Spirit of God, a special season of mercy.[23] In a small, localized way, he had been privileged to see such a season at Wycliffe Chapel in 1839.

Over the following years Andrew Reed was heartened to hear of fruit coming from the publication of the *Revival of Religion*. In Tewkesbury, he heard of a Congregational minister who had publicly read the work to his congregation and urged them to respond. The church had set itself to pray, and a religious awakening had followed, through which fifty-eight people had been added to the church. Similarly, a Baptist minister near London reported fifty-seven additions to his church following the public reading of the *Narrative*, and a Wesleyan minister reported 1,600 new members in his circuit as a result of the stimulus given to his ministry by reading *Revival of Religion*.[24] Reed was called on to explain events to a number of meetings of ministers, and each time he emphasized his conviction that it was the use of the ordinary means of church life that God had extraordinarily blessed.

After the revival

Gradually the revival faded; such scenes were not again repeated in Wycliffe Chapel during the ministry of Andrew Reed, although there continued to be significant numbers of conversions through his preaching ministry in the years that followed. But the toll on Reed and others was considerable, and he was ill through part of late 1839. Samuel Plumbe, who had become his right-hand man in the work, also fell prey to illness. Plumbe, who seemed to have been raised up specially for this season of blessing, was never able to return to his former work.

Another loss was that of William Milne, who had been instrumental in the work amongst the young people during the revival. Milne, who soon after the revival sailed to China to serve as a missionary, was one of the orphaned sons of the missionary Dr William Milne whom Elizabeth and Andrew had welcomed into their home after their father's death. Young William had been like a son to Andrew Reed, and he confessed that those months of revival in Wycliffe Chapel had done far more to prepare him for a lifetime's service in overseas mission than any college course. His brother Robert was also called into Christian ministry, and became a minister in Whitehaven in 1841.[25]

Those glorious months in 1839 were the high point of Andrew Reed's ministry at Wycliffe Chapel. He had witnessed revivalism in America, much of which he did not like, and what had happened at Wycliffe Chapel was not revivalism. The week of planned services had been quickly overtaken by spontaneous events, and yet the means God had chosen to bless were the ordinary, regular, church activities — prayer, Bible reading, faithful attendance at service, faithful witness. It had begun with his deep sense of longing for God to do a new work in his life and the personal reviving of his spiritual life that had followed. This blessing had then been shared by the church. Reed was convinced that for seven months God had worked in their midst in an extraordinary way. His heartfelt and oft-repeated prayer, that he might do something useful for God, was answered. It closed a remarkable decade. In the years between 1832 and 1841 Wycliffe Chapel saw 913 new members join its ranks.

16.
Preacher of the Word

'There is that about his whole deportment and preaching which must convince everyone he is in earnest'

(An observer, commenting on Andrew Reed's preaching).

16.
Preacher of the Word

To Andrew Reed the preaching of God's Word to God's people was his principal calling. It was a most serious business: the minister was entrusted with the 'cure of souls and the honour of the Redeemer'.[1] This brought great responsibility: it was the duty of the minister on behalf of others to guard and uphold the faith, 'that *good thing*, that inestimable treasure'.[2] The preacher dealt with issues that were of infinite importance — they were eternal: 'It relates to the soul; and relates to her in her immortal interests.' The task was also supremely urgent — multitudes were constantly passing from this world and when the minister failed in his duty, the result was appalling: 'The effect will be extreme, everlasting, infinite! The lost soul must live for ever; and will be the wretched and imperishable monument of his negligence, infidelity, and guilt.'[3] The vital necessity of the work brought a committed response from Andrew Reed. Through his preaching thousands found spiritual sustenance and pastoral help, and episodes of revival were experienced.

The early days

Although used to giving short talks as part of his Sunday school work, Reed delivered his first formal sermon in daunting circumstances. Preached before a committee of senior ministers, on it rested the decision as to whether he would be accepted by

Hackney College for ministerial training. He took as his text, 'And Noah walked with God' (Genesis 6:9), speaking for about fifteen minutes. As he delivered his message he had a strong sense of God's presence. The committee agreed with this assessment and accepted him for the college.

One aspect of his college studies involved preaching in churches around London and the Home Counties. His first sermon as a ministerial student was delivered on 19 July 1807 at Wooburn, in Buckinghamshire. The awesome responsibility of preaching God's Word weighed heavily on his mind, and he felt totally unworthy of the task. He was desperately disappointed with his first efforts, but then things improved, as he recorded in his journal: 'In the morning, so miserable that I could scarcely utter one word after another, and, in the evening, unexpectedly enabled thoroughly to enjoy the exercise.'

As he grew in experience and confidence over time he received an increasingly positive response from his hearers. Preaching remained an activity through which he longed to glorify God, and into it he threw his heart and soul. Yet he was never entirely free of the fears that beset many preachers — the fear of failing in his duty, the fear of not making the gospel clear and attractive, the fear of attributing any success to his own abilities. He longed to be an instrument in God's hands. His cry was simple — to be useful to God. Yet he recognized that his own intellect and talents were insufficient on their own: for him to be of service to God 'it will be nothing less than a miracle of Divine grace'.[4]

The preacher's task

While utterly convinced of his need to depend on God, Reed was also aware of his responsibility to invest time and effort in the task to which he had been called. The first qualification of the preacher was that he should be a converted person: he believed that 'The glory of our nonconformist churches is found

in a regenerated ministry.'⁵ The minister of the Word was then
to give himself 'with all diligence to reading, to meditation, to
prayer ... he is the best teacher who is the best scholar'. The
preacher was not just to be a student of the Word, but also of
the wider world: 'Everywhere he should seek knowledge; and
as he acquires it, he should bring it into the sanctuary, and
dedicate it to the honour of God and the benefit of mankind.'⁶

From the beginning of his ministry, he exercised great care
over every aspect of his preaching — it was that by which he
was to stand or fall. He carefully planned his sermons, giving
them a coherent structure and ensuring that there was a strong,
but clearly expressed, doctrinal component. His tone and
manner of delivery were particularly appealing, and the words
he used carefully chosen. Above all, from the outset of his work
at New Road the congregation sensed that God was blessing
Andrew Reed's pulpit ministry.⁷ For all his diligent study, there
was a spontaneity and openness to the Spirit that characterized
his preaching. His watchword was: 'Preparation first, and then
freedom in the use of it.'

He also recognized the interaction between congregation
and preacher which helped in the delivery of a sermon. The
response of the congregation could bring liberty or discouragement: 'I cannot get on except I can take them with me, and
sometimes one trifling person will put me out. I was for a long
time troubled by a man with a stony face who sat before me;
and thankful I was when he disappeared.' He aimed to speak
especially to those who appeared most distant and unmoved —
if they responded, he knew he had succeeded with the rest.⁸

Reed lamented over preachers who strove to be intellectual;
his aim in preaching was rather to be of service to God. Effective preaching grew out of a sincere, steady walk with God and
love for his Word. Reed believed that 'The best interpreter of
Scripture is a humble spirit; and nigh to it is common sense.'⁹
He was shocked to hear a preacher report how, during a period
of over thirty years of ministry, he had known no instance of a
conversion during his morning sermons. He believed preachers

should be deadly serious in what they were doing. They were to preach with absolute conviction, coupled with deep, reverential emotion, demonstrating '*deep earnestness* of the soul, which is created by the truth *strongly perceived* and *entirely* believed'. The minister was to be well versed in both the text and the needs of those to whom he was preaching.[10] Yet the awesome majesty of the truth of God was not to be in any way minimized to accommodate it to modern ears: 'We must not bring down the majesty of truth to our tastes, but elevate our tastes to its majesty.'[11]

Preaching engagements away from home

As his reputation as a preacher grew, Reed was increasingly called upon to preach in different parts of the country, especially at anniversary meetings, the opening of chapel buildings and the induction of ministers. He remembered some of these occasions as times of great blessing, and ministers and their congregations wrote to show how they had been particularly encouraged. A number of Reed's sermons on special occasions were printed, and letters reached him containing indications of how his published sermons of the 1820s and 1830s had been helpful to their readers.[12]

These preaching visits around the country were sometimes undertaken at considerable risk. Travel by railway could be uncertain and dangerous in the 1840s. In one series of preaching engagements, during which he covered some 1,500 miles and opened six new chapels, three accidents occurred to trains on which he was travelling, including one in which four people were killed and eight injured. A very major disaster was only just avoided while he was a passenger on the Midland Counties line, when a viaduct collapsed moments before the train on which he was travelling started to cross it. A signalman with a red flag frantically waved a warning, and the driver threw the engine into reverse to bring it to a halt just before it plunged over the gaping chasm. Although the passengers were badly shaken, no one was seriously hurt.[13]

Such accidents were not only a hazard of rail travel, but also of boat and horse-drawn coach journeys. On a return visit from preaching in the Isle of Man in 1843, he lost his footing when transferring from a small boat onto the side of the steamer. Reed was left dangling by a rope just above the boiling sea, and it was several minutes before the sailors could pull him over the side to safety. He knew it was a special deliverance: 'The Lord saved me from the very jaws of death.'

In that same year he visited Edinburgh and hoped to sail back to London the following day, but found that the only ship available, the *Pegasus*, was leaving that very evening. Reed was unable to be free of his commitments by then, so the ship sailed without him, and he travelled the next day. He was stunned on reaching Hull to hear that the *Pegasus* had sunk the previous evening with the loss of all passengers. Only a few of the crew survived. He rejoiced in his providential escape, but deeply mourned the death of so many passengers, including John Mackenzie, whom he knew well and who was reportedly last seen kneeling on the deck of the stricken vessel, surrounded by terrified passengers, for whom he was praying.[14] With such remarkable escapes, Reed could only conclude that he had been spared by God for some special work. He threw himself more thoroughly into personal evangelism after this escape.

The content and style of his preaching

The evangelistic element of Reed's preaching was clear and urgent, his constant fear being that those who had heard him might not respond. On the ninth anniversary of beginning his ministry, he characteristically pleaded with the New Road congregation: 'May you *now* listen to a voice you have so much neglected. May your heart be *now* softened into peni-tence and prayer by the grace of God... All time is on flight!

Eternity is at hand! The judge is at the door! Prepare to meet your God!'[15]

It was this aspect of Reed's preaching that attracted the notice of an observer in the 1830s, when he was at the height of his preaching powers: 'There is that about his whole deportment and preaching which must convince everyone he is in earnest.' The range of language used by Reed was also noteworthy: to the sinner it was 'glowing and heart-stirring'; to the believer seeking comfort and consolation his tone conveyed 'all the kindness of a parent, and the affection of a friend'. At the root of his ministry, the observer believed, lay Reed's commitment to prayer: 'He appears to breathe the spirit of prayer in every movement of his life,' a commitment matched by that of his congregation.[16]

The range of Reed's preaching becomes apparent from the evidence of one faithful Wycliffe Chapel member, Richard Jolly (1784-1872). In his pocket book, covering the years 1846 to 1851, he recorded the texts used for the sermons each week, with comments as to what the hearer found particularly helpful.[17] It provides a unique glimpse into what it was like to sit under Reed's ministry, and the profound affection in which he was held. Jolly refers to Reed as 'our dear pastor', and 'our invaluable pastor'. Andrew Reed usually preached twice on a Sunday, and once on a Wednesday evening, making up for this demanding schedule with extended breaks during the summer. His return from holiday, or travels abroad, was always greeted by Richard Jolly as an occasion for great joy.

Reed usually preached from an individual verse of the Bible, and his choices indicate a preference for the New Testament, although a range of Old Testament texts were also used. Sometimes Reed preached a consecutive series of messages — in February 1846 three sermons on grace, based on 2 Peter 3:18. The Lord's Prayer was covered in seven sermons in June and July 1846. In October 1847 he preached twelve sermons on the Beatitudes. The longest series in these years was of fourteen sermons on John chapter 10. Andrew Reed was still preaching expository sermons in the 1850s — one notable series was on Ephesians 1:17–23. Reed loved the themes that this passage opened up, and brought the series to a close with some sadness.[18]

Many sermons were preached with the unconverted in mind, but the preaching of the gospel message proved to be a blessing to believers as well. A sermon on 'What must I do to be saved?' (Acts 16:30) was thought by Mrs Jolly to be 'sublime', and Jolly himself declared the sermon on John 19:30 'powerfully affecting and truly good'. The New Year's Eve message for 1846 on 'The end of all things is at hand' (1 Peter 4:7) was to Richard Jolly a 'sublime sermon indeed'. There was also a healthy pastoral range to Reed's preaching: evangelism, encouragement to holiness, repentance, the wonders of Christ, perseverance and suffering were all themes to be found in his pulpit ministry. On 4 January 1846 Reed preached on a subject dear to his heart, the longing for revival. Working from the text of Habakkuk 3:2, 'O Lord, revive thy work,' he challenged his hearers to three things: the duty of the church to show 'conviction of sin by true penitence'; earnest effort in prayer for those around the church, and zeal and untiring efforts for the salvation of others. There was an earnestness and urgency about his preaching. In January 1846, as he led the communion service, he urged those who were present as spectators not to always 'halt between two opinions', but 'with earnest wrestling and prayer to decide to give themselves to the Lord'.

Reed's style was to begin slowly, carefully introducing his subject and establishing its importance. He explained his theme thoughtfully, choosing individual words deliberately. There is a distinctive elegance to his language, but his phrases became more clipped as he moved towards challenging application. In his London Missionary Society anniversary sermon of 1831, 'Eminent Piety Essential to Eminent Usefulness', as he begins to apply his text, his challenges to devotion to the missionary task become searching: 'Can we pretend, with the apostolic example and scriptural standard before us, that we have rightly and fully

respected the claims of this service? ... Have we ever laboured
in this cause with the zest and aptitude with which we have
pursued our temporal interests? Have we ever sorrowed over
man's spiritual apostasy and misery as we have lamented a
personal or a relative calamity?' His conclusions conveyed the
urgency of his theme, and built to a dramatic climax. He ended
this anniversary sermon with the longing of the church for the
return of Christ: 'Thy saints are waiting for thy coming! Hell is
moved at thy coming! Heaven is silent for thy coming! Come,
Lord Jesus, come quickly.'[19]

The effect on his hearers

Reed's preaching and teaching ministry inspired and encouraged a strong personal devotional life amongst his regular
hearers. When Richard Jolly was unable to attend church
because of a cold, he still read the Scriptures and prayed at
home, as he recorded, 'I trust with a penitent spirit'. The
preaching of Andrew Reed was hard to match and when he
was absent on holiday, Jolly and his wife took the opportunity
to listen to leading preachers elsewhere in London, including
Independent, Baptist and Methodist churches. Visiting preachers to Wycliffe Chapel were often tutors or students at Hackney
College, or missionaries on home assignment. On 11 January
1850 Jolly recorded that the sermon was given by Mr Pinning-
ton, a black preacher.[20]

Reed's powerful preaching ministry encouraged others to
follow his example. He advocated high standards in the ministry
and became a valued supporter, and then trustee, of his former
college. A number of students from Homerton and Hackney
Colleges attended Wycliffe Chapel during the period of their
studies, and Reed sought to involve them in the working of
various institutions connected with the congregation.[21] The
daughter churches established by Wycliffe Chapel, the Christian
Instruction Society and the work at the 'preaching stations' and

Bible Classes associated with the church gave many opportunities for lay members, and ministerial students, to develop their
gifts in public speaking and preaching. Andrew Reed's oldest
son, Andrew, became a successful Congregational minister, and
other chapel members went into pastoral ministry or became
missionaries.[22]

His theology

His sermons indicate that, from the theological point of view,
Andrew Reed stood in the Calvinistic tradition, but that this was
a Calvinism modified by the influences of the eighteenth-
century Evangelical Revival. This gave his work a distinctive
emphasis on the authority of the Bible and the urgency of
evangelism. At the heart of his ministry lay the certainty that the
Bible was the Word of God. It was to be studied by the
preacher thoroughly: 'Every part of truth has an important
bearing on the great subject of salvation.'[23] His preaching was
also strongly evangelistic, his sermons making a direct appeal to
the heart, while relying absolutely on the grace of God for
conversion. In this way Reed followed the pattern set by the
evangelical Calvinism of George Whitefield.

The book *The Advancement of Religion the Claim of the
Times* consists of a series of lectures Reed delivered before the
season of blessing experienced by Wycliffe Chapel in 1838. Full
of references to the cross and earnest, fervent, longing for the
spiritual welfare of those whom he addressed, the addresses
give a glimpse into the evangelistic heart of Andrew Reed.[24]
What Reed saw in terms of the advance of the gospel around
the world through mission effort, and the tremendous growth he
saw in his own church, filled him with optimism as to the future
advance of the gospel: 'Virtue shall subdue vice, religion,
ungodliness; and where death and sin abounded, there grace
and life shall much more abound... That feeble light which rose

like a star over Bethlehem, shall expand into a sun, and shall fill the whole earth with its glory.'[25]

An influential figure in shaping Reed's theology was Samuel Lyndall, under whose ministry at the New Road Chapel he was converted. Lyndall inclined to high Calvinism, emphasizing strongly the sovereignty of God in absolute predestination, and was wary of making appeals to the unconverted to accept Christ. If those moved by his ministry were of the elect, he believed God would bring them to himself without the need to appeal to the human will. What Andrew and his mother particularly found attractive about Lyndall was his simple and direct style, and also the spiritual vitality in his preaching, with an emphasis on the reality of Christian experience. Lyndall would never deliver 'a lifeless essay on divine things'.[26] For a while Reed adopted Lyndall's high Calvinism, but under the influence of his mentors Matthew Wilks at the Moorfields Tabernacle and George Collison at Hackney College, he began to emphasize the role of human activity in proclaiming the gospel, and the responsibility of those who heard the message to repent and believe it, while still strongly believing that those who responded to the gospel did so because God enabled them so to do. He saw no conflict between human responsibility and divine sovereignty. His Calvinism therefore became a vital force, filled with energy and optimism, stressing the importance of preaching as the means by which people came to believe.

This was further enhanced through the development of his thinking on the topic of revival. His trip to America in 1834 was particularly influential in this. Reed came to stress even more firmly that humans had a responsibility to proclaim the gospel, and a duty to believe it when they heard it preached. However, a careful balance was maintained: he believed any tendency to underplay divine sovereignty and overstress human action led only to 'unwarrantable extravagance'.[27] He argued that this balance was present in the preaching of the apostles: 'Mark how they command all men to repent and believe the Gospel, and yet maintain that these deposits are the gift of God.'[28] Reed saw no incompatibility between urgent evangelism and the doctrine of election: 'Since we know not who are the persons that shall receive the truth to their salvation … it is imperative in duty, that we should proclaim the will of God to all men; lest if we willingly neglected a single individual, we might, in that individual, be passing by a subject of mercy for whom Christ died.'[29]

He also believed that the death of Christ was for a specific purpose, designed for, and applied to, those who were 'chosen by God to salvation before the foundation of the world'.[30] However, while he was convinced of the doctrine of limited atonement, he did not speak in terms of a double predestination — of some being predestined to heaven and others to hell: 'None perish but those who perversely refuse to slake their thirst at those overflowing waters which are ever welling forth from the living fountain of Mercy.' If a person was lost, the responsibility was that of the individual, not God's.[31]

The need for Christians to strive after holiness was stressed by Andrew Reed; there was no place to simply wait for God to do this work. All of life was to be lived to please and honour God. The great charitable enterprises in which he was involved were an outworking of his theological views; a constant theme for Reed, and one which he found delightful, was the 'rich and spontaneous grace of God';[32] from the experience of this amazing grace of God was to flow a life filled with good works, pleasing to the Saviour. It was the inevitable spiritual response to what God had done in salvation. The grace of God did not make a Christian inactive, but inspired an outflow in the person's life, through urgent evangelism and holy living. As Reed declared, 'Now that redemption is accomplished, make haste to proclaim the Saviour as the rightful Sovereign and to establish His kingdom over the whole world.'[33] Those most convinced of the sovereign grace of God should be the most fruitful in his service. Between what Andrew Reed said in the pulpit, and what he did in the establishing and running of charities designed to help the most needy of individuals, there was both continuity and consistency.

17.
Starting again

The ability of Andrew Reed to arouse the sympathy and compassion of ordinary … people, as well as wealthy benefactors, was striking. His Christian compassion for the weak and helpless was infectious.

17.
Starting again

When a recently bereaved widow decided to ask the Baptist C. H. Spurgeon's Stockwell Orphanage to care for her son, her local Anglican vicar promptly wrote to inform her that it would be 'the height of cruelty to hand over your poor boy to the Baptists'; to him such a step was akin to abandoning the Christian faith.[1] As a committed Nonconformist Andrew Reed was determined that such discriminatory attitudes should not be allowed to deny orphan children the help they so urgently needed. The traumatic events of 1843, culminating in the separation from the Infant Orphan Asylum and then from the London Orphan Asylum, left Reed bruised and discouraged. His hopes that charity could operate on the basis of Christian compassion for those in need, without sectarian or denominational rivalries intervening, appeared to have been dashed. Sadly the hostility between Anglicans and Nonconformists remained intense in some quarters. As the dust settled after his decision to separate from the Infant Orphan Asylum, a new plan began to formulate in his mind. It was for an orphanage that would transcend denominational divides and which would be open to children from all backgrounds, especially those from families who did not want their children's religious education to be exclusively Anglican in form.

The conditions for admission to the new orphanage

On 15 March 1844 Reed met together in his study in Hackney with four resolute friends who had worked in his earlier charities. Together they discussed his proposition for a new orphanage 'to receive and bless the fatherless infant, without distinction of sex, place, or religious connexion'. The salutary lessons of the Infant Orphan Asylum were learned: although the education of the children was to be 'strictly religious and scriptural', it was explicitly stipulated that 'no denominational catechism whatever shall be introduced, and that no particular forms whatever shall be imposed on any child, contrary to the religious convictions of the surviving parent or guardian of such a child'.[2]

While it was recognized that this scheme would prove less attractive to Anglican supporters and that the Dissenting constituency was smaller and less affluent, Reed was greatly encouraged when £1,200 was quickly pledged. As the project for the Asylum for Fatherless Children began to take shape, a provisional committee was formed on 15 May 1844. Yet there were some who opposed the move, claiming that it would adversely affect the work of the orphanages at Wanstead and Clapton. Reed preferred to see it rather as supplementary to those efforts. He argued that Wanstead was now closed 'to the child of the widowed Nonconformist, except upon condition of his learning the Catechism of the Church of England'. On behalf of other Nonconformists, he argued that 'We must commit the crime, when help is refused from others, of helping ourselves. We will bear the wrong, but we will not be driven from our duty to our principles.' He was determined to contend 'meekly and firmly for liberal things' and, whatever happened, he was resolved not to 'carry uncharitableness into the work of charity'.[3] The religious opinions of parents, or distinctions of religious party, were not to be a barrier to children benefiting from the help of the asylum.

Rather than using a liturgy or a catechism as a defining religious principle, the new charity was based upon 'the great, solemn, and holy truths on which, as Christians, we are all agreed'. Reed was delighted that prominent figures such as Lord Dudley Stuart, Lord Robert Grosvenor, Miss Burdett Coutts and the wealthy Nonconformist Gurney and Morley families were willing to unite on such a basis in the cause of Christian compassion. Most of them were present at the official formation of the charity in the Hall of Commerce, Threadneedle Street, London, on 15 May 1844. A board of twenty-seven members was appointed and the first child was admitted. Baron Lionel de Rothschild was to become a vital supporter of the orphanage, in the capacities of trustee and treasurer. Initially Andrew Reed did not take a formal public position, but his guiding hand was evident in all aspects of the charity's operations.[4]

Children eligible for assistance were those who had been bereaved of both parents, or of their wage-earning father. Orphans who had tragically lost their father before birth and whose mother died during, or soon after, childbirth were to be instantly admitted to the care of the charity.[5] A child whose father was physically or mentally handicapped and unable to support his family was also deemed eligible. The children eligible for support were to be 'destitute' — i.e., without family or friends capable of maintaining them. Sadly, as with the other orphanages, there were simply insufficient resources to care for children with severe infirmities or disabilities. However, their plight was never forgotten by Andrew Reed, as future events were to prove.

Growing numbers admitted

Almost immediately cases of great need were brought to Reed's attention, and by the end of July 1844 there were six children in the care of the charity. In August of that year a house in Richmond was rented to accommodate the children, with a matron appointed to care for them. Soon after this the children were moved to a larger house in Hackney Road, much nearer to Reed's home in East London.

Now freed from his commitments to the other orphanages, Reed was able to give his full philanthropic attention to the new project and, as the numbers of children seeking help increased, the search began for still larger and more suitable premises. Negotiations for a second property led to a large mansion on Stamford Hill being secured in 1845, but in consequence the financial pressures on the charity quickly began to mount. Reed arranged a series of meetings with churches and individuals, visiting towns in the Midlands and the north of England. Liverpool, Manchester, Bradford, Leeds and Derby were taken in during a whirlwind tour to promote the charity and raise funds. He returned with £1,180, and the charity's future secured.[6] Cases of need continued to multiply, and continued expansion followed, with a further house near to Abney Park Cemetery in Stoke Newington being leased for the care of the infants.[7]

It was possible for the wider family and friends of orphans to scrape together funds to pay for a place in the asylum. £200 would allow the support of a child from the age of three until he or she was fourteen, but such cases were rare. Most friends and relatives were unable to afford such sums, and the majority of children were accepted through the election system favoured by the other charities. A subscription of half a guinea secured the right to cast a vote in an election; one guinea gave two votes.[8] This system, used in the other charities, was again believed to give the supporters of the charity a strong say in its running, and a role in deciding who would benefit from its work. Elections were held twice a year, places available being dependent on the number of vacancies created by children who had left during the previous months, and on the resources available to support them. The buying and selling of votes between subscribers was not permitted. The names of children were allowed to appear on the election list for three years, or for six elections, and votes previously cast were accumulated. The method had its limitations, it being easier for those with affluent supporters to secure the requisite number of votes. However, the most needy candidates were usually quickly accepted, and the board had the right to admit emergency cases where a child had no parents or relations.[9] This system was to persist in the orphanage until 1939, when the onset of the Second World War led to its suspension, and the board took on the task of selecting suitable candidates.

The New Poor Law and its effects

The Asylum for Fatherless Children was established ten years after a major change in the provision of social care in England, brought about by the introduction of the New Poor Law in 1834. This new regime took an even more rigorous attitude to poverty, with its 'less eligibility test', founded on the belief that most poverty was created by improvidence, drink and careless living. Ostensibly designed to make people more responsible for their actions, ultimately it sought to discourage them from claiming assistance and denied any payments to those who stayed in their own homes. Help was restricted to those who entered the workhouse, and these places were made as grim and unattractive as possible, while those who sought help were even more harshly stigmatized as 'paupers'. Within the workhouse the sexes, including married couples, were kept separate at all but mealtimes, which was greatly distressing, especially to the elderly.

Although the New Poor Law was enforced with varying degrees of rigour in different parts of the country, the weaknesses of this system were obvious, especially for orphan children, whose descent into poverty and dependence could hardly be blamed on their own fecklessness. George Müller found children begging on the streets of Bristol in the 1830s, some of whom he took to the poorhouse before he started his orphanage in 1836. In his novel *Oliver Twist* in 1837, Charles Dickens described the orphan of the workhouse as a 'humble

half-starved drudge; to be cuffed and buffeted through the
world — despised by all, and pitied by none'. The New Poor
Law, and the problems it created for children who, through no
fault of their own, were plunged into poverty by family bereavement, made the need for charities such as the Asylum for
Fatherless Children all the more real. Reed longed to spare such
children further suffering and permanently being labelled as
'paupers'. However, the charity was not able to accept children
already being provided for by the Poor Law: those who were
helped came mainly from 'respectable' working-class families
who were considered 'deserving'.

The need to establish the charity was made all the more
urgent by the economic difficulties of the time. The 1840s have
been called 'the Hungry Forties'. At a low point in the economic
cycle between 1837 and 1842, recession hit the country,
resulting in high bread prices and high levels of unemployment.
Social observers increasingly reported on the problems of poor
housing, poor water and sanitation, crime and disease in the big
cities. Economic and environmental problems added to the
numbers of people on the margins of subsistence; the death of
one or more parents left children struggling for survival.

Christian compassion that was infectious

Behind the huge investment of time and effort involved in
starting another philanthropic project from scratch lay the
undiminished compassion of Andrew Reed for children. He
delighted to see them happy, and was deeply distressed at their
suffering.

On his visits to the home he would readily join in their fun
and games, but this light-heartedness led to a serious accident
that occurred to him in 1848. Soon after he joined in a game of
chase with the children in the garden at Stamford Hill, a small
child tripped and fell straight in front of him. To avoid running
into the little boy, Reed threw himself to one side and crashed

heavily to the ground on a gravel path. Now aged sixty-one, the philanthropist seriously injured his right arm in the fall, and it was many months before he regained its proper use. There followed an agony, not only of pain, but also of frustration at the limitations imposed on him. His inability to engage in full-scale fund-raising and supervisory operations was his main concern. However, he was thrilled when the following year friends began to speak of the need for a permanent home for the orphanage, and a building fund was launched.

Another key development was the appointment of the Rev. Thomas William Aveling as secretary of the charity. An Independent (Congregationalist) minister like the founder himself, Aveling worked closely together with Reed. 'As a son with a father, he has laboured with me in this work,' Reed later commented. Aveling was a highly respected figure in the Congregational Union and was to become its chairman in 1876. By the time of his death in 1884, his influence on the Asylum for Fatherless Children had been very significant. In honour of his work, the church that had been built alongside the school in 1878 was renamed the Aveling Memorial Church.[10]

In December 1849 a building fund for the charity was opened, but progress in fund-raising was slow,[11] and it was not until 1853 that a site for the new asylum was purchased, for the sum of £3,895.[12] The committee chose a breezy, leafy hillside at Coulsdon,[13] Surrey, a little beyond the point where the Caterham branch line dropped away from the main London to Brighton railway, south of Purley. Ever conscious of the importance of fresh air and rural scenery in sustaining the health of children, and scarred by the memories of the early tragedies of the Infant Orphan Asylum, when infectious disease had swept through the children in their cramped accommodation in the unhealthy East End of London, Reed demonstrated his desire to give the orphans the best start in life by his choice of site. He longed for them to enjoy something of the happy childhood he himself had spent roaming the Surrey countryside.

Some three miles from the nearest town, Croydon, the spot was at the time a little isolated, yet it was hoped that this would reduce the incidence of infectious diseases amongst the children. The site was also quite steep, but afforded views away to the distant South Downs. The air was fresh and the rural aspect attractive. The site was also believed to give the charity national prominence; situated on a hill above the main London to Brighton railway line, it was passed by thousands each day as they travelled by train to and from the capital. The estate was larger than the asylum needed, which gave scope for selling on part of the land for other purposes.

By September 1853 preparatory work had started, although the slowness of progress in fund-raising meant that it was August 1856 before the foundation stone was laid.

As a non-sectarian religious institution, the new orphanage did not readily attract the number of Anglican supporters who had given their money to the Infant and London Orphan Asylums. However, Reed triumphed again in securing the support of the royal family — a tribute once more to the esteem in which his philanthropic work was held. He was not rejected by royalty on account of the part he had played in the campaign for the religious liberties of Dissenters.

Queen Victoria's father, the Duke of Kent, who died in 1820, had taken a deep interest in the work of the London Orphan Asylum, and his daughter was to offer valuable support to the Asylum for Fatherless Children. In 1851 Queen Victoria purchased for His Royal Highness the Prince of Wales, then aged ten, a life nomination for the

Queen Victoria

sum of £262, 10 shillings. The prince exercised his right to nominate an orphan child to the care of the institution throughout the life of Andrew Reed and afterwards, and a succession of children were nominated, their names duly recorded — Charlotte Sharpe, Charles Weston, Elisabeth Baker. With this donation Queen Victoria became patron of the institution, a role continued by the Prince of Wales when he became King Edward VII on his mother's death in 1901.[14] Royal patronage brought great prestige to the charity and was seen by Reed as a seal of approval on the bold non-sectarian stance adopted after his withdrawal from the Infant Orphan Asylum and the London Orphan Asylum in 1843 and 1844.

Other benefactors included the wealthy Bradford factory owner and philanthropist Titus Salt, who donated to the charity £525 of the fortune he made from weaving alpaca wool. Salt was a Congregationalist, and the list of church collections for the Asylum for Fatherless Children is dominated by Congregational and Independent Chapels. Sadly, the religious mood of the times was reflected, and only a few Anglican churches offered donations.[15]

The ability of Andrew Reed to arouse the sympathy and compassion of ordinary working and middle-class people, as well as wealthy benefactors, was striking. His Christian compassion for the weak and helpless was infectious. In appeals on behalf of those orphaned of father, or both father and mother, Reed stressed that they were innocent of any blame for their plight. This made the condition of these children all the more pitiable. The model he constantly appealed to was that of Jesus Christ, who 'pitied, loved, and sheltered such little ones when He was Himself on earth'.[16]

The new building

It took two years to complete the building of the Asylum for Fatherless Children, during which period Andrew Reed was frequently at the site, ensuring that work was carried out to the highest possible standards. For an architect, Andrew Reed again turned to William Moffatt, who had worked jointly with Gilbert Scott on the Infant Orphan Asylum project. Moffatt's design for the Asylum for Fatherless Children was in the Italianate, or Osborne, style. The tender price of £16,480, plus £970 for using Devonshire stone, reflects the more limited resources available to the charity.

The foundation stone was laid on 5 August 1856, and construction began. The steepness of the Coulsdon site required significant terracing work to level the site for the main building. The imposing frontage included three towers; under the main tower a flight of steps led to a lofty entrance hall, and behind each tower a wing stretched back towards the hillside. The wings included dormitories for boys, girls and infants, together with classrooms, playrooms, washrooms and staff accommodation. To the rear of the building were laundry and boiler rooms.[17]

On 23 June 1858, as Reed approached his seventy-first birthday, the committee were able to rejoice that all the children were transferred from their cramped and increasingly unsuitable accommodation at Stamford Hill and Stoke Newington to the green spaces, fresh air and wide views of the Surrey hills.[18] The opening on 14 July 1858 of the building, which was capable of accommodating over 300 children, was an occasion of great celebration, with guests travelling from London by special train to a station temporarily constructed on the estate for the purpose. It was an idyllic, cloudless summer's afternoon, as children lined the route from the station to the new orphanage, and dignitaries and supporters processed up the hill behind the band of the Coldstream Guards. After a celebratory dinner in the refectory decorated with flags and banners, there were speeches by Lord Raynham, Andrew Reed and the Earl of Carlisle. Then the incoming Lord Mayor of London declared the new asylum open.[19]

The Asylum for Fatherless Children

The building suffered from the limitations of the days in which it was built. Water had to be pumped from a well; lighting was by candlelight until a gas supply was laid in the area in 1869, and attempts to centrally heat the building only began in 1866. However, the improved environmental conditions in the fresh Surrey air quickly proved beneficial, and instances of illness became far less frequent. Sadly, as Andrew Reed had learned by previous painful experience, it was never entirely possible to rest secure in the achievements of the past.

A cruel and heartless act

Soon after the building was opened, the charity stared near ruin in the face. In any charitable institution with significant sums of money being handled, the fallibility of human nature was an ever-present problem. It was discovered that the sub-secretary and collector of the charity had defrauded it of funds to the tune of over £900. For the times, the loss was enormous. Reed's charities did all they could to guard against such a proceeding by requiring paid officers to provide sureties, but this was no absolute guarantee against fraud.

When he discovered what had happened, Andrew Reed was devastated — the action amounted to stealing bread out of the mouths of the children. It was an act so cruel and heartless he could hardly bear to speak about it. When news of what had occurred filtered out, the asylum was subjected to severe and unwarranted criticism by a writer in one public journal. Reed was shocked by the unfairness of the attack on the charity when it was at its weakest moment and most in need of assistance. Subscriptions and donations began to dry up. Tired by the fruitless controversies of the past, Reed chose to make no reply and let the quality of its work prove the worth of the charity. In time events proved the rightness of the policy. Leading support-ers of the charity rallied round to cover the deficit, but it was eight years before the collector's relatives were able to repay what had been stolen.[20]

An enlightened policy

The lessons learned from the admissions policies of both the Infant Orphan Asylum and the London Orphan Asylum were evident in the approach adopted by the Asylum for Fatherless Children. There were to be no barriers of admission based on age, sex, or denominational background. Reed argued for love and respect for all, without discrimination on the basis of rank, race, sex or religion: the charity was open to orphaned children of Jew or Gentile, Anglican or Nonconformist.

At first children were accepted until they were eight years old, and then the committee decided on their future care on an individual basis. In 1851 the policy was clarified, with boys from the point of their admission being accepted until the age of fourteen, and girls until the age of fifteen. This was considered an appropriate school-leaving age, the threshold of adulthood, when young people were ready to enter further training or apprenticeships. At a time when many children received little or no education, it was an enlightened policy.[21] Boys and girls were equally welcomed, although slightly more boys than girls gained admission. Numbers being cared for rose steadily. In February 1852 there were eighty-nine children 'on the establishment', with fifty-eight in the house at Stamford Hill and twenty-six infants in the house at Stoke Newington; a further five little infants were fostered out with wet nurses.[22] The opening of the new home at Coulsdon allowed for a significant increase on these numbers: by 1868 there were 144 boys and 105 girls in the care of the institution.[23]

The charity came to the assistance of families hit by the terrible tragedies that had inspired the foundation of the London Orphan Asylum thirty years earlier. These were still all too common in the middle of the nineteenth century. Henry Breton, who was elected to the charity in 1860, at the age of four, had lost both parents and, along with three other children, had been left with no means of support. Horace Fisher's father had worked at the Clerkenwell Hospital and on his death he had left five children in the care of his widow; Horace was six years old when he was received by the charity. Elizabeth Carter's father had been a boatman and had left six children dependent on their mother; she came into the orphanage in 1858 at the age of four.[24]

A wide-ranging education

The Asylum for Fatherless Children was much more than an orphanage, having a strong educational component, with separate schools for girls, boys and infants aged between three and a half and eight years old. Significant resources were invested in the education of the children. For a short period between 1854 and 1857 some of the older boys were sent to Reigate Grammar School, but the practice was promptly terminated when one of the boys was believed to have been mistreated there.[25] After this the orphanage supplied a wide-ranging education for the children, pitched at grammar school standard.

Those who visited the home to assess the education it provided commented on the good quality of the textbooks and the ability of teachers to amplify and explain the material further to the children. In an era of low-quality and unimaginative teaching methods, it was reported that the style of the teachers was never dictatorial or dogmatic, but involved asking children questions and stimulating their participation. The teachers were considered to be putting far more into their preparation than would be the case elsewhere. It was found that those who had entered the orphanage at a very early age, and had benefited from the infants' schooling, reached higher levels of attainment than others. A special emphasis was placed on teaching the children about the Holy Scriptures, and for their work in this area the teachers were especially commended by visitors.[26] The curriculum was well rounded, extending beyond the basics of reading, writing and arithmetic to include history, geography, drawing and singing. Music was also taught (with opportunities to learn how to play brass instruments and the harmonium), gymnastics, swimming, cricket and gardening, and needlework for the girls.

With such a fully-rounded education, children leaving the orphanage were well equipped to find employment when formal education ended at the age of fourteen. Of 150 boys who had progressed through the school by 1868, the largest number (forty-two) gained employment as office clerks. In 1868 one former pupil became a reporter on the *Christian Times* newspaper; others went to work in the offices of lawyers, bankers, or architects, or entered retail trades working for drapers, chemists, or warehousemen. Seven emigrated to take up fresh opportunities in the colonies.[27] Girls found employment as teachers or governesses, working in shops, or as dressmakers, telegraph clerks, or nursery maids.[28]

A happy home

Supporters of the charity believed that the regime instituted by Reed, and maintained after his death, succeeded in producing a 'Happy Home', where Christian faith and character were cultivated.[29] In the infant school, hours of study were limited to allow plenty of time for healthy recreation, with the aim being to help children feel they were in a home rather than a public institution.

After leaving the orphanage, children frequently kept in touch with staff, fondly remembering the home as 'dear old Reedham', or 'Blessed Reedham'. After leaving one girl wrote, 'The home and benefactors of my childhood can never be forgotten.'[30] The desire of Reed's heart that the children should not only learn about Christianity, but come to personal faith in Jesus Christ, was fulfilled in many cases, and frequently leavers took up places in local churches as Sunday school teachers.

One girl, approaching the age for her departure from the orphanage, became seriously ill with heart disease. She died with her mother at her bedside, expressing a 'firm though simple trust in the Saviour she learned to love'.[31]

Recognition of Andrew Reed's achievements

By the time the children were established in the new building, Andrew Reed was in his seventies, and there was a growing recognition of the significance of what he had achieved in his lifetime. Attempts were made to honour him for what he had done. One such came in 1858, when the Board of Management of the Asylum for Fatherless Children made the decision to change the name of the estate on which the building stood from Coulsdon to Reedham. The founder protested against this, but the board pressed ahead regardless, and to this day passengers on the railway line that runs along the Chipstead Valley, south of Purley, can still alight at the first station, Reedham.

When in 1861, the year of his ministerial jubilee, the Asylum for Fatherless Children proposed raising a testimonial fund in his honour, Reed at once refused to allow this to take place. However, when he heard Wycliffe Chapel was proposing a similar gesture, he surprisingly agreed to it, as long as it was of money, not silver plate. On the 27th November the church duly presented him with their tribute, the very large sum of £500, and he immediately forwarded it to the Asylum for Fatherless Children with the instruction: 'Take it, and make the best of it for the fatherless.'[32] For all the philanthropic work he undertook, Andrew Reed constantly rejected any suggestion of receiving recompense. He discountenanced anything that might take money away from the children. When told of various proposals, his reply was simple: 'Tell them that I am well repaid: I only want to know that they will not let the poor orphans forget me.'[33]

18.
The missionary call

'A Christian must learn
to part with everything
he is required to be, and
to content himself with
what he is in the sight of
God, and God alone.
Till then, he is not free'
(Andrew Reed).

18.
The missionary call

That Andrew Reed had a heart for mission is without doubt. From his earliest work as a Sunday school teacher, he was powerfully motivated by the need to present the Christian message to those who had not yet heard it. This concern was not just for those in Britain who were unreached with the gospel; he was also convinced that the need for overseas missionary work was 'immediate and imperative', and that the church should respond urgently. Although believing firmly in the sovereignty of God, Reed argued that the church should not expect the conversion of the nations to come about simply through special divine intervention. It required 'human instrumentality'.[1] Reed longed to be just such an instrument in God's hand.

As with his philanthropic work, the seeds of his interest in overseas mission were sown when he was young. As a boy he had been taken by his mother to early meetings of the London Missionary Society. Rev. Matthew Wilks, one of Reed's mentors in ministry, was among the founders of the society, and it was through this body that most of his endeavours were to be channelled. In the years after he had become established in his ministry at the New Road Chapel, Andrew Reed was invited to serve on the society's committee. Founded in 1795 to promote the preaching of the gospel to the heathen, the London Missionary Society was not originally intended to be identified with any one denominational system, but over time it came to

be the missionary body most closely associated with the Congregational churches.

Links with overseas missionaries

As a result of his ministerial work and association with the
London Missionary Society, Andrew Reed was brought into
close acquaintance with some of the leading figures in the
missionary world. One such was John Philip, who arrived in
the Cape Colony (later South Africa) in 1819, where he
became superintendent of the London Missionary Society.
During the thirty years he held the post, Philip insisted that the
expansion of Christianity should be a catalyst for raising the
social and moral standards in the colony. He set himself
resolutely to defend the interests of the black population,
preaching the equality of black and white before God, and
asserting that this should be reflected in the laws of the colony.
Philip's representations to the British Colonial Office helped
secure a liberalization of the legal position of the native population, which paved the way for the adoption by 1853 of a
non-racial constitution.

Through the development of education and free commerce,
Philip sought to oppose the inroads of slave traders into the
colony, and he challenged the oppressive attitudes of many
European settlers, insisting that, with equal opportunities of
education and training, Africans would prove themselves to be
the equals of the white population. The stance of John Philip
and other missionaries in defending the interests of indigenous
tribes against white settlers was controversial, and was a factor
behind the Great Trek, or Voortrek, as Boer settlers rejected life
under British rule and, after 1830, formed communities across
the Orange River in what became the Orange Free State and
the Transvaal. When Philip returned to Britain in late 1826, to
plead his cause in public and to raise funds, he received an
enthusiastic welcome from many in the wider populace, but the

response in some missionary circles was cooler. Andrew Reed did all he could to support Philip and encouraged others to give generously towards his work, and he travelled with him to attend meetings in Holland and Germany. On Philip's return to South Africa a farewell prayer meeting was held at Wycliffe Chapel. A warm friendship developed between the two men, maintained by correspondence over the following years, and Reed was asked to help see through to publication Philip's book *Researches in South Africa*.[2]

By exposing the horrors of the slave trade, and by linking Christianity with an extension of civilizing forces, Philip was to have a profound effect on Thomas Fowell Buxton, William Wilberforce's successor in the campaign to abolish slavery and, later, on David Livingstone.[3] Andrew Reed's strong endorsement of Philip drew him into a public role with the London Missionary Society, which grew more prominent as a storm of controversy broke over the publication of *Researches in South Africa*. Philip was sued for libel in South Africa for one part of the book, and found himself facing a bill for damages of £200 and costs of £900. The board of the LMS were unable to use their funds in Philip's support, so in October 1830 Reed stepped forward to arrange a series of meetings in London Congregational churches to help raise the money. Reed believed that the action against Philip was nothing less than an attempt to silence his protests against slavery. Although the slave trade in British ships had been abolished in 1807, the ownership of slaves continued. Reed ensured that the meetings to support Philip included strong condemnations of the practice and calls for the 'early and total abolition of slavery throughout the British dominions'.[4] These meetings became part of the renewed campaign to abolish the holding of slaves, which finally culminated in the bill passed in 1833 to emancipate slaves in the British colonies.

The link with John Philip was directly continued in later years when his son moved into the East London area and began to attend Reed's congregation with his family. At the age

of seven his little daughter experienced a remarkable conversion. She was admitted to the membership of the chapel at the
age of ten, after Andrew Reed had met her and been convinced
of the soundness of the work of God in her life. She was to be
the youngest member Reed ever admitted to membership of
Wycliffe Chapel.[5]

Another strong link with the work of overseas mission came
through the Scotsman William Milne, who in 1813 arrived in
China to work with the London Missionary Society as the
colleague of the missionary statesman Robert Morrison. William
Milne died tragically in 1822, aged just thirty-seven, leaving
three sons and a daughter. When the Milne children returned to
England to be educated, the Reed family welcomed them into
their home, and they came to treat Andrew as a second father.
Milne's daughter became a member of Reed's congregation,
although, sadly, she died when still a young woman. The two
eldest sons, William and Robert, became great helpers in the
work of Wycliffe Chapel, went on to study at Aberdeen University and then Homerton College. Eventually William returned to
China to continue his father's work as a missionary, and his
brother became a minister in the north of England.

Other leading missionary figures were regular visitors to the
Reeds' home in Hackney, including Robert Moffat, father-in-law
of David Livingstone, and John Williams, later to be martyred
for his faith in the South Sea Islands. It became the custom of
Andrew and Elizabeth Reed to spend an hour in prayer each
Saturday evening for their many friends scattered across the
world engaged in missionary work.[6]

Preaching engagements on behalf of missions

On 11 May 1831, Andrew Reed was invited to preach the
annual London Missionary Society sermon at Surrey Chapel,
London. Attended by a large congregation, including many
eminent preachers, the sermon was the high point of the annual

missionary gathering, and a great honour to the invited preacher. Reed was at the time recovering from a period of illness, during which he had completely lost his voice, and he was advised by his physician to cancel the engagement. Feeling that it was his duty to fulfil the engagement, he ignored medical advice and pressed ahead with his preparations. However, as he started the sermon, Reed was alarmed to find that the first sentences he spoke were barely audible. He was relieved that, as the sermon unfolded, the full range of his voice slowly returned.

He took as his text 'This kind goeth forth but by prayer and fasting,' and entitled his sermon 'Eminent Piety Essential to Eminent Usefulness'.[7] Reed ranged through Scripture, and commented on the current state of missionary endeavour, before building to a searching call in which he unburdened his heart as to the urgency of the missionary task, speaking with earnest compassion of the multitudes around the world who did not know Jesus Christ: 'And still they are dying: now, while I speak — while you listen, they are dying! See how they pass along, melancholy, sad, and speechless, sinking down into endless night! Oh! If they would but stay till we could make one attempt for their salvation! No! they would, but they cannot; they are gone — they are gone! We shall meet them next in judgement. O Thou Judge of all, how shall we meet them? How shall we meet Thee then?' Many in the large congregation were greatly moved by his stirring message, and the sermon continued to have an impact when it was subsequently published. Some wrote to tell Reed how their spiritual commitment had been deepened through reading it.[8]

A steady stream of invitations was sent to Andrew Reed to preach sermons on behalf of local auxiliaries of the London Missionary Society. In his own congregation too, the missionary interest was strong. Wycliffe Chapel was generous in its giving, the annual missionary budget running to nearly £400 during 1841. Reed's own giving was similarly generous, and extended beyond the LMS to include gifts to the Baptist Missionary

Society and other agencies for the extension of the gospel.[9] The more Reed saw and heard of the work of mission, the more he was excited at what was being done, and what it might signify, as he declared in one missionary sermon in Manchester: 'When we see a thousand agencies put in busy operation, and all of them scattering the good seed of heavenly truth over the face of all the nations, shall we not say even with superior confidence — *the kingdom of heaven is at hand?*'[10]

A new foreign secretary for the LMS

With such an extensive range of involvement, there was every likelihood that Andrew Reed might become a very major figure in missionary affairs. Such expectations seemed about to be fulfilled when in 1830 the foreign secretary of the London Missionary Society, William Orme, died suddenly. Some members of the committee, led by the Congregationalist minister John Clayton, informally approached Andrew Reed about becoming Orme's successor in this prestigious position.

With a very busy pastorate, and extensive commitments to two orphanages at the time, it was probably unwise even to consider the proposal, but Reed felt constrained to do so. He agreed that his name could be discussed, but only if there was absolute unanimity on the committee as to the matter. The role demanded considerable skills of diplomacy and tact, treading a careful path between different interest groups, in an already well-established and successful organization. This was different from Reed's philanthropic work, where he was used to acting in pioneering and entrepreneurial fashion and, from that leading position, drawing about himself a team of able and supportive workers. Yet he was attracted to the significance of the post and felt that through it he could contribute in a major way to advancing the kingdom of Christ over the world.

When others on the committee heard that his name was being mooted for the post, they resisted the suggestion. Reed then withdrew his name and the post was promptly offered to Rev. William Ellis, a former missionary in the South Seas and Madagascar. There is no doubt that this was something of a snub to Andrew Reed. Tensions between Reed and the London Missionary Society directors were to resurface in the following years, as he felt increasingly constrained to speak out on matters of the board's policy with which he disagreed.[11]

One such issue arose soon afterwards, in relation to the position of William Hankey, the wealthy treasurer of the London Missionary Society between 1816 and 1832. Andrew Reed consistently took a principled and resolute stand against the practice of slavery, as shown in his support for John Philip. When it became known that part of Hankey's considerable wealth included a property which he had inherited in the West Indies, and upon which he owned and employed slave labour, the news provoked outrage amongst some LMS supporters. Hankey protested that the property was inherited and that he could not unilaterally free his slaves. He also argued that he was caring for his slaves in an enlightened way. Andrew Reed wrote to William Hankey in a frank but moderate way, pointing out the inconsistency of being a slave owner and holding high office in a missionary society whose workers were doing so much to oppose slavery. Eventually, in 1832, Hankey gave in to the pressure, and resigned his position. In subsequent years he was amongst the first to emancipate his slaves voluntarily.[12]

'I am prepared to go'

Andrew Reed's visit to America in 1835 convinced him of the need for the best of Britain's ministers to serve overseas. In a dramatic speech delivered at the anniversary meetings of the London Missionary Society in the Exeter Hall, London, in May 1835, he urged that some of the ministers present should be prepared to volunteer themselves to the missionary task, including those present on the platform. He then made the

Exeter Hall
Reproduced by courtesy of Professor Donald Lewis

sensational pronouncement: 'I am prepared to go', although he added a qualifying note, which many ignored, that the final decision should rest with a committee of his fellow ministers, who would need to be satisfied that the cause of Christ could be better served by his going overseas than by his staying at home.

The effect on the audience was electrifying, but at Wycliffe Chapel the proposal caused consternation. The deacons were divided over the idea, although some offered to abandon all to go and serve with him, wherever it should be. Some ministers began to express concern over the prospect of uprooting him from his successful church and philanthropic work. Reed subjected the decision as to whether it was advisable for him to serve in overseas mission to his old friend and tutor George Collison and instructed him to form a consultative committee to assess a call should one ever come.[13]

His trip across the Atlantic had also left Reed shocked at the lack of effective religious provision in the colonies, and in September 1836 he urged the London Missionary Society to take an active interest in such areas. To his growing frustration, for eighteen months the mission board hesitated over the matter, debating whether it was legitimate to extend their operations beyond 'heathen' countries. Reed pressed them hard, but it was eventually to be the Congregational Union that took the project on board, a move that deeply disappointed him. The newly founded Colonial Missionary Society was therefore left with what Reed called a 'crippled and dependent existence', before it eventually became an independent body. For a time he served as one of the honorary secretaries, but his growing philanthropic commitments meant that he had to withdraw from active involvement.[14]

Then in early 1837 came the missionary call he had declared his willingness to embrace. The need for a Congregational minister in the growing city of Toronto was reported to the Colonial Missionary Society, and leading Congregationalists such as Thomas Binney, Robert Vaughan and Arthur Tidman all recommended Andrew Reed for the post. As he had promised, he referred the matter to George Collison and his committee, declaring his willingness to abide by whatever their decision was. The committee declined to accept responsibility for uprooting Reed, but suggested a shorter stay, in order to get the work in Toronto established. A term of nine months was agreed, but when this was put to the membership of Wycliffe Chapel, they protested, fearing that he would never return. The whole process took almost five months and ended in frustration for Reed.[15] Sadly, recriminations were to follow. Some ministers complained that he had never been willing to go in the first place, and that his comments at the Exeter Hall were a grand, but empty, gesture.

The Advancement of Religion

The need for urgent evangelism at home was seen by Andrew
Reed as inseparable from the need for the extension of the
gospel to lands which had never had the opportunity to embrace the good news. After 1829 he served on the committee of
the Home Missionary Society, which promoted the preaching of
the gospel, the distribution of religious tracts and the running of
Sunday schools and prayer meetings in parts of England
destitute of the gospel.[16]

In 1838 he delivered a series of lectures on 'The Advancement of Religion', which were well received, and in 1842 he
began the work of turning the lectures into a book of practical
divinity. The process was to be a profoundly moving one for
him. The recent years of revival in his chapel seemed to have
passed and, as he revised what he had said four years before,
he became convinced that in his own life he was falling far short
of the standards he had set before others. He even began to
wonder whether he should step down from the ministry, fearing
that he had been unfruitful and unworthy of his calling, but he
found strength to carry on and assurance that there was yet
more work for him to do. The chapters on the 'Advancement of
Religion' — in the person, in the family, in the church, in the
nation and in the world — are influenced by this internal
struggle. One of these chapters was printed as a tract and
circulated amongst the congregation.

When a 'Sermon to Young Men' was announced by Reed,
regular chapel-goers voluntarily decided to hold back from
attendance to allow young people to attend, and on the Sunday
evening 1,500 young men crowded into the building. Further
services were demanded, and in all fifteen were held. The
events took Reed back to the scenes of revival in his congregation in 1839 and he was again at the chapel every night of the
week offering pastoral counsel to those affected — many of
whom had been converted.

These periods of awakening and blessing on his ministry only deepened in Reed's heart the sense of obligation to do something for those still in spiritual darkness around the world. At the communion service on the first Sunday in 1843 Reed quietly gave himself up to God — 'to be wholly at His disposal, happy if He would accept any service from me'. His congregation knew nothing of the struggle that was going on within his heart.[17]

The call of China

Throughout this period of inward spiritual conflict in 1842, the call of the mission-field had again been stirring within him. This time his thoughts turned towards South-East Asia. His interest in that vast and populous region had been kindled years before. Andrew Reed's sister Martha had been a close friend of a young woman named Maria Newell, and after Martha's death, Maria had helped teach the Reeds' children. She subsequently became the first single woman to be accepted as a missionary by the London Missionary Society and was sent to Malacca, where she worked as a teacher amongst the large Chinese community resident there. There she met and married the missionary pioneer Dr Charles Gutzlaff. Sadly, after a few happy years of marriage Maria died, but the connection with the Reeds remained strong, and when the somewhat eccentric Dr Gutzlaff visited England he stayed with them. Gutzlaff persuaded Andrew Reed to edit and to prepare for publication his works, *History of China* and *China Opened*. In his preface to *China Opened*, Reed expressed his longing that the work would awaken interest in communicating the Christian faith to the most extensive people on the face of the earth.[18]

As he edited the books, and saw them through to publication in 1838, it became clear to Andrew Reed that Gutzlaff was communicating matters of vital importance to the Christian church: China was opening up not only to trade, but also to the gospel. The signing of the Treaty of Nanking in August 1842 appeared to support Gutzlaff's contention and brought great excitement in missionary circles. Supporters begged missionary societies not to be bound by financial constraints and to embrace this opportunity. The London Missionary Society Annual Report echoed these calls: 'The voice of God to his church is distinctly uttered by his Providence as though we heard it from the Holy Oracle, "Behold I have set before thee an open door, and no man can shut it. Go forward." '[19]

Reed was stirred by this appeal. His editorial work for Gutzlaff made him feel he knew China well and he felt impelled to offer himself for work there, believing he could still give ten years of service to the work of mission. Matters were at this time coming to a head which would lead to his withdrawal from the leadership of the London and Infant Orphan Asylums. He wondered whether this was God providentially opening the door to render him finally free enough to respond to the missionary call.

Unsure of his judgement in the matter, he again sought the guidance of a committee of other ministers. Their decision came in February 1843, just at the time when his mind was in turmoil over his decision to resign from the committee of the Infant Orphan Asylum, with its building almost complete. Once more, the committee's recommendation was in the negative: they felt it was inappropriate to recommend that Reed leave Wycliffe Chapel. He was deeply disappointed. For eight years he had wrestled with the idea of a call to overseas service, but now he realized that the door had closed.

There is no doubt that his failure to put into effect his offer made in the Exeter Hall led to significant loss of face in the missionary community. Perhaps he had been too taken with the romance of the missionary role, and had been unrealistic enough to imagine that he would be allowed to give up the important work he was doing in London. He comforted himself with the thought that the word 'disappointment' did not exist in the dictionary of faith: such events were simply indications of the will of God. He was determined that he should never cease to regard himself simply as 'a poor penitent at the foot of the Cross'.[20]

The controversy over Tahiti

The legacy of unhappiness over his opposition to William Hankey and the offer of missionary service that never came to fruition were not forgotten by some of the other board members of the London Missionary Society. Andrew Reed was to find these matters raked up again a few years later in 1846 when an unseemly controversy, into which he was drawn, engulfed the society.

Extensive pastoral and philanthropic work meant that Reed was unable to attend all the meetings of the directors, which were sometimes as many as thirty in a year. In 1841-42 he managed to attend just ten, and only thirteen in 1843-44, and he indicated to the society that he was not available for sub-committee work. Some failed to appreciate what his extensive pastoral and philanthropic commitments demanded of him and were unhappy at his attendance record, although, with a board numbering over fifty members, Reed was not the only one who failed to attend all the meetings. Increasingly, as with other heavily committed senior ministers, his presence on the London Missionary Society board became symbolic and the everyday running of the society fell to paid officials.

Although he could not give the attention to the society that he wished, his role on the board left him frustrated with the way it was conducting its affairs and with some of the decisions being made. Matters came to a head over the conduct of the London Missionary Society on the Polynesian island of Tahiti, which had become one of the great success stories in the work of the mission.

Work had begun on Tahiti in the late 1790s, but had faced enormous difficulties, and for the first fifteen years had yielded almost no fruit. The small band of missionaries had struggled on, with their lives frequently under threat, and their numbers being steadily reduced by the often fatal ravages of tropical disease. When a number of the indigenous population embraced Christianity, some were murdered by their fellow islanders. None the less, a native Tahitian church was gradually born through the faithful, heroic perseverance of the early missionaries. That church began to grow steadily, especially after the pre-eminent chief, Pomare, threw away his idols and asked for Christian baptism. The change that followed was demonstrable: when in 1835 Charles Darwin visited Tahiti on the ship *The Beagle* he noted the evidence of a moral transformation on the island, of real faith and prayerfulness amongst the population and a genuine joy that marked out the inhabitants. This appeared strikingly different from the constant wars, bloodshed, infanticide, dishonesty and intemperance that had been reported on the islands before the arrival of Christianity. From the royal family down, the island largely embraced the Christian faith and became, in both name and law, Protestant.

However, this settled state of affairs was challenged in 1836 when two French priests, avoiding islands where there was no Christian presence at all, landed covertly on Tahiti. Without the requisite permissions this was an illegal act. They sought to befriend a group of native chiefs who were unhappy with the new state of affairs on the island and to win them to Roman Catholic, and French, influence. When their presence was discovered, three of the London Missionary Society missionaries asked them to leave, because their landing contravened the law of the island. The priests refused and barricaded themselves in their hut, whereupon the roof was removed by the representatives of the Tahitian government, and they were 'conveyed' back to their vessel. It was claimed that this had been done without harming them or their possessions. The six other LMS missionaries later registered their disapproval at the stance of their colleagues. The two priests persisted in their efforts to settle on the island, and returned to Tahiti, but were again refused admittance.[21]

News of these events only slowly filtered out. The LMS took no action on the matter, but Andrew Reed protested against what had happened. Although he opposed the teachings of Roman Catholicism, he argued that, just as Nonconformists appealed for religious liberty in Britain, they should support and maintain religious liberty in all other countries, even if it meant allowing the dissemination of views with which they did not agree. Matters began to deteriorate when the two priests took a complaint about their treatment to the French government in Paris. In August 1838 a French frigate was sent to the island, demanding an apology and reparations from the Tahitian authorities, and requiring protection for any French citizens who should visit the island. The Queen of Tahiti, under duress, agreed to such conditions but appealed to Britain for help. No assistance was forthcoming. Attempts to outlaw the promotion of Catholicism met with stern resistance from the French authorities, and in 1841 they began to install their own government.

The position of the London Missionary Society was compromised in this incident by the actions of the three missionaries in ordering the priests to leave. Its role was further confused by the fact that one of its workers, George Pritchard, had been appointed British Consul on the island in 1837. Sent out by the LMS, Pritchard had arrived on Tahiti in 1824 and, although by trade a brass founder, he had risen to the position of principal in a seminary on the island, before in 1837 accepting office with the British government. On their assumption of control in Tahiti, the French temporarily imprisoned the consul, exiled the widow of the pre-eminent chief Pomare and restricted the activity of the Protestant church.

When Pritchard was eventually released, the LMS took an appeal against his treatment to the British government, who promised that the matter would be investigated. However, as an employee of the government, he was ordered to remain silent on the matter. Pritchard privately approached Andrew Reed and sought his advice. Reed was a strong supporter of religious freedom, and was willing to allow the activity of Catholic priests on Tahiti, but was not prepared to countenance a French takeover of the island, along with what appeared to be repression of the Protestant church.

Through his charitable work Reed knew a number of leading figures in the government and was aware that they were waiting to gauge public reaction to events before deciding what action should be taken. He advised Pritchard to ignore the government's order and, as a mission worker, to take to the public the plight of the native government of Tahiti and its Protestant church. The raising of a storm of popular protest would be to the British government a signal that it must challenge strongly the French action in occupying this island. Buoyed up by the successful Nonconformist campaign against the education clauses of the 1843 Factory Bill, Reed was confident that opposition from an outraged public would have a similar effect, and the government would have no choice but to act. When, a little before the events on Tahiti, American missionaries on the Sandwich Islands had been similarly threatened by French incursions, the United States government had responded quickly and their missionary work had been protected. Reed had no doubt that Tahiti could be similarly spared, while lamenting that the LMS leadership had not foreseen a similar eventuality.[22]

However, the LMS directors, not wanting to antagonize their friends in the government, refused to countenance any such mobilization of public concern, and contented themselves with writing to the government and sending a deputation to Lord Aberdeen, the Foreign Secretary. They also ordered Pritchard to say nothing in public on the matter. Reed later learned that the government read the supine response of the LMS as a sign that no further action was needed. Although protesting at French policy, Lord Aberdeen was anxious to avoid any confrontation. The British government decided to sacrifice Tahiti to the entente cordiale it was at the time strenuously trying to maintain with France. Pritchard was repaid for his silence with a consul's post elsewhere, and Andrew Reed was left indignant that nothing had been done to defend the rights of the infant Protestant church in Tahiti, built up at the cost of the lives of many missionaries. Believing that strong pressure from the British government would have forced the French to back down, he lamented that the island, once a jewel in the crown of Protestant missionary efforts, was now in the hands of Catholic France, with 'homes and churches forsaken'. He was also frustrated that because of his charitable commitments he had not been able to attend all the relevant committee meetings and little account had been taken of his views.

Eventually, when in November 1846 the directors of the LMS issued a circular about their work in Tahiti, Reed felt constrained to respond publicly. In early 1847 he wrote to the *Patriot*, a religious newspaper, to alert the Christian public more fully to what had happened. Suddenly the directors of the LMS were roused to action, but their anger was directed not at the policy of either the British or French governments, but at their fellow director who had chosen to criticize their action in public. A short, and at times bitter, exchange of public pamphlets followed. The directors' responses to Reed were written in a highly combative tone and were deeply personal attacks. His performance as a director of the LMS, the issues surrounding the decision not to appoint him as its foreign secretary and his failure to take up a missionary post after his public offer were all used against him. The endeavours of his church in sending out missionaries were also publicly questioned. For his part Reed criticized not only the policy over Tahiti, but also the running of the LMS and its failure to make effective use of the society's jubilee for fund-raising. He was clearly unhappy at a number of cautious decisions the society had made, including the appointment of a home secretary who was also working as the minister of a church. He believed that such decisions smacked more of retrenchment than of urgently responding to growing opportunities for world mission. The controversy was a boiling over of simmering frustrations and resentments on both sides, and was deeply unfortunate. Busy with other commitments, Andrew Reed was ill-suited to the intricacies of a pamphlet war. He saw the bigger issues and focused on them, but did not spend enough time researching details and preparing carefully worded contributions for publication. Some of the statements he made proved inexact and were incorrect in minor details. This gave the LMS directors scope to pick holes in his arguments and quibble over his facts, and thereby to divert criticism from their policies. It is hard not to be a little shocked at the tone the directors adopted in responding to Reed's criticisms: he was accused of making 'empty boasts of self-confidence', of being 'deficient in ingenuousness and candour' and of 'egregious inconsistency'.[23]

Little was achieved by the controversy, which broke out when it was too late to do anything about Tahiti. Reed might have done better to resign quietly and throw himself into his other important projects. His criticisms cost him a number of friends. He found himself ostracized by the London Missionary Society Board; some whispered that by his actions he had stolen the bread from the mouths of the children of missionaries. The matter was raised at the London Board of Congregational Ministers, and even at the board of his own beloved Asylum for Fatherless Children, then still in its early and vulnerable days. Through the harsh response to his criticisms, Reed felt his reputation had been taken from him and trampled upon. Yet he saw God's hand in this, and sought to learn lessons for his own spiritual growth from the events. Giving up time, talents, money to the cause of Christ was easy, but more was needed: 'A Christian must learn to part with everything he is required to be, and to content himself with what he is in the sight of God, and God alone. Till then, he is not free.'[24] Emotionally he felt crushed by the vilification he received: on his return from a summer break after these events he found himself in tears in his vestry.

He threw himself anew on God's mercy, and confessed his 'boundless necessity and boundless unworthiness'. Reed was determined to see only God, not his troubles: 'I must see His face in His Son, or it will trouble me. I would think, prepare for the field of life and service, — think as Thou wouldst have me, do as Thou wouldst have me, suffer and be what Thou wouldst. Oh! That my mind might apprehend Thee, — my heart rest on Thee, be full of Thee, satisfied in Thee, exult in Thee!' His congregation readily understood what he was going through and steadfastly stood by him. Unbeknown to him, they took up a collection and, with the funds raised, struck a gold medal in honour of his work, which he found lovingly laid on his desk when he returned from one of his trips away from London.[25]

In the controversies in 1842-43 over the use of the Anglican catechism in the orphanages he had established, Reed had chosen to withdraw quietly from the charities, rather than lead a public campaign that might adversely affect the care of the children. In the case of the LMS the matter was not one of broad Christian compassion, but the conduct of world mission by the Congregational churches, a body in which he was a leading figure. On matters of principle relating to the spread of the Christian gospel, Reed could be unshakeable. For the sake of this cause he chose to take his campaign to the public, believing that this was the way to bring about change for the good in missionary endeavour. Reed became impatient with the cautious LMS policy and was shocked to find that, rather than the directors throwing their efforts into resolving the problems he had identified, they directed them into attacks on their one-time friend now turned critic. When John Philip, whose work Reed had championed in the 1820s and 1830s, had adopted an overtly political stance (coupled with a somewhat domineering style) he too had found himself disowned by the LMS. Nor could the society accommodate the radical dynamism of the great David Livingstone, who was ultimately to end up working independently in Africa.[26]

There were faults on both sides. Reed learned the hard way that it was impossible to be a busy minister, active in philanthropic activities, and a missionary statesman. The resource of his time was limited; he needed to restrict the ongoing commitments he accepted. He had probably been unwise to offer himself as a missionary candidate when he had vital philanthropic work to complete at home. The events of 1847 proved deeply bruising to him, and several bouts of illness later that year appear to have been connected to the stress he had been placed under. Reed was open to his faults, and to the fact that he was unduly concerned about his reputation. In his journal he cried out his prayer to God: 'Hide me from the effects of my own folly and sins... Help me; for I have neither wisdom, grace, nor energy without Thee.'[27]

The fact that one of the directors' charges, that Wycliffe Chapel was not active in sending missionaries, was without foundation was proved in January 1848, with the farewell service for William Hill. Hill had been converted through the work of the church and had been a loyal member during the years of his studies at Hackney College. For all the criticism that the society had heaped on Reed, he still recommended Hill to the London Missionary Society, and was delighted when he was accepted and sent forth into missionary labours. The young man was deeply attached to Reed, who in turn commented, 'I have joy in him!'[28]

Yet out of the legacy of hurt and disappointment came good. In their *Memoir* of their father, Reed's sons indicate that a number of his chief suggestions were eventually adopted by the LMS, indicating the wisdom of what he had proposed, if not the way in which he had raised the matter. Freed of his commitments in the field of overseas mission, he was able to concentrate on other key benevolent projects that he was at that time developing, particularly one of crucial importance for those with severe learning disabilities.

19.
Caring for the most needy

As he neared the end of his life Reed ... recalled, 'I have always had their *souls* in view. Who was it once asked me if idiots had any souls...? Yes, and I remember that little fellow at Highgate who said, "I love God."'

19.
Caring for the most needy

The 1840s were years of difficulty and sadness for Andrew Reed in a number of aspects of his public life. Early in the decade he felt he had no choice but to sever his connections from two orphanages he had been instrumental in founding, and later came the years in which his relationship with colleagues on the board of the London Missionary Society was strained to breaking point as he urged changes in their policy. Yet the 1840s were also a decade of new beginnings as he refocused his efforts in Christian compassion. In 1844 he responded to the continuing desperate needs of orphaned children with the commencement of the Asylum for Fatherless Children on explicitly non-sectarian grounds. Although now in his late fifties, Andrew Reed was at this time freed from some of his wider concerns and decided to embark on two more major philanthropic projects before his death. The first of these was aimed at those who, alongside orphan children, were the most needy and vulnerable in society — children with severe learning difficulties.

The need assessed

In the eighteenth and early nineteenth centuries a number of lunatic asylums had been built for those declared insane. However, for those with severe learning difficulties little was formally done. On his many preaching visits around the country

Andrew Reed had sometimes seen them chained up along with prisoners, or the insane, in the common pound, or village lock-up. Others were chased from one community to another, hounded by crowds of jeering, taunting children, or even adults. In 1840 Reed had confided in his journal the hope that he might do something for those whom society classed as less than human, but concerning whom he firmly insisted that 'The Divine image is stamped upon all.' This conviction of the fundamental human dignity of those with severe learning difficulties was a crucial motivation to this major work.[1] To one who loved natural beauty, those disfigured by physical or mental handicap were particular objects of compassion. Yet Reed's hopes took many years to materialize into concrete proposals.

By 1846, however, his resolution to take action was firm: 'Now I will go to the lowest.' Before launching a scheme, Andrew Reed knew he needed to undertake thorough research and planning. Although a small pioneering work was begun at Bath that same year by the White sisters, who had started a school for mentally handicapped children, Reed knew he needed to travel to Europe to undertake investigations into the latest work of leading practitioners. When he found this was not immediately possible, he entered into correspondence with the key figures in the understanding and treatment of those with mental handicaps, particularly children. He sought the views of the French physician Dr Jean Itard in Paris, a pioneer in the field, who had successfully treated Victor, the 'Wild Boy of Aveyron', in the early nineteenth century. He also consulted Dr Saegert in Berlin, and Itard's pupil, Edouard Séguin, who had established a school for those with severe learning difficulties at the Bicêtre Hospital in Paris. Reed sought support for the view that children with mental handicaps could be educated, and spared a life of absolute hopelessness and inactivity. He read all the literature available from Britain and overseas. A close friendship was also formed with Dr John Conolly, England's leading expert on mental handicap, and Conolly was to become a central figure in the asylum that Reed was to establish. In 1847 Reed had the long-awaited opportunity to visit some of the leading centres in Europe, in an endeavour to learn from best practice elsewhere. He was particularly impressed with the asylum established in 1839 by Dr Guggenbühl at Abendberg, a beautiful location above Interlaken in Switzerland with views towards the Jungfrau.[2]

Reed returned armed with a vast array of information, and with the benefit of having seen at first hand the successes and failures in attempts at care and treatment. He also gathered statistics from England and Wales which suggested there were over 30,000 people suffering from serious mental handicaps, although there was no formal attempt to distinguish between mental handicap and mental illness. He found that many were consigned to live in workhouses, or were mixed with those who were mentally ill in lunatic asylums. Others were in a state of absolute destitution, or were cared for by relatives who had very low incomes. Reed's research was extensive and thorough, all undertaken at his own expense. Although it was time-consuming, his work ensured that he was operating at the cutting edge of research and practice into the care and treatment of those with mental handicaps.

Time to act

Again, it was acute pastoral need that confirmed to Reed that the time was right to act. Mrs Anne Plumbe, a member of his church, came to him seeking advice as to where her son Andrew, who had severe learning difficulties, could find support and care. She had read of the pioneering work of the Bicêtre in France, but this was too expensive, and she urged her pastor to help in some way. When all the other avenues Reed tried failed, he saw this as God's providential leading — now he should move his own project forward.[3]

He spent June 1847 drawing together a provisional committee, before visiting Paris and Berlin again to gather further detailed information. This informal committee included Samuel Morton Peto, the railway baron, John Wilks MP (son of Andrew Reed's early mentor Matthew Wilks), James Nisbet (the publisher), William Howitt (a Quaker writer), William Champneys (the evangelical Anglican vicar of Whitechapel) and Reed's loyal supporter from the Asylum for Fatherless Children, William Monk. In July, Reed made his report to the committee and explained his plan. The object of the institution was set out as being 'to take care of, and, by skilful and earnest application of the best means, to prepare, as far as possible, for the duties and enjoyments of life' those with mental handicaps. No restriction as to age, sex, or country of origin was to be placed on those admitted. Reed was the first subscriber to the charity, and Anne Plumbe was the second.[4]

Drawing on all his previous experience of founding charities, he launched himself into an exhausting round of visiting and letter-writing, urging the assistance of individuals from all ranks — noblemen, clergymen, bankers, merchants and ordinary lay members of churches. At a public meeting on 27 October 1847, presided over by the Lord Mayor of London, Sir George Carroll, the charity was formally launched.[5]

Sadly, over the years words change their meaning, and the name chosen for the institution, the 'Asylum for Idiots', would not be appropriate today. However, in the 1840s the word 'idiot' was merely a medical term to describe a person with a particular type of permanent mental handicap from birth or an early age. It was used by doctors, alongside words such as 'imbecile', 'cretin', 'fatuous' and 'lunatic' (all of which have since degenerated into terms of abuse), as terms designed to distinguish different degrees of disability, and to differentiate between mental handicap and mental illness. According to one Edinburgh medical doctor and lunatic asylum superintendent, writing in 1837, 'idiocy' referred to the condition of a person whose mental capacity had only partially developed. Some in

this condition were able to recognize people, attempt communication — which was often incoherent — and demonstrate
affection, but the capacity to reflect or reason was in the main
considered to be absent. Such children often possessed limited
mobility and spent much time asleep, or sitting rocking back-
wards and forwards in a chair. Tragically, as this doctor observed, when they were given liberty in wider society, they
became 'the sport of fortune or of their own imperfect instincts
and ill-regulated passions, the prey of the designing, the butt of
the idle or the cruel'.[6] Andrew Reed had come to the view,
radical for the time, that children with such moderate to severe
learning difficulties could be helped by education and by
appropriate physical exercise to overcome at least some of their
mental handicaps. This made him one of Britain's pioneer
thinkers in the field.[7]

In his original address to the public meeting in October
1847, Reed urged the vital necessity of the charity. 'Idiot'
children were uncared for: this was the yawning gulf in Britain's
charitable provision, for they were the most needy. The address
declared: 'We plead for those who cannot plead for themselves.' Reed expressed his higher spiritual hope that not only
would the children be educated for life, but also that they might
have the opportunity to learn of Jesus Christ, 'and look beyond
our present imperfect modes of being to perfected life in a
glorious and everlasting future'.[8] It was this hope for the spiritual
well-being of the children that particularly inspired him.

The October meeting showed that Reed's preparatory work
had been thorough: his reputation as a philanthropist went
before him, and leading figures in society readily lent their
backing to the charity. In addition to the support of the Lord
Mayor of London came that of Lord Palmerston (foreign
secretary and later prime minister) and Lord Dudley Stuart, all
of whom were appointed presidents. Of the twenty-one vice-
presidents, who, as with the Asylum for Fatherless Children,
included Baron Rothschild, twelve were members of Parliament. The directors of the charity included Andrew Reed, who

was honorary secretary, William Champneys and John Wilks MP from the early committee, and Dr John Conolly. The joint secretary with Reed was the Rev. Dr James Holloway.[9]

The aims of the charity

The charity was concerned not only to provide care for the young people it accommodated, but to take seriously Reed's views as to what could be achieved by education. Poverty was not to be a barrier to entry: admission was granted to those who were destitute of all means (although it did not admit those already cared for by the Poor Law), as well as those whose families could make a modest contribution. Most of those helped came from low-income working-class families. Age was to be no barrier to admission, although the committee understandably favoured those deemed 'most likely to profit by the course of treatment and education to be adopted', which in most cases meant children aged between eight and fourteen. This assessment rested in part with the doctors who were required to examine cases before admission. The board of the charity had authority to admit cases in an emergency, but the usual system of acceptance was through the half-yearly elections in April and October. Again repeating the pattern established in the previous charities, Reed insisted that candidates were not present at the election, to shelter them from the process. A half-guinea subscription gave the right to one vote, the number of votes increasing with additional donations. Candidates who were unsuccessful in one election could have the votes they accrued carried forward for a further two elections, giving a considerable likelihood of eventual entry. The system was a way of ensuring that donors had a say in the admission of those the charity sought to help, and it proved highly popular, soon attracting thousands of subscribers, most of whom paid modest amounts of between half a guinea and five guineas.[10]

Park House

Efforts to find a suitable property for the asylum were spear-headed by Andrew Reed, who devoted much time to the endeavour. Eventually Park House, standing in sixteen acres of gardens on Highgate Hill, was secured for the charity in early 1848, on an eleven-year lease at £250 per annum. Preparations were made for the admission of the first inmates in April 1848, with Reed expending considerable efforts in purchasing suitable furniture and appointing William Millard as headmaster, together with a gymnastics teacher and a singing teacher. When the asylum opened on the 26th April, seventeen young people were admitted, ranging in age from twenty-five years down to eight years, the circumstances and health of each having been carefully investigated. The following month, the stables of Park House were converted into a gymnasium, to facilitate the emphasis on physical exercise in the care of the patients. A washing room, workshop, playroom and infirmary followed soon afterwards.[11]

To an observer without the eye of faith, the scene in Park House in the first few days after the arrival of the first inmates was not a promising one. It illustrated the need for the home, but also the challenges ahead. The carers had little experience in treating those with severe learning difficulties, many of whom were not used to living in a structured or restricted community environment. Reed described the early scenes vividly: 'Some had been spoiled, some neglected, some ill-used. Some were clamorous without speech, and rebellious without mind; some were sullen and perverse, and some unconscious and inert. Some were constantly making involuntary noises from nervous irritation, and others hid themselves in corners from the face of man as from the face of an enemy. Windows were smashed, wainscoting broken, boundaries defied, and the spirit of law-lessness was triumphant.' Some supporters, though well-meaning, found the spectacle shocking and one for which they were utterly unprepared. Many despaired at any prospect of success in what they had taken on.[12]

However, others were far more visionary. Among these were members of the royal family. One early supporter was the Duke of Cambridge, uncle of Queen Victoria, who became a frequent visitor to the home in Highgate until his death in 1850. Another was Prince Albert, who visited the asylum in 1849 and, after returning the following year, donated 250 guineas to endow, in the name of the Prince of Wales, a bed for a child 'in perpetuity'. The following year Andrew Reed rejoiced to hear that Queen Victoria had granted her patronage to the charity. These leading figures added huge prestige to the project, and their support gave a great boost to fund-raising efforts.[13]

Lord Shaftesbury and the Commissioners of Lunacy

It had been hoped to enlist the support of Lord Shaftesbury, the leading evangelical politician of the day. From early in his Parliamentary career he had embraced the cause of the treatment of those who were mentally ill, and had been appointed one of Her Majesty's Commissioners of Lunacy. He had played a key role in improving standards in lunatic asylums, and in establishing proper criteria upon which patients were admitted to a mental asylum. However, as an inspector of such facilities, he wished to preserve his independence from any charity, and he therefore declined the opportunity of any personal involvement in the project. Instead he surprised the committee by insisting that the commissioners, who were keen to assert their authority over any new development, had the right to visit and inspect the new asylum. This was steadfastly resisted by members of the committee, especially Dr John Conolly, who stressed that the patients were not lunatics, and that the work of the charity was more educative than medical.

In such a pioneering work the commissioners had no specialist knowledge of their own upon which to draw. The committee took the opinion of a Queen's Counsel on the matter, but were disappointed that this upheld the view that Park House, Highgate, should be viewed as a lunatic hospital. Andrew Reed was delegated to meet with Shaftesbury and mediate in the matter. While agreeing that the commissioners had no experience in inspecting or regulating institutions of this nature, Shaftesbury was unshakeable in his opinion that the charity was running a hospital, not a school, and that a resident medical officer was required to be appointed, even though this was not explicitly stated by the Act of Parliament. Reed was disappointed that his visionary view that 'idiot' children were young people with learning difficulties, rather than patients requiring treatment, was rejected. However, he did extract from the 'Poor Man's Earl' a promise that the commissioners would 'rejoice to assist us in every way to make so desirable and important an experiment'.[14] The relationship between the charity and the Commissioners of Lunacy was to be an uneasy one in future years, with the inspectors producing a number of critical reports that often failed to take account of the experimental nature of the work, in which there were bound to be teething problems and a need to learn from mistakes that would inevitably be made.

The committee complied reluctantly with the commissioners' request that a resident medical officer be employed, and in October 1848 Dr Foreman was appointed, at an initial salary of £200, with promises that this would increase in proportion to the number of patients. He was given a significant role in the care and management of the 'family', as the children and staff were called. He was to supervise the exercise regime of each child and to be in attendance at mealtimes, for proper diet was considered key to the care of the children: much depended not only on the food that they were given, but also on 'the manner in which it [was] received and masticated'. The doctor was to keep proper records of the progress of the residents, from the time of their arrival to their discharge. He was also to oversee the appointment and training of suitable staff. This was an important matter, for within two months of the arrival of the first cases, one male assistant had to be dismissed because of 'harshness and violence of temper'.[15] Andrew Reed encouraged bringing over a specialist nurse from the pioneering work at the Abendberg in Switzerland, who sought to establish best practice among the staff and to ensure continuing high standards.[16]

Life in the asylum

The daily regime adopted by the asylum indicates the emphasis placed on education and exercise in the care of the children. Three hours each morning were allocated to education and physical exercise, and a further two hours in the afternoon. In addition to mealtimes, two hours each day were given to free play, and one hour in the early evening to occupational training, such as gardening, carpentry and mat- or basket-weaving. This reflected Reed's hope that the residents might one day be able to find useful employment in the community, as well as improving their motor skills. Wednesday and Saturday afternoons were visiting times for friends and families. High standards for the clothing and cleanliness of the pupils were established, with both showers and aromatic baths available.

Andrew Reed stressed that the diet for the residents should be plentiful and wholesome. Meat was served every day at lunchtime — beef, mutton and bacon, together with vegetables, rice, fruit or some other dessert. Breakfast was usually porridge, and supper was bread with cheese, or treacle. All, it was stipulated, was to be of the 'very best quality'. The attendants were to ensure that all were well satisfied, that food was chewed properly and that the pupils were not allowed to gorge themselves. Any thought that their diet should be 'allowanced' was utterly rejected. By the standards of the day, the menu was varied and nourishing. Many working-class families lived at the time largely on bread and potatoes, with meat and green vegetables being a rarity, and those cared for by the Poor Law system were subjected to a poor-quality diet, which in some places was chronically deficient, if not approaching starvation level. At the Rotherhithe workhouse in London during this period, children were fed mainly on bread, potatoes, suet, with some meat, but no milk; bread and flour were usually of poor quality and heavily adulterated. In one terrible incident in the Wendover workhouse, the inmates were found to be so badly fed that they had resorted to eating the mouldy bones they had been given to crush as part of the work assigned to them. Only by the 1860s were workhouse standards beginning to improve.[17]

An important aspect of the care of those in the asylum was the provision of religious instruction. This was delivered at a level appropriate to the capacity of the children, and focused on simple Scripture texts, the Lord's Prayer, the Ten Commandments and the Creed. Andrew Reed ensured that there was to be no repetition of the problems of 1843 by inserting a clause in the constitution of the asylum that families and friends should be consulted as to their wishes in this matter: 'Nothing shall be done in violation of their conscientious convictions.' Decisions about the materials used in the religious education of the children were kept in the hands of Andrew Reed and the other honorary secretary.[18]

Under such an enlightened regime a number of the children began to respond positively. Reed was thrilled with any signs of progress, and noted in his journal: 'We have advanced steadily. I will do what I can for it by the help of God.'[19] He continued to search out best practice, and gave over his holidays in 1849 to visits to leading mental asylums in the country, at Hanwell, Lancaster and York. Reed hoped for significant improvement in at least one in three of the children accommodated, and any signs of progress were carefully noted. One small boy was admitted who had been unable to walk, and could only slide about on the floor on his stomach. Through the work of the staff in patiently exercising his muscles, Reed was delighted to see him first stand, then walk and then run. The development of his physical potential was matched in other areas: he gained the power of speech and began to make educational progress.[20]

Birds and animals were kept in the grounds to amuse the children. As the care of the staff brought improvements in the physical and mental condition of the children, many of whom had previously been left to vegetate, or run riot, the chaotic scenes of the first few weeks were replaced by a more settled and harmonious routine. Children began to speak, read, write and do simple arithmetic. They responded particularly well to music. By the end of 1849 Reed also discerned signs of increased spiritual awareness in the children, and more active participation in simple services of worship.[21] The following year he could report that 'Windows are now safe; boundaries are observed without walls; and doors are safe without locks. The desire now is, not to get away, but to stay. They are essentially, not only an improving, but a *happy family*.'[22]

Meeting challenges

Some of the children progressed more rapidly than expected, and attention had to be given to providing future training opportunities for them. This was not a simple matter. Although some of them helped the gardener, or with carpentry and mat-making, the reports of the visitors from the Commissioners of Lunacy challenged the staff at Park House to do more to add variety when offering training in 'useful occupations and employments'.[23] Such efforts cost money, and fund-raising was a continuing challenge.

Less than a year after Park House had been opened, the charity was stunned to find that the crime committed in the Asylum for Fatherless Children had been repeated here. One of the officials in the charity's main office had stolen a large sum from the funds of the charity. His dismissal swiftly followed, but Reed and other committee members were required to make up a significant shortfall to meet ongoing running costs.[24]

In 1850 a further blow came when Dr Foreman also resigned. Finding suitable medical staff was always a problem to
charities and workhouses alike, and those appointed were often
younger men who had not yet established a private practice,
and who accepted the role as a way of enhancing their reputation, sometimes without any deep commitment to the charity
itself. As their private practices grew these usually took the best
part of their attention.[25]

Dr John Conolly

A key adviser to Andrew Reed and an active supporter of the
charity was Dr John Conolly. The decision to seek his support
was most important — Anne Plumbe had consulted him in her
attempts to get help for her son. He was probably Britain's
leading expert on the diagnosis, care and treatment of mental
handicap and mental illness.

Although a brilliant pioneer, he was also at times a controversial figure. As an expert he was frequently called upon to
diagnose cases where mental illness existed and, where necessary, to sign certificates of insanity. This was a very serious
business, for those who were committed to an asylum could
lose their liberty, their reputation and even their property.
Conolly appeared as an expert witness in a number of major
trials. There were very real fears of unscrupulous doctors being
persuaded, or even paid, by family members to commit to
lunatic asylums people who were not in fact mentally ill. Some
doctors were also proprietors of asylums, and stood to gain
from the admission of patients. In 1830 Conolly wrote his
Inquiry Concerning Insanity, in which he opposed the practice
of doctors making money by committing patients to their own
asylums, and in 1845 an Act of Parliament was passed to stop
the practice. In the book he made the startling claim that 'The
crowd of most of our asylums is made up of odd, but harmless

individuals, not much more absurd than numbers who are at large.'[26]

Conolly was no mere theoretician, but was a distinguished medical doctor who for two years was Professor of the Nature and Treatment of Diseases at the University of London. He then became the superintendent of the Hanwell Asylum in Middlesex, one of the country's leading institutions. Under his direction Hanwell became a model asylum, particularly in the use of non-restraint methods in the treatment of the mentally ill. He dispensed with the whips, chains, manacles and straitjackets which had characterized previous treatment regimes, preferring at worst a cold shower as punishment for violence to staff or other patients. For his enlightened regime he has been called by some 'the patron saint of English psychiatry'.[27] Conolly was pleased to lend his support to Reed's work in the Park House project, and was delighted that the asylum had created a 'happy family not by coercion but by desire'.[28]

The creation of publicly funded asylums for the insane, where proper treatment and care could be provided for those in need, was a cause Conolly campaigned for. He also stressed that they should be of manageable size: if they were too large patients lost their identity and were not properly cared for. This proved an area of difficulty for him at Hanwell, which had been built to house 300 patients. Over a period of time the local magistrates had gone over his head in repeatedly extending the asylum until it could accommodate up to 975 patients. Eventually he resigned in protest at the decision of the magistrates to place Hanwell under the supervision of a lay administrator, which robbed him of much of his authority in the asylum.[29]

This resignation left him in financial difficulties and forced him into something of a volte-face on his earlier views when he was forced to open his own private asylum and take on the position of consulting physician for another. Controversy followed in 1858, when he committed a patient to an asylum for which he was also paid to do consultancy. The patient then

brought a successful legal action against the asylum's owner
and Conolly for false imprisonment, even though the doctor
protested that his involvement had only been indirect.[30]

In working so closely with Conolly, Reed allowed his name
to be joined to that of a colourful and controversial character,
but one whose ideas on the nature and treatment of mental
illness were deeply compassionate and far-sighted. Conolly did
much to restore the status of personhood to those suffering from
mental illness, believing deeply in a therapeutic model of
treatment, rather than a regime of physical coercion. In 1851,
on the death of the Rev. Dr Holloway, Dr Conolly accepted the
role of joint secretary along with Reed, and became a key figure
in the operation of the charity. Reed had the vision to embrace
Conolly's pioneering approach, adding to it his own strong
religious convictions that those with mental handicaps possessed innate dignity because they were made in the image of
God.

Essex Hall, Colchester

The success of Park House brought immediate interest from
families caring for children with severe learning difficulties, and
a growing demand for places. In late 1849 the charity was
approached with a significant proposition by one of its wealthy
supporters, a railway baron and prominent Baptist, Sir Samuel
Morton Peto. He had been developing a home in Colchester for
children with learning difficulties, upon which he had spent
some £1,400, and he now proposed leasing the building to the
Asylum for Idiots at a modest rent, and offering an interest-free
loan of £1,000 and an annual donation of £200. Impressed by
what Reed had done, Peto wanted the two charities united for
the good of their common cause. The proposal was gladly
accepted, and in January 1850 twenty-eight children and five
adults were transferred to Essex Hall in Colchester.[31]

Essex Hall, Colchester

Andrew Reed, who became one of the trustees of the property, was delighted at this extension of the work. It could easily have been viewed as a solution to the growing need for a permanent home for the asylum, but Reed believed that this should be built much nearer to London. Instead, his vision was much wider: joining the charities together would be a temporary step and, over time, he hoped that local charitable interests in Essex would embrace the hospital and support it as their own. There were some on the board who believed that this was too far-sighted, and that all their efforts should be concentrated at Highgate. In the meantime it was decided that the younger children should be moved to Colchester as a temporary measure.

Within a few weeks of their arrival in Colchester, there was near tragedy. On the 7th February a terrific storm swept across East Anglia, shattering windows in Essex Hall, stripping slates from the roof, and blowing down two chimney stacks, which crashed through the roof and several floors beneath. The children were terrified by the experience, but fortunately none of them were injured. The next morning Reed hurried to the building to inspect the damage. The staff gathered together with Andrew Reed and thanked God the Preserver, before scouring the county for plumbers, glaziers, carpenters and builders to repair the damage.[32] A month later he was able to report to the board that 'all was pleasant and satisfactory at Colchester'.[33]

Andrew Reed was now aged sixty-three and he had added to his daily church commitments, his visits to the Asylum for Fatherless Children and to Park House, Highgate, a further project that involved travelling at least once a week to Colchester by train. As with the asylum in Highgate, he did not simply visit the institution; he met the children, ate with them, patiently spent time helping them try to walk, or letting himself be led by the hand to see a favourite pet, part of the garden, or piece of school work. Christmas Day 1851 was spent with the children at Essex Hall. They had decorated the asylum themselves, and the day was spent eating, playing games, singing and watching a magic-lantern show. Reed was with the children from morning till evening when, exhausted by the excitement of the day, the little ones retired to bed and slept 'without a care for the past or a thought for the future'.[34]

Not all visitors were capable of Reed's ready sympathy and compassion for the individual. The novelty of the experiment in working with such needy children attracted a variety of notable figures in the land wishing to observe what was being done. Some who were curious merely came to stare; others were genuinely compassionate. A number compiled reports which helped with fund-raising and encouraged benevolent individuals elsewhere to ponder whether a local scheme could be started in their area. Reed and the committee tried to control what was happening, to stop any intrusive behaviour. A few reports were critical. Some objected to the regimented nature of the daily life of the children, and undoubtedly there were times when exercise could become drill, and learning a matter of merely repeating answers without understanding them. Yet these were the results of the limited level of understanding in

Reed's day as to the care and treatment of children with severe learning difficulties, rather than the fault of the institution. These were believed to be the ways in which discipline and structure could be maintained.

A permanent home for the asylum

Burdened with a sense of the importance of this work, Andrew Reed became convinced that a permanent home for the asylum was needed — one that was of national significance and that showed the compassion of the British people for those with learning difficulties. He watched the Crystal Palace slowly taking shape in Hyde Park, to house the Great Exhibition, and he felt shame that while money could be expended on this, the capital lacked a major home for those most neglected and uncared for by the nation.

Despite the constant struggle to support Park House on a day-to-day basis, the charity took a step of faith in December 1850 by agreeing the purchase of the Earlswood estate near Redhill in Surrey. The property was bought from a judge, Mr Justice Talfourd, who had planned to build a house for himself there. When he heard that the charity was interested in the property, he gladly changed his plans, and even made a donation of £50.[35] The first payments were made in March 1851 and at the annual dinner, where Charles Dickens was one of the speakers, nearly £3,000 was raised, which seemed to confirm the rightness of the venture.[36] But the pressures on Reed were becoming intense as he spearheaded yet another major new venture.

Suddenly, in 1851, he received a reminder of his increasing age and the demands he was placing on his constitution. Sitting on the train on his way to conduct business for the charity, he felt his right side go numb and his arm go limp. He immediately knew the problem was serious, but with characteristic fortitude he resolved not to let anyone see what had happened, and battled through his day's engagements before seeking medical advice at home. His prayers were deep and fervent; with the Asylum for Fatherless Children and the Asylum for Idiots still struggling in their infancy, he prayed that he might be spared to see them settled to maturity. Then he cried out to God: 'Thou didst not need me; but perhaps thou wilt condescend to use me. I will endeavour to be more diligent in my work, more faithful in my trust, and more cheerful beneath the burdens and trials of my service!'

His doctor ordered total rest, and then a trip to Europe to convalesce. With typical determination that no time should be wasted, he turned his European trip into a tour of inspection of the latest developments in the care of children with learning disabilities in Germany, Denmark and Sweden. He returned home determined to press on in the cause, no matter how slowly: 'Better to walk than to creep, but better to creep than to stand still.' He prayed earnestly that God would open the hearts of a few benevolent men to lead the way in raising funds for the much-needed hospital.

In December 1851 these prayers were answered. A legacy of £2,000 was left for the charity, and Andrew Reed built on this with a plea to the Corporation of London for help. The corporation followed with a gift of 200 guineas, and other public bodies offered significant sums, as Reed's hope that the charity might become a national institution, attracting national support, gained ground.[37] The care of children with mental handicaps was now at the forefront of national charitable concern.

The committee of the asylum gave the task of drawing up plans for the Earlswood Hospital to William Moffatt, who had worked with Gilbert Scott on the Infant Orphan Asylum, and who was now working on his own. As in previous building projects, Andrew Reed took an active role in overseeing the plans, arranging the layout, selecting appropriate stone and materials. Prince Albert laid the foundation stone in the summer of 1853, and the band of the Coldstream Guards played during the ceremony. Building work proceeded all too slowly for

Andrew Reed, who was dismayed to see that the premises remained unfinished as 1855 began. As donations to the charity slowed, some began to urge the closure of Essex Hall in Colchester, in order to enable resources to be consolidated at Earlswood when the building was completed, but Andrew Reed would countenance no such retrenchment.

In the aftermath of his stroke in 1851, his family became increasingly concerned about his health. He was now in his sixties, ministering to a congregation of up to 2,000 at Wycliffe Chapel, developing the work of the Asylum for Fatherless Children, which bought land for a new asylum in 1853 and began building work in 1856, and undertaking his extensive engagements with the Earlswood Asylum. One compensation was that the sites of the Earlswood Asylum and of the Asylum for Fatherless Children, although at a distance from Hackney, were in close proximity to each other. Remarkably, as we shall see, he had also taken on yet another major philanthropic concern in the 1850s.[38]

In late 1855, Reed calculated that, between 1851 and 1855, he had visited Earlswood four hundred times, to attend board meetings and house committee meetings and inspect the building work. Each visit took a day to accomplish. Reed laughed off concerns about his personal well-being, joking that it was like driving a coach-and-four. He believed that God's hand was behind these new developments, and that disappointment would not follow: 'God, who has given the mind to plan, and the will to resolve, will not now withhold the hands to do, and the courage to dare!'[39]

Eventually the frustrations over the delays in the building process were over. In the summer of 1855, Prince Albert again returned, this time to officially open the impressive building, and Samuel Wilberforce, the Bishop of Oxford, led a short religious service of dedication. In September 1855 the residents were moved from Park House to Earlswood. There was great sadness in parting from a building that had seen such success in the early years of the project. It also meant leaving a place filled with reminders of his childhood, of scenes where he had played with his sister, and made his early vow to 'serve my God and love my neighbour'.[40] It was a vow he had most faithfully kept.

The Earlswood Asylum

The Earlswood Asylum was a very large and prestigious undertaking, and as a building project had many complexities. On a prominent site visible from the London to Brighton railway line, and designed to accommodate up to 500 children, it was intended to be a statement to the nation as to the national significance of the project. Yet, as with the Infant Orphan Asylum, it appears that the completion of such a contract to specification was fraught with difficulties. Again the builder had underestimated the cost of the project and on a number of occasions attempted to withdraw from his obligations. The charity had negotiated a fixed price of £29,440, with no additions permitted. With 210 men employed on the contract, the builder sought ways to cut costs, and in consequence much of the work proved to be unsatisfactory. Then he withdrew his workmen before the architect had approved the work, and there were inevitable disputes about payment at its conclusion.[41]

The new building suffered from problems with damp in the early years, and facilities such as the toilets did not work adequately at first. A major difficulty was the inadequacy of the water supply, which came from a brook above the building. Supply was plentiful, and on the whole the quality was good, but at times of heavy rain the stream could be filled with leaves, and the water became discoloured and tasted unpleasant. Filtering the water did not solve the problem, and in 1860 a well had to be bored to yield the 6,000 gallons a day required. The lawns, paths and flowerbeds were incomplete when the building opened, and took time to become established, initially being unusable, especially after prolonged periods of rain. In consequence the children were unable to play outside as often as anticipated and when they did, they returned caked in mud. This hampered the policy of mixing education with plenty of physical exercise and fresh air.

Visiting the new hospital soon after it opened, the Commissioners of Lunacy immediately picked up on the faults with the building and the water supply, taking little account of the fact that they were teething problems in a new building, then accommodating 314 children. Early relocation from Highgate to Earlswood was in part an attempt to reduce costs at a time when income to the charity had slowed, but it also brought problems with the daily management of the newly recruited staff. The Commissioners' Report of 1856 was sharply worded, declaring that the everyday running of the asylum 'does not in our opinion properly carry out the benevolent intentions of the founders and subscribers'.

Such a report was clearly embarrassing to the committee and to Andrew Reed, and in part reflects the difficulties the latter was having in regularly attending the asylum because of the distance of Earlswood from his Hackney home. As he approached his seventieth birthday, and suffering from increasing infirmity, he remained determined to resolve these early difficulties. By 1861, the problems had largely been addressed, and the medical officers who visited the asylum declared their 'most unqualified admiration', observing that the building was 'clean, well warmed, and thoroughly ventilated', with an air of 'neatness and cheerfulness' and that the children were 'happy and healthy'.[42] With its own farm, gymnasium and cricket ground, it was an attractive location. Delighted with the progress her daughter was making at Earlswood, the mother of one child wrote to Reed, describing how happy the little girl was: 'She laughs when the sun shines.' It was the founder's heartfelt wish that the sun would always shine on Earlswood, and that the building would always be filled with laughter.[43]

The Earlswood Asylum

The Eastern Counties Asylum

Essex Hall in Colchester was also a very significant charity in its own right. In its early years it was heavily dependent on the parent London charity, and the workload consequently created was considerable, with 181 children under its care in 1855.[44] Andrew Reed's vision for Essex Hall to become the Eastern Counties Asylum, and to exist independently of Earlswood, was fulfilled in 1859 after many setbacks. From this point onwards, Reed's visits to Colchester became less frequent, although he calculated he had travelled some 30,000 miles in ten years on the Eastern Counties railway line to assist with operations there. Reed hoped that this would be the first of a chain of asylums that would spring up across the nation, from London to Edinburgh and Dublin. His hopes were not in vain.[45]

A visionary approach

Andrew Reed's involvement at both Earlswood and Essex Hall placed him at the forefront of work with those with severe learning difficulties. His visionary approach made him one of the most important figures helping to change attitudes to the care and education of such children. Others had a vital role in this work, and made Earlswood a world leader in its field. One key decision was that to appoint John Langdon Down as resident medical superintendent in 1858. Like John Conolly, he was both gifted and controversial, but he undertook outstanding work in the treatment and classification of patients with mental disability and Down's syndrome is named after him.[46] Yet at Earlswood only a small beginning had been made, and it took many years for its enlightened approach to spread. In 1881, nearly twenty years after Reed's death, of 30,000 'idiots' known to be living in England, less than 1,000 were receiving appropriate care.[47] Of the rest, many continued to suffer the cruelties and abuses that had so moved Andrew Reed to action.

Increasing age brought a growing emotional susceptibility to Andrew Reed. He found witnessing the handicaps and suffering of the children harder to bear, and he was less able to hold back the tears. What sustained him was the demonstrable improvement in the health and abilities of many of the children. He remembered the mother who came to visit her child, who had entered the asylum in a state of near immobility. When the child ran to greet her, she emphatically asserted, 'This is not my child.' She needed to look again to see that indeed it was her child, but the improvement was so great it was hard to recognize him.[48] Emma Garnett entered the institution in 1859 at the age of thirteen. At first her behaviour was very disruptive, and she did not speak, but within two years she had become more settled, and had begun to speak, and read short words. When she left the hospital she could read a little, and hem and sew garments neatly.[49]

The letters of thanks written by parents or guardians on the discharge of their children are filled with expressions of gratitude and appreciation for the work of the institution. Many refer to the improvement in the children, far beyond what they imagined possible; others, sadly, saw little progress — but all expressed thanks for what the charity had done. The happiness and contentedness of the children was frequently stressed, as was the kindness of the staff. William and Ann Morgan reported that their son James had been made 'more happy under your fostering care than any parents could, even under prosperous circumstances in life'.[50]

News of such physical and mental improvements delighted Andrew Reed, but what thrilled him above all was that there were indications of a growing spiritual awareness in many of the children. He once came across a gentle little boy quietly sitting by a fireside. When Reed asked him what made him so comfortable, the lad spontaneously replied, 'My Saviour.' Reed persisted, asking, 'What did He do for you?', and the boy expressed his simple, but real, faith: 'Died for me, for my sins, that I may go to heaven.' As he neared the end of his life Reed

looked back on his ultimate motivation in the work, which was
that the children might through this work of compassionate care
learn of God and come to love him. He recalled, 'I have always
had their *souls* in view. Who was it once asked me if idiots had
any souls...? Yes, and I remember that little fellow at Highgate
who said, "I love God." — Nothing that loves Him shall perish.
No, they shall not die. I shall meet them soon in heaven.'[51]

20.
Family and friends

`It has been a blessed thing to me, that I ever knew Dr Reed. It was a blessed thing to do anything in conjunction with him'
                    (Samuel Plumbe).

20.
Family and friends

To originate, and see through to successful establishment, one major project per decade was a tall order for Andrew Reed to maintain, yet he successfully followed this pattern throughout his ministry. The pressures of such work on his physical constitution, let alone on his family, were considerable. The success of Andrew Reed owed a great deal to the enormous contribution of his family, particularly his wife Elizabeth, and that of his close friends and associates.

Elizabeth and hymn-writing

Andrew's marriage to Elizabeth Holmes was a deeply happy one. At the time of his proposal of marriage to Elizabeth, as the minister of a not very prosperous Independent chapel, Andrew had struggled hard to convince her father that he was a suitable match for his daughter. One stumbling block was the Holmes family's adherence to the Church of England, although they had for a while attended the Countess of Huntingdon's Chapel in Spa Fields, and shared Reed's evangelicalism. Finally, after a number of years of courtship, and with prospects at New Road rapidly improving, permission was given for them to marry.

Elizabeth Reed was a woman of considerable ability. She was well educated, and among her accomplishments was fluency in French. During a visit by the Reeds to Rev. César

Malan, leader of a reforming movement amongst the churches in Geneva, they were given some of his Swiss tracts. Elizabeth undertook the task of translating into English these religious tales, written with the purpose of encouraging the spiritual life. The translations were published in 1822, and Andrew provided a foreword.[1]

Congregational worship was very important to Andrew Reed. He emphasized that every member should participate in this activity, rather than entrusting it to a choir. He argued that there was 'nothing half so fine as the concurrent voices of a thousand persons, pouring forth their grateful sentiments in holy psalmody'.[2] To promote this worship, he wrote a number of hymns, the best-known of which still features in some modern hymn books:

> Spirit Divine, attend our prayers,
> And make our hearts Thy home;
> Descend with all Thy gracious powers.
> O come, great Spirit, come!

It is a hymn filled with longing for the reviving touch of God on the worship of the church, with each verse containing an echoing call for the Holy Spirit to visit the congregation in its worship: 'Come as the fire… Come as the dew… Come as the dove… Come as the wind…' Reed remembered how he had never seen a congregation in England so moved in worship as during the revival in Wycliffe Chapel in the 1830s.[3]

In 1817 Reed published a selection of hymns, designed to supplement the much-loved and widely used *Psalms and Hymns* of Isaac Watts. A number of the items were his own compositions, with others simply marked 'Original'. In 1841 a combined edition of his psalms and hymns under one cover was published, for the benefit of his congregation and to reduce the inconvenience of using two separate books. The sections indicate the matters foremost in Reed's mind at the time: 'Divine Praise', 'Christian Experience' and 'The Revival of

Religion' (including 'The Church — its decline' and 'The Church — its revival'). In the preface to the hymn book Reed stressed the value in a service of good hymns, well chosen, particularly after the ministration of God's Word, as a way of carrying conviction to the heart: 'Nothing is so likely to subdue and sanctify the heart as a hymn well chosen, well read, and sung not with display, but with earnest feeling.' He had observed a great difference in the way people sang at times of awakening in the congregation, yet he had struggled to find hymns that were suitable to the occasion. Reed also hoped that the words of the hymns might be a means of converting people to God.

A number of the hymns marked 'Original' in the 1817 book had in fact been written by his wife Elizabeth, but religious sensitivities in the early nineteenth century with regard to women taking a lead in writing hymns had precluded their true origin being revealed. In the later editions Andrew insisted that her name be ascribed to her compositions. Elizabeth's poetic gift had been evident from an early age, and some of the hymns were written before her marriage. The final edition contains twenty-four hymns attributed to Elizabeth.[4] They reveal the depth of her religious devotion, being filled with spiritual longing and hope. Her own yearning after a deeper knowledge of the Saviour fills the verses:

I would be Thine, O take my heart
And fill it with Thy love.

The happiness of Elizabeth in her home life shines through, but far stronger is her absolute delight in Jesus Christ, and his sovereign ways in her life, despite the tragedies of the death of several of their children in infancy:

This world has many charms for me,
But these, my God, compared with Thee
Are dust upon the scales.

Reed's hymn books proved very popular with the large Wycliffe Chapel congregation, but amongst the wider body of Congregational churches Josiah Conder's *Congregational Hymn Book* was more frequently used as a supplement to Isaac Watts.

His children and the family finances

The children born to Elizabeth and Andrew also proved extremely gifted and were extensively involved in the weekly activities of Wycliffe Chapel. They all gained their first experiences in Christian work by teaching in the Sunday school. Most of their father's Sunday was spent at the church, and when old enough the family gladly joined him there. It was a happy time, although their father carefully instructed them that their 'conversation must be suitable to the sacred character of the day'. Young Charles Reed remembered the sense of thrill in his heart at seeing over 1,000 people joining together on the last Sunday of each month to share communion, with a further 1,000 looking on from the gallery.[5]

In 1833 came news that delighted Andrew and Elizabeth. Their oldest son, Andrew, then aged just sixteen, had for some twelve months been showing signs of having undergone a deep spiritual change. His parents watched patiently, longing to find out whether it would prove real and lasting. Young Andrew was encouraged to speak to a local minister, who talked the matter over with him, and soon all were agreed that he had been truly converted and had devoted himself to the Saviour. His father was delighted and also relieved; the sense of responsibility for the spiritual welfare of his children weighed heavily on Andrew Reed, aware as he was that the work of church and charity often took him away from home.

The change in young Andrew was so marked that the other children noticed, and concern about their own spiritual need was also awakened. It was the supreme joy of Andrew and Elizabeth to see all their children converted to Christ and in turn applying and being accepted as members of Wycliffe Chapel. Although in later years, through marriage and employment, they were to move to other parts of the country, all testified to the influence of their godly parents on their continuing Christian commitment. They had seen God at work in the church, and had often lingered in the vestry in the midst of numbers of people anxiously enquiring as to the way of salvation. Into their home had come church members, other ministers and missionaries, all of whom had been welcomed and encouraged. In the Sunday school they had made their first tentative ventures into Christian work. The reality of what they had witnessed in times of awakening in the church had been impressed deeply on their hearts and minds. Growing up in a godly home, and in a church vibrant with Christian life, had proved a formative blessing to them spiritually. They might have seen their father less often than they wished, because of his church and philanthropic work, but they accepted this because of the evidence that God was at work all around them.

In that work they took their full part: Andrew lovingly described his children as 'the companions of our daily life, and helpers in our daily work'. Yet he was not content to rest in the knowledge that they had made professions of faith. Other responsibilities fell to parents of Christian children — to present a pattern of daily discipleship, and to set a clear and consistent example: 'When our children begin to run the heavenly race, we should be quickened, lest we be outrun.'[6]

Much of the daily burden of the care of the children fell on Elizabeth, a responsibility she took on with great seriousness and skill. Working quietly to support and advise Andrew, she was at one with him in his desires to give himself to the help and support of the most needy. She gave freely of her available time, whether it was serving on ladies' committees for the charities, working in the Sunday school, or opening her home and heart to orphan children from the streets of London. Gladly she and Andrew welcomed into their home the orphaned missionary children of the Milne family when they had to return from China.

Elizabeth's parents lived in Reading at the time of her marriage to Andrew, but they later moved to Blackheath. Their children remembered happy holidays spent with their grand-parents. Elizabeth brought money to the marriage, which increased with the death of her merchant father. This was invested wisely, and enabled her and Andrew not to place great demands on the church financially — his salary of £500 was modest by many standards, especially in the light of a congrega-tion numbering 2,000. Comprised largely of the working people who lived in Stepney, it was not an affluent body, and the salary was reduced to £400 in 1855 and, with Andrew's deteri-orating health, it was further cut to £200 in 1859. Andrew and Elizabeth resolved not to become preoccupied with complicated savings and investment schemes, but to devote surpluses to philanthropic work. They lived a comfortable middle-class life, but no more than that, and in his will Andrew was able to leave some £2,400 to the charities on his death. Including what was given during Andrew's ministry, in all they gave £4,540 to the charities, a very large sum at a time when many people earned between £100 and £150 a year.[7]

The resources that Andrew and Elizabeth had did not mean that they were immune from the realities of economic life. In 1840 a major bank in the United States failed, resulting in a drastic reduction in the value of some securities in which he had been advised to invest. It was a blow, yet Reed could note in his journal, 'My loss has not cost me an hour's sleep. I would fain *have*, that I may *give*. When I give, let me say "A debtor still"; and when I lose, I will add, "God is sufficient still." '

Worse was to follow in 1842 when further economic turmoil in America completely wiped out the value of the investments. The family tightened their belts and went without an annual holiday that year, but Reed was untroubled. He had no doubt that if God gave them a 'lighter purse', it was that 'they may enjoy a weightier blessing'.[8] Such problems were all too common in the nineteenth-century financial world in which money markets were ill-regulated. Churches and charities faced similar financial problems. When a church in Market Harborough was saving funds to build a new chapel, it deposited the £1,500 in a local bank. When the bank failed, all the money was lost. The church began fund-raising again, but still had a debt of £400 when the building was opened by Andrew Reed. At the services he challenged those present to rise to the occasion, and by the end of the day the debt was cleared.[9]

Andrew Reed sought to include his children not only in the life of the local church, but also in his charitable work. They were frequently taken to visit the orphanages, and in the children there was fostered a love for the benevolent projects with which their father was associated and a deep sense of duty to care for those with real social need. Their oldest son, Andrew, remembered being taken as a young boy to the London Orphan Asylum every Saturday, where he helped his father arrange for the laying out of the grounds. Their second son, Charles, became particularly closely involved in the work of the Asylum for Fatherless Children and the Hospital for Incurables.[10]

The education of his own children was a matter over which Andrew Reed took great care. Andrew was educated at Mill Hill School, a Congregational foundation, before attending London University, where he gained his BA in 1837. Charles went to Hackney Grammar School, which his father had helped to found, before moving to the Congregational Silcoates School in Yorkshire. Martin remained closer to home, and was taught by a ministerial friend in Totteridge.

Gradually, young Andrew's mind turned towards following his father into Christian ministry. Reed was very careful not to encourage these desires too early; he wanted to be sure that Andrew had been truly called, as he wrote in his journal: 'I would not, for the world, that he should run *unsent*.'[11] Andrew junior did indeed prove to have been truly called, and served for forty years in pastorates in Norwich, Preston, London and St Leonard's-on-Sea, faithfully preaching the gospel of God's grace, so beloved by his father. He was active in many of the causes dear to his parents, including the British and Foreign Bible Society, the London Missionary Society and the London City Mission. He died in 1899, at the age of eighty-one.[12]

Charles Reed served a business apprenticeship with a woollen manufacturer in Leeds, before in 1842 becoming a partner in a printing company in London. He became his father's right-hand man in many projects he undertook. He was secretary of the London committee formed to oppose the 1843 Factory Education Bill, and he campaigned widely against the dominance of the Church of England in the provision of education. Together with the wealthy Congregationalist businessman Samuel Morley, he helped to found the Congregational Board of Education. His grounding in educational matters came through experience as a Sunday school teacher, and later as superintendent of the Wycliffe Chapel Sunday School. In 1844 he joined the committee of the Sunday School Union, and frequently addressed deputation meetings on their behalf — sharing the gift of communication possessed by his father and older brother. Charles married Margaret, the youngest daughter of Edward Baines, the leading Nonconformist from Leeds who, through his family newspaper the *Leeds Mercury*, had played a prominent part in the campaign against the 1843 education proposals. When, in 1868, Charles was elected Liberal MP for Hackney, his maiden speech was to introduce a bill exempting Sunday and ragged schools from the requirement to pay rates. He was also active in the work of the British and Foreign Bible Society, the Religious Tract Society and the London Missionary Society. Charles Reed became chairman of the London School Board, and for his distinguished public service he was knighted in 1874. His son, Charles Edward Baines Reed, became secretary of the British and Foreign Bible Society.

Andrew and Elizabeth's daughter Elizabeth married Thomas Spalding, from a wealthy family of stationers. The Reeds were, indeed, a gifted family. Three of Andrew and Elizabeth's grandsons have entries in the *Dictionary of National Biography*, and of these three two were sons of Charles.[13]

His friends

Deep personal friendships were formed with many families in the Wycliffe Chapel congregation. When the Jolly family moved to London from Cornwall early in Reed's ministry, they became committed members of his congregation. Richard Jolly was a successful ship's chandler in Wapping and owned several merchant ships; his nature matched his name — he was a jovial man with red cheeks and a twinkle in his eye. His sister, Sarah, became a leading figure in the Sunday school, and was much respected for her work. Both Richard and Sarah were deeply devoted Christians and greatly admired Andrew Reed's ministry.

By 1850 Sarah was running the Wycliffe Chapel Bible Class of older teenagers, amongst whom 'serious attention' was noticed. From Sarah Jolly's Bible Class came many converts and a number of future Sunday school teachers. She was also secretary of the girls' day school.[14] Her devoted work did not pass unnoticed, and in the midst of his busy pastoral and philanthropic work Andrew Reed took time to honour her contribution to the church. Well remembering the significance of faithful Sunday school work in his own spiritual development, in 1852 he presented her with a small writing desk. The inscription demonstrates the regard in which she was held: 'In testimony of long continued and self-denying service which though they cannot be appreciated should be very gratefully acknowledged.'[15]

Others were treated with similar kindness. Each Christmas a group of elderly widows were invited to dinner with the Reeds; those unable to come were sent special gifts. Even those employed as doorkeepers and stewards in the chapel were frequently remembered with personal gifts.[16]

Among others for whom the Reeds had great affection were the Plumbe family. Samuel Plumbe's business had brought him to London from the West Country, and he became a deacon at Wycliffe Chapel, where he served as an unofficial assistant to Andrew Reed for a number of years. The love and respect that grew up between Samuel and his pastor was very great. He once wrote, 'It has been a blessed thing to me, that I ever knew Dr Reed. It was a blessed thing to do anything in conjunction with him.'[17]

The life of Samuel Plumbe's young son was retold by Andrew Reed in a short work, *Rolls Plumbe: An Authentic Memoir of a Child*, published in 1832. The boy shared his father's first name, Samuel, so was affectionately known by his second name, Rolls. He died at the age of eleven after a long illness, in the course of which he had demonstrated a deep and growing faith in Christ. Andrew frequently visited the family on his pastoral round and was deeply moved by the courage and the mature faith of the little boy, with his face pale and pinched with pain and his body dreadfully thin. When one day Andrew asked him how he should pray for him, he replied, 'I have no wants that the world can supply. I want more love to my Saviour, more faith in God's Word... Pray that I may have patience to be made perfect through suffering.' As he neared death, Rolls' trust in Jesus Christ was undaunted, as he told his aunt: 'I am going to glory! O, the joy, the joy unspeakable... I do believe in him! And I do love him! Because he first loved me.' His death came gently and peacefully, with his parents and brothers and sisters gathered around his bed.[18] Andrew was so moved by such real faith in one so young that he sought the permission of Rolls' parents to publish an account of the boy's short life aimed at children, with an evangelistic challenge at the end as to whether readers shared a similar faith and assurance.

Eight years later the Plumbe family suffered further sorrow when Samuel himself became seriously unwell. After several months it became clear that he was terminally ill. When the news of the gravity of his condition was brought to Andrew

Reed after one Sunday evening service, he was deeply moved: 'All I could do was, to lay myself down in silence at the footstool of the Divine mercy.' Samuel Plumbe's death two weeks later brought the loss of a co-worker so efficient and beloved that Reed felt him to be irreplaceable. Coming as it did towards the end of the time of spiritual awakening in the church in 1839-40, it was a severe setback. At his memorial service the chapel was packed as Reed preached on the text: 'Weep not for me, but for yourselves.' A prayer meeting was held after the service, attended by 2,000 people.[19]

A devoted family man, Reed gladly opened his home to orphans, whether from the streets of London, or from the mission-field in China. He also opened his heart to his children, involved them in his work and nurtured in them compassion and love for the friendless and needy. Amidst the huge pressures of church and charitable work, with the unflagging and devoted support of Elizabeth, Andrew won and held the deep and abiding love of his own children. They all chose to follow the one to whose service he had devoted his life. That was the delight of his heart and the answer to his most earnest parental prayer.

21.
A home for the incurable

'Among the innumerable medical charities with which this country abounds, there is not one for the help of those who, of all others, must require succour, and who must die, and do die in thousands, neglected and unaided'

(Charles Dickens).

21.
A home for the incurable

The deep Christian compassion of Andrew Reed drew him consistently towards cases of the greatest disadvantage and suffering. His response was not simply one of sympathy and fellow feeling, but of a steady determination to do something that would improve the conditions of needy individuals, in the conviction that each person was made in the image of God. He found that few seemed to care for those with severe learning difficulties, and he was determined something should be done to help them. During his researches into that cause, he became increasingly aware of another group of needy individuals whose plight was equally tragic.

Hospitals in the nineteenth century

The hospital system of London in the mid-nineteenth century was a complicated mixture of voluntary hospitals, funded by charitable donations and subscriptions, and workhouse hospitals for the very poor. High-quality health care and medicine were available only for the wealthy, and even for them the treatment on offer was restricted by the limited level of medical knowledge. Some of London's hospitals, such as St Thomas's and St Bartholomew's, had been founded in the medieval period and were funded by permanent endowments, but in the eighteenth century a series of great hospitals were founded as voluntary charities, dependent on donations and subscriptions for their work. These hospitals, such as the Westminster, the Middlesex and the London, were intended to assist those unable to afford to pay for medical help. They were not aimed at those who were already destitute, who could obtain medical help from the Poor Law Infirmaries, but at those who were in danger of becoming destitute through no fault of their own — through an accident or sudden onset of serious illness. Much medical knowledge was rudimentary, and experimental, and there is some debate as to whether the work of hospitals in the eighteenth and nineteenth centuries actually increased life expectancy, or in fact reduced it![1]

Hospitals combined the functions of medical school, general hospital and welfare agency. The work of the major voluntary hospitals was aimed at acute and curable cases, and in dealing with these they had some success. Those with long-term, degenerative, or incurable illness were simply discharged and left to fend for themselves, with no practical support. Often they were so disabled that they were unable to look after themselves, let alone attempt to earn a living. Many were utterly destitute and friendless. Their last years were frequently spent in pain and misery, as the bleakness of a lonely death slowly closed in upon them.

Others ended their days without dignity in the grim, prison-like Poor Law Infirmaries, with little medical care and often surrounded by alcoholics, dropouts, the senile and the mentally deranged, for in the middle of the century by no means all workhouses had separate wards for medical cases. Forbidding on the outside, inside these places were characterized by an overwhelming smell of whitewash, over-boiled cabbage and urine. Cases were reported in the Poor Law Infirmaries of patients found lying on filthy bed-sheets with undressed, festering sores. In 1865 *The Lancet* declared that 'The work-house system is a disgrace to our civilization.'[2] Even in the 1870s, when there was a prospect that his aged father would be sent to a workhouse, Joseph Arch declared, 'I'd sooner rot under a hedge than he should go there.' Yet in the mid-nineteenth century, of those who had been in the workhouse for more than five years, 42% were there because of old age, 11% because of physical handicap and 35% for reasons of mental illness.[3] Such statistics confirm the need for Andrew Reed's two last major charitable works.

Many staff in the workhouse infirmaries were paupers themselves. Ill-educated and with no training for nursing work, they were often ignorant, incompetent or abusive. Many were found drunk on duty, indifferent to the needs of patients, ignoring their desperate cries for help, or were themselves suffering from illness. Such doctors as could be found were usually those who could not obtain employment elsewhere. Poor standards of hygiene and nursing care, with sick patients scattered indiscriminately around the general Poor Law wards, led to shocking conditions. In the early 1860s Florence Nightingale declared the Liverpool workhouse infirmary to be 'worse than Scutari'. In another she found an elderly female inmate, with an ulcerated leg and cancer of the breast, acting as a midwife to mothers in labour and caring for the newborn babies, many of whom, unsurprisingly, had a raised temperature and were in poor health.[4] To be discharged from hospital as incurable, and to know that future years of declining health would have to be spent in such terrible conditions, was an awful prospect, and one faced by many.

Reed embarks on one final project

Through the work of caring for the children in the orphanages, Reed's eyes had been opened to the suffering of families with a father, and major wage-earner, who was severely disabled or terminally ill. When the Asylum for Fatherless Children had been established he arranged for the charity to accept children whose father was in such a condition. As he passed his sixtieth birthday, Reed was increasingly aware of his advancing years, and growing infirmity. In 1848 he began to look to one further work in what he expected to be the last decade of his life: 'Oh! I have suffered with those I saw suffer! Away then with sloth and ease, and the fear which hath bondage; and bravely run another course. I must begin to move in double quick time; for the noiseless foot of death is behind me, and before me there are some faint streaks of morning light.'[5]

Yet this sense of needing to act quickly as his own life moved on did not lead to precipitate action. As usual Reed considered his strategy very carefully, and undertook thorough research. With the building projects for the Asylum for Fatherless Children and the Earlswood Hospital in full swing, it seems incredible that Reed had time to even think about another major charitable work, let alone for detailed planning, but in 1849 his prayer was clear: 'May the last be best!'

The statistical evidence he compiled revealed a serious gap in the medical provision of his day. At St Thomas's Hospital, in the very centre of London, 4,000 patients were admitted each year; 2,400 were discharged as cured, but 176 without cure. At Guy's and St Bartholomew's the numbers admitted were larger, but a similar proportion were discharged as incurable, and at the Brompton Hospital an even larger number left without any prospect of being cured. Reed also visited hospitals in Europe, where the evidence he found was even more compelling.[6]

As he compiled the statistics to support the new project, he was approached by a merchant in the City of London. What this man had to say surprised Reed, but he saw it as confirmation that the project was something God intended him to pursue. Unaware of the research Reed was currently undertaking, the merchant offered him £500 to start a home for people diagnosed as incurable.

Then came another event which appeared to be a further signal to move ahead. In 1850 an article appeared in the magazine *Household Words* written by the great novelist Charles Dickens, declaring it a fact almost inconceivable that

'Among the innumerable medical charities with which this country abounds, there is not one for the help of those who, of all others, must require succour, and who must die, and do die in thousands, neglected and unaided... Hopeless pain, allied to hopeless poverty, is a condition of existence not to be thought of without a shudder. It is a slow journey through the Valley of the Shadow of Death, from which we save even the greatest criminals.'[7]

Notwithstanding all the encouragements to move forward, the pressures on Reed to delay action were great. Fund-raising and construction work at the Asylum for Fatherless Children and the Earlswood Hospital progressed frustratingly slowly, and frequent trips to the Eastern Counties Asylum at Colchester were required, together with his regular pastoral work, although he had now been freed from the demands of involvement in the London Missionary Society. His family were increasingly concerned about the philanthropist's physical condition. His doctor advised him strongly not to embark on a further project, and in 1851 came the stroke that hampered his activities for some time. To such warnings, Reed was deaf — the needs of those suffering and dying in poverty and loneliness were far greater than his desire to preserve his own health. He did, however, recognize that he needed to see matters more settled at Coulsdon and Earlswood before he could begin in earnest: 'When my hands are free, then I have it on my heart to do it, or to sustain it if it shall be done by others.'[8]

The article by Charles Dickens prompted others to think seriously about the needs of those with incurable illness, and a number of rival schemes sprang into life. Aware of these developments, Reed bided his time, preferring to have a well-researched and well-formulated plan before bringing anything into the public arena. He took no satisfaction in hearing the news that the three other schemes had only briefly sprung into life and then expired before achieving anything. Rivalry, internal dissension and indecision ruined the other projects, and

Reed was determined that the same should not happen to what he had planned.

By November 1853, £2,000 had been pledged towards the scheme, and he felt the way was becoming clearer. In July 1854 he was ready to start, and in his journal he gave thanks to God: 'Proposed Asylum for the permanent care and comfort of those who, by disease, accident, or deformity, are hopelessly disqualified for the duties of life. Bless Thou the springing thereof!'[9] He followed his usual practice of calling a meeting of his closest friends and associates in charitable activity, and on 7 July 1854 he set before them what he believed God had laid on his heart. Once convinced of the need for a particular project, Reed invariably became a powerful and compelling advocate for it. His personal commitment was sufficient to persuade others of the need, and the discussion quickly turned from whether the scheme should go ahead to how it was to be done.

By the time a second meeting was held on the 13th July, an advertisement for the charity had been sent to the newspapers, and an *Appeal* was being printed. Andrew Reed saw the charity as the final achievement of his life: 'The hospital is an offering to the Lord, and I may not offer that which costs me nothing.' He described in his diary how family and friends urged him to slow down, but how he disregarded their calls; he was driven forward by the urgency of the task: 'I hear a voice they do not hear, I see a hand they do not see: onward is the word — forward is the hand. Remember me, O my God!, for good, concerning this also, and spare me according to the greatness of thy mercy! If I may, I will do this, and then die.'[10]

The *Appeal*

The *Appeal* Reed issued was powerfully argued — he calculated that London's twelve hospitals were each year discharging 1,500 patients as incurable, the result of accident, chronic illness, congenital disease or degenerative conditions. Once these patients were deemed incurable, hospitals refused to readmit them for further treatment. What Reed longed for was not just another hospital, but a home, 'where every comfort may be enjoyed to mitigate affliction, and where the best medical skill and care may be had, with the hope of making disease something less than incurable'. It was to be a place of skilful and sympathetic care, a place of tranquillity, surrounded by the therapeutic qualities of the beauties of nature. It was, above all, to be a place where the comforts of the Christian faith were to be ministered, bringing consolation and hope in the face of diseases 'otherwise beyond remedy and all but intolerable'.

Reed reminded his readers that accidents or sudden illness resulting in a chronic and incurable condition could befall anyone at anytime, and rob the victims not only of health and the capacity to enjoy life, but also of the means to support themselves. Recognition of this mutual state of vulnerability should awaken sympathy and concern for others: 'Our condition is essentially one; let our sympathies be one. Have we health? Let us relieve the sick. Have we wealth? Let us help the poor. Are we strong? Let us uphold the weak. Are we happy? Let us feel for the miserable. Let us bear each other's burdens, and so fulfil the law of Christ — the law of kindness and of love.' He urged those who were wealthy to see that the riches entrusted to them by God were used wisely. Using the biblical parable of the rich man and Lazarus in Luke 16, Reed urged a response: 'What, then, shall be done for the many, who, equally worthy with ourselves, are languishing at our feet, and whom disease and despair are dragging down to the grave?' Drawing on another biblical parable, that of the shrewd manager, he urged, 'Let us make to ourselves friends of what is too often "the mammon of unrighteousness" that when all else fails us, health, friends, life, hope, they may welcome us into everlasting habitations.'[11]

A disappointing start

The second meeting of the charity began unpromisingly. Reed had made himself available in the hours before the meeting for private consultations, but few people came. However, in the formal proceedings, a provisional committee was set up, in which Reed accepted the role of secretary (a post for which, as with the other charities, he received no remuneration). Although this meeting was billed as one for free discussion, and any plans were stated to be merely tentative, Reed quickly demonstrated the leading role he would take in the project, and the fact that his ideas were well advanced. The first resolution was passed, summing up his charitable philosophy learned and worked out, sometimes bitterly, in the experience of the other charities: 'Resolved, that the design shall be carried out with Christian kindness and liberality, apart from all party distinctions whatever, whether political or religious, and in the spirit of that love which cometh down from heaven and is the bond of perfectness.' Reed also jotted down a motto for the charity: 'All the good for the good of all.'[12]

The rest of the week was a whirlwind of activity, in the stifling heat of the summer of 1854, when temperatures soared to over 80°F, but the fruits of his arduous labour were not particularly promising. Arrangements were made for a formal public meeting on the 31st July at the Mansion House, where so many other charities had been launched on the public, with the Lord Mayor of London taking the chair. Reed also wrote to Queen Victoria, appealing once more for her support in what he was convinced would be his last charitable venture. After such great success in securing royal patronage for his previous charities, it came as a great disappointment when a positive response from the queen was not forthcoming. This made Reed's frequent references to the charity as the Royal Hospital for Incurables somewhat premature.[13] It transpired that the queen was reluctant to have her name attached to a charity whose intention was to offer only palliative care and support rather than cure. The public meeting in the Eygptian Hall at the Mansion House was also disappointing, and although the Lord Mayor presided over proceedings, he did it with an evident lack of enthusiasm. At the meeting it was announced that £2,000 had already been pledged to the charity, but even this promising situation was not to last for long.

On the following day one prominent supporter, who had promised £1,000, wrote to Reed attaching so many conditions to his support that Reed was constrained to decline the offer of money. He did not think it right that the charity should be hamstrung in such a way, but it was a deep blow, for the sum had been earmarked for the support of the first patients in a rented home that was already being planned. With characteristic generosity, Reed promptly cancelled his summer holiday, and from his reserves scraped together a further £300, in addition to the £100 he had pledged the evening before, and earnestly asked others to give generously. He was delighted that amongst those who gave most freely, members of the medical profession were to the forefront.

Supporters rally to the cause

The names of those involved in the early meetings of the charity show how well Reed's network of friends and supporters of other charities had rallied to the new cause. Samuel Gurney from the Quaker banking family, already involved in the Asylum for Fatherless Children, was appointed treasurer. The first board of directors included old friends from earlier charities: Alderman David Wire, former Lord Mayor of London, William Monk and William Millard. Lord Dudley Stuart was an early donor. Three medical men were on the board, including Thomas Calloway, of the Royal College of Surgeons, and John Conolly, who had proved such a pivotal figure in the Asylum for Idiots.[14] This set the Hospital for Incurables in advance of

other major London charitable hospitals, which at the time
generally did not include medical men on their boards.[15]

Admission to the hospital

The constitution of the charity, which was drawn up in these
early days, set out the tragic plight of those it sought to help. It
was not intended to rival the work of other hospitals, or give
temporary help: 'It will not deal with the hopeful case, but with
the hopeless, and provide, in a hospital, a final home for such
as would otherwise be the rejected and outcast of mankind.'
Designed to help those unable to work or care for themselves
because of disease, accident, or physical deformity, it was to fill
a gap in the provision offered by existing medical charities. That
it was to be a Christian charity was also clearly spelled out: 'The
Design shall be carried out on the broad principle of Christian
kindness, and liberal charity, in the hope of uniting all the goods
for the good of all who really need help; in the spirit of that
wisdom and love, which "cometh down from above", and
which is "the bond of perfectness", to the exclusion of all party
and sectarian influences whatever.'
      There was a degree of flexibility in the scheme that Reed was
proposing. Where patients were capable of being cared for at
home by their families, they could be treated as 'extra-patients',
or outpatients, and would receive a monthly allowance in
addition to medical visitation and attendance. Such a flexible
arrangement allowed patients to find support, 'without destroy-
ing the most natural sources of comfort'. At a time when the
Poor Law had formally drawn back from offering out-relief to
those not resident in the workhouse — although locally the
practice did continue — this was an enlightened policy. Those
without family or friends to care for them would receive full
relief; the hospital was to be their home. Although their illnesses
were incurable, they were not to be considered as 'hopeless'
cases; they were to be treated by the 'best medical science

hopefully', rather than being abandoned to an inevitable and lingering death.[16]

The patients were to be admitted to the hospital through the election system adopted by the other charities Reed had started, although urgent and destitute cases could be accepted in an emergency, pending their later election by subscribers. The names of patients could be put forward at up to six elections, and votes cast in their favour at previous elections could be accumulated to their advantage. The board also had the power to receive cases without resort to the election system provided that 75% of its members agreed. Once elected, incurable patients had the assurance of knowing they would be supported for the rest of their lives. As in Reed's previous charities, participation was possible for those of modest means. Subscription of half a guinea brought the right to vote in an election. Those who subscribed thirty guineas could attend board meetings, and a subscription of 100 guineas brought the right to be a governor for life. It was also possible for families to pay for the support of their relatives in the hospital: for those of limited means £25 per annum was required; £50 for those who were more affluent. Those seeking admission by the payment system were very much in the minority — just sixteen out of the first 100 applicants, the rest being by election.[17]

It is all too easy to criticize the use of the election system for a charity of this nature, but this method for selecting candidates was operated by the orphanages and many other medical charities. Entry to most of the major London hospitals required a letter which could only be obtained from a subscriber, certifying that the patient was a 'proper object' of charity. A subscription of three guineas to these hospitals brought the right to recommend three inpatients and six outpatients in one year.[18] Only in cases of serious accident, or extreme emergency, could this system be bypassed, and repeatedly the governors fought hard to resist any diminution of the rights of subscribers. Patients in the London hospitals were also required to provide sureties, or a deposit, that should they die in hospital their body would be removed — a precaution hardly likely to inspire confidence in the treatment they were about to receive! The hospitals admitted those who were acutely ill, but treatable. However, the chronically ill were resolutely excluded.[19]

Unless it was an absolute emergency, patients were admitted on different days — Tuesday at St Thomas's, Wednesday at Guy's, Thursday at St Bartholomew's. With up to 100 patients seeking admission at any one time, the hospitals were often full and the disappointed had to seek a subscriber's letter for admission elsewhere, or to wait on in pain to try again on the next admission day.[20] The lack of available beds to meet the demands of patients led to tragedies, such as that which befell the eighteen-year-old girl found dying on the steps of St Andrew's Church, Holborn, because she had been unable to gain the necessary subscriber's letter to secure admission to a hospital. As a result, William Marsden, the doctor who discovered her, was inspired to found the Royal Free Hospital in 1828, where no subscriber's or governor's letter was required for admission. The Metropolitan Free Hospital followed in 1837, but these were pioneer ventures.[21] The Hospital for Incurables was to follow suit with the founding of a free ward.

The pattern of operation that the Hospital for Incurables was to follow was already well established. The London charitable hospitals were run by boards of governors, made up of individuals who had made large donations, or subscriptions, but day-to-day management was left in the hands of a much smaller group who had the time and energy to attend weekly meetings.[22] Hospital governors, limited in the care they could provide by the amount they received in subscriptions and gifts from supporters, rigorously excluded the chronically sick, and sought to return pauper cases to the workhouse infirmaries, for it was argued that the latter could already obtain medical support, even though it was only in the workhouse infirmaries. Even for urgent cases there were waiting lists.[23]

The charity is set up

In spite of the disappointment over the way the Mansion House meeting in July 1854 was conducted, and the loss of a major donor soon afterwards, Reed remained encouraged by the progress he had made. His prayer was that he might be equal to the unfolding task: 'Let Thy love dwell in my heart, and sanctify my heart! Make my path plain! Prepare me for the work Thou hast given me to do, that I may finish it!' By September the charity had an office in the heart of the City of London, on the Poultry, where there were also offices for three of Reed's other charities.

He also made the case for the need for the charity more forcefully in a second appeal, outlining in emotional language the tragic plight of the patient who was deemed incurable: 'At the very moment in which the sufferer is told that his affliction is hopeless, he also finds that the gates of mercy are closed on him for ever. If not hopeless before, his treatment now seals his fate. He is spirit-broken; and like the stricken deer, he steals away from the abodes of humanity, to an unnatural and cruel solitude, to sob, to languish, and to die.' Drawing on images from the parable of the Good Samaritan, Reed begged for help to be given to the incurable: 'We may not pass by "on the other side", and *look* the other way; we must look on him, *consider* him ... mitigate the sufferings we cannot cure, by medicine, and love which "doeth good like a medicine"; cleave to him, comfort him to the last, and point his rising spirit to "the better land" which excludes the sorrows and sufferings of earth and of time for ever.' His final challenge was urgent: 'Is he not our brother?'[24]

Strong support from the medical fraternity was a feature of the early days of the charity. In 1854 Reed secured a statement from leading London medical men asserting that the new project would not in any way detract from other existing medical charities, but was an essential addition to the 'General' hospitals of London, and would complement their work, relieving them of the pain of discharging incurable patients with nowhere to go, and no one to care for them. It was signed by thirty-nine eminent physicians and surgeons from the major London hospitals, including Sir James Clark, 'Physician in Ordinary' to Queen Victoria.[25]

In November 1854 a property in Carshalton was rented, and the first of the six-monthly elections of patients was held on the 27th of that month, Andrew Reed's birthday. The house, which was owned by the treasurer Samuel Gurney, had at one time been used as a workhouse, and then as a convalescent home, but was now empty. The election passed off well, but Reed realized that a terrible mistake had been made in allowing the patients seeking election to attend on the day. He was re-minded of scenes in the New Testament where those with incurable diseases crowded round Jesus Christ seeking help. To the election meeting came prospective patients doubled up with rheumatism, some without limbs, some unable to walk, others paralysed and one who could only crawl along the floor. While Jesus left none in need, Reed was deeply distressed at the disappointment of those who were unsuccessful and went sadly away. The scenes served to inspire him to expand the work of the charity so that more could be helped.

The first patients were admitted in 1855, and received every attention as they settled into the home in Carshalton, with books, nourishing diet, nursing support and companions to visit, befriend and read to the bedridden. Rooms were made homely by bringing in treasured items from the patients' homes — a favourite old clock, picture, or item of furniture. Soon the rented home was filled, but cases of need continued to be brought before the charity. The generosity of the public also increased steadily.[26]

Those who applied for admission were subjected to medical examination; careful enquiry as to their personal financial circumstances was made, and the recommendation of a sub-scriber was sought. Because they were already receiving at least some form of help, those being supported by the Poor Law or other charities were not to be admitted. The checks were by no means foolproof, and the early residents of the Carshalton home were astonished to find one of their number being arrested by the police on suspicion of being an accessory to a robbery![27] Chronic neurological disease was the most common condition suffered by those who applied for admission in the early years, usually due to an injury to the spine, or abnormality from birth. Other cases included those disabled by chronic rheumatism, cancer and severe epilepsy.[28]

Plans for a permanent home

It was not long before Andrew Reed and the board of the new charity had resolved that a permanent home for the charity should be built. The Carshalton property was not suitable on a long-term basis, being too small and cramped, with poor ventilation. Within two years of the home opening, over forty patients were crammed into the restricted space. The level of interest in the charity was growing appreciably — Sarah Plumley, the candidate gaining the highest number of votes in the 1855 election, received 1,368, and monetary receipts that year were very encouraging, totalling £1,874.[29]

Many sites for a permanent home were considered, including ones in Wimbledon and Slough, but on each occasion the charity was outbid at auction. Eventually Reed negotiated for a plot of twenty acres of land, part of the site of the Asylum for Fatherless Children at Coulsdon, Purley, to be sold to the hospital for £2,500. It became his dream that these two vital institutions, one for children rendered homeless by the loss of their parents, and one for those declared incurable by the medical profession and thereby ineligible to occupy hospital beds, should stand side by side on the Surrey hills, as a tribute to national compassion and benevolence.[30] The land was considered suitable for a number of reasons: the beautiful location amidst the Surrey hills would be beneficial to the health of the patients, and its being next door to the extensive grounds of the orphanage meant that there would be no problem with future building work encroaching on the area. The site was beside the London to Brighton railway line, accessible from London in half an hour, and it was a location that would give to the charity the national prominence that had been similarly sought for the orphanage.

Reed had every expectation that, with the supporters the charity had already attracted, the funds to make it a major British institution would be forthcoming. At the annual dinner in May 1857 Charles Dickens took the chair. He described his visit to the home in Carshalton: 'In all the inmates of this house whom I saw, — there was not only a hopefulness of manner, but a serenity of face, a cheerfulness and social habit, that perfectly amazed me.' Dickens described the misery from which the forty-three patients had been delivered, and how many of them would have had no alternative, on being discharged from hospital, but to lay their weary and suffering bodies down outside the Poor House door and wait for admission. He longed for the day when the only requirement for entry to the home would be the presence of an incurable disease.[31]

By the end of July 1857, alternative and much larger premises at Putney House, in Richmond Road, Putney, had been rented for £225 per year, on a lease running from three to five years. In fact the charity was to remain at Putney House until 1865.[32] Meanwhile fund-raising for the building project at Coulsdon was under way.

The charity was becoming extraordinarily successful, with the demand for places far outstripping supply. Influential figures had come to lend their support to the charity — the Bishop of London, Lord Shaftesbury and Lord Raynham, who took a prominent role. In 1855, vice-presidents included the Duke of Devonshire, the Duke of Bedford and the Duke of Leeds, two marquises, four earls and three viscounts; Lord Palmerston, who became prime minister in 1855, was also a vice-president. The involvement of figures with wealth and influence was highly necessary, for large-scale charitable hospitals were notoriously expensive to run. In the late eighteenth and early nineteenth centuries the major London hospitals suffered repeated shortages of funds, and on occasions problems reached such a crisis that they had to close wards or restrict the medicines being used.[33] Charities competed for funds, and launched repeated appeals. The charity dinner and festival was a commonly used means of raising money, and securing notable guests and speakers was considered essential.

None to be excluded

Andrew Reed shared the fear hinted at by Charles Dickens in his speech that places in the new hospital might be filled by those who had relatives able to pay the modest charges for payment cases, and that those who had no means of financial support, or who required expensive diet or intensive nursing support, might be excluded.

Reed was also determined that no case should be treated as beyond care and support. Again, the model was to be Jesus himself, who excluded none: 'If we cannot *heal* all, we must soothe, help, and comfort all, and to the last. I cannot endure that any sufferer of the human family should be excluded from human sympathy.' The matter increasingly distressed Reed as the weaknesses of the election system were beginning to be exposed. On occasion the poorest and most deserving cases failed in the election when at the last minute friends of some less acute cases bought more votes than the poorest could muster. Others were troubled by the same problem, and a group of benevolent ladies approached Reed about the possibility of starting a free ward exclusively for the poorest patients of all. He was delighted by this proposal. The scheme brought a ready response from the wider public, and £2,000 was raised between February and May 1859 for the exclusive purpose of admitting the urgent cases amongst the poorest applicants.[34]

The Hospital for Incurables, Putney House

The home at Putney

In 1860 there were eighty-four patients in the home at Putney, and sixty-two outpatients were also being supported with an allowance of £20 per year towards their maintenance, care and medical needs. Some received further supportive gifts in addition to this.[35]

Patients frequently wrote to Reed expressing their gratitude for what was being done. It was believed that the general health of the patients had improved considerably, and this owed much to the high standards of medical and personal care and the sense of security that came from their knowing that they were to be supported for life. Leading doctors regularly visited the patients, and after 1857 the hospital had its own medical officer. On occasion the charity could even report that patients admitted as incurable had in fact, with such high standards of care, recovered and been discharged as cured. For others the charity could bring no cure, but distressing symptoms were alleviated, and comfort and support offered as life drew to a close. One woman nearing death passed a note to the matron addressed to Andrew Reed. She wrote of the home in heaven to which she was going, and added, 'I should have had no home but for this, and no friend to watch by my dying couch and comfort me. May God bless those who instituted and keep up this home! Will you tell them what a pleasant place this has been, and how grateful I am for all the kindness I have received?'[36]

Reed regularly visited the patients, and spent time listening to their comments and concerns; those resident in the hospital were always referred to as 'the family', reflecting an atmosphere of welcome, acceptance and commitment achieved by the staff and directors. Although they were a much-afflicted family, it was repeatedly observed that they were a 'happy family'.

Everything possible was done to spare terminally ill patients the lonely death to which they might otherwise have been consigned. With a policy that pre-dated by many years the enlightened work of the modern hospice movement, staff members normally sat with patients as they neared death, to minister a caring presence and comfort in their last moments of life.

To recruit and train staff capable of such high standards of care was a considerable achievement. In 1867 Florence Nightingale, a redoubtable campaigner for improved standards of nursing care, described the nurses in the workhouse infirmaries as 'too old, too weak, too drunken, too dirty, too stolid, or too bad to do anything else'.[37] It was into the care of such individuals that many of the patients at the Hospital for Incurables would have fallen had the charity not existed. Reed wanted to do all he could to spare the incurable or terminally ill such a fate. Nurses in the voluntary charitable hospitals were usually of a higher standard, and matrons and sisters were often well educated, with increased opportunities for training being made available as the nineteenth century progressed.[38] Securing good-quality staff was a high priority.

Controversy over the Coulsdon site

Andrew Reed consistently attended the board meetings, which were held at least every month; it was October 1857 before he missed a meeting. He repeatedly urged that building work at Coulsdon should start immediately, but opposition to the proposed site was mounting, led in particular by one individual who had not been on the board in the early years of the charity. The founder believed that some directors were being excessively cautious in requiring most of the money to be in hand before building work could commence. In 1859, now over seventy years old, he was conscious of time running out and that he was losing the strength for the fight. He needed to rest more than ever on the strength of God. He prayed, 'O Lord, be a comfort to mine age! I have sought to work righteousness and charity on the earth; forgive my great offences, and help me, now that I am old and grey-headed! Make my work easy to me and delightful!' His other charities were by now well established and running and he asked of God the strength to complete this one last thing. Yet opponents on the board were becoming more vociferous. It was argued that the Purley site was too far from London for family and friends to visit, and the undeveloped nature of the area meant that there was no accommodation available locally where they could stay if travelling from a distance. Reed's opponents claimed that because the land bought was on a breezy hillside it was unsuitable for those who had difficulties walking, or those with pulmonary or respiratory diseases. The water supply was also believed to be inadequate.

With failing powers, Reed did his best to counter their arguments. He was convinced that the fresh, rural air of the Surrey hills would greatly benefit the health of the patients, that a levelled site could be created, and he commissioned a doctor to investigate the water supply, who declared it entirely suitable for the purposes. In 1861, in the later stages of the controversy, the advice of the heroine of the Scutari hospital in the Crimean War (1854-56), Florence Nightingale, was sought. She declared the location 'well chosen', and appropriate for the intended purposes. She offered advice on the amounts of air and light required by patients, the size of wards and the need for day and exercise rooms.[39]

In his steadfast adherence to the Coulsdon site, Reed was not simply following personal preference; he was in fact acting on prevailing medical opinion, which stressed the harmful effects of exposure to the unhealthy environment of most urban areas. It was in the cities that the worst problems of polluted air and water, lack of drainage, bad sanitation and overcrowding were to be found. With limited understanding as to how disease was spread, many feared 'miasmata', the unhealthy influences that were believed to hang in the atmosphere, penetrating buildings and carrying diseases. To counter these, doctors stressed the importance and health-giving properties of natural light and ventilation. Medical experts urged that hospitals should be moved out of the polluted city centres, where they were usually located, and that they should be designed as low-rise buildings on expansive sites, in open-pavilion plan to cut the risk of cross-infection, with natural ventilation and fresh air freely available on all sides. The location and construction of a number of hospitals was believed to be detrimental to the health of many patients, as Florence Nightingale pithily observed in her *Notes on Hospitals*: 'The first requirement in a hospital is that it should do the sick no harm.'[40] Such opinions weighed heavily with Andrew Reed, who saw in the location, aspect and elevation of the Coulsdon site the ideal way of fulfilling what best medical practice aimed for.

Those unhappy with the move to rural Surrey expected to be able simply to sell the land at Coulsdon, and purchase another, more convenient, location. Against Reed's wishes they entered into negotiations with the Warehousemen and Clerks' School, who were interested in purchasing the site. To their dismay they found that, during the purchase of the land, Reed had insisted on adding a restrictive covenant that, if the plot were ever to be sold, the sale required the consent of the trustees of the Asylum for Fatherless Children, and that it could only be used for the purposes of a hospital. His intention had been to preserve the neighbouring orphanage from encroachment by unwanted building development should the site be sold on in the future. Reed's opponents on the board were outraged at what he had done, and demanded to know why they had not been told. Reed calmly answered that the deeds had been available at two board meetings for all to inspect, and nobody had objected on those occasions.[41]

Matters reached a head at a special board meeting in February 1860 at which a decision to proceed with building at Coulsdon was defeated by just one vote. Further special board meetings were called in the following months as an impasse between the sides was reached, but Reed, now seventy-three years old and increasingly frail, could not bear to attend. The strain of these unhappy events told heavily on him. Both sides obtained the opinion of a Queen's Counsel, and some spoke of litigation in the Court of Chancery over the matter. Reed began to expect the defeat of his plans, and even quietly contemplated his own independent scheme, which he much preferred to taking the case to court. In the end his supporters, led by his son Charles, rallied to his side at the annual general meeting, and reinstated the decision to proceed at Coulsdon, but the fall-out from the controversy was bitter.[42] Led by Lord Raynham, the treasurer and chairman of many of the board meetings, and two vice-presidents, around a dozen board members resigned from the Hospital for Incurables and began their own scheme, which became the British Hospital and Home for Incurables, initially located in Clapham and later in Streatham.[43] Reed likened the split to that between Abraham and Lot in the Old Testament. He similarly longed that there should be no lasting strife and maintained that, with the whole land before them, there was ample room for both charities. None the less, although the board members who resigned were soon replaced, the dispute over the Coulsdon land was a setback, springing from an unfortunate series of events.

There were faults on both sides. Reed had something of a conflict of loyalties between the Asylum for Fatherless Children and the Hospital for Incurables, and his well-intentioned desire to protect the orphanage was to the detriment of the hospital's scheme. There was a greater need for orphan children to be away from infectious diseases and to have the freedom of the countryside than there was for patients who were seriously disabled. The Coulsdon site, set on a hillside, was certainly far from level and was not ideal for wheelchair users. Although terracing work would have corrected much of the problem, this was expensive. Its location made it difficult for visitors to reach easily. Reed acted in the independent and entrepreneurial fashion that had got things done in the past, and in what he believed was the best interests of the charities, but, on the issue of inserting the restrictive covenant, he should have consulted more widely and shared information more freely. However, amongst the new faces on the board there appears to have been a lack of respect for Reed's historic achievement in the founding of the Hospital for Incurables and other charities. Their approach should have been less confrontational and insensitive; some were from an aristocratic background and simply expected their will to prevail. For all their frustrations, an amicable solution could have been found. Sadly, the severe stresses of these years can only have served to hasten the end of Reed's life, and taken something of the gloss off his marvellous achievement.

Much of the remaining strength Reed possessed was thrown into making the hospital a success. The generosity of the public was not diminished by the division in the board, and the high regard attached to Reed's name played an important role in this. He withdrew as much as possible from the regular activities of the other charities, and worked on plans for the new building at Coulsdon. Instructions to architects were issued, and specifications set down — emphasizing that the needs of the disabled should be paramount, with ramps, lifts and hoists being freely used. Reed wanted the needs of four types of patient to be identified and specifically catered for: those who were bedridden; the less disabled who needed some nursing assistance; those who could live semi-independently with regular support; and those who could live with a degree of privacy without the need for constant attendance.[44] One of his last and wisest decisions was to recruit Henry Huth to replace Lord Raynham as treasurer. It was under Huth's fine leadership that much of the continued success of the Hospital for Incurables was achieved.

On 24 October 1861 Andrew Reed attended his last board meeting. Soon afterwards he was himself confined to his room through growing infirmity, although he still found the strength to dictate the draft of the Annual Report for that year. He did not live to see the construction of the longed-for building for the last great charity he had inspired. Indeed, it never was built at Coulsdon as he had so desired. After his death the questions about the suitability of the land would not go away, and in 1863 the decision was made to search for an alternative site and to seek to sell the land back to the Asylum for Fatherless Children. Instead the Hospital for Incurables purchased for £18,000 the twenty-five acre Melrose Hall estate, at the crown of West Hill, Putney Heath. Its parkland setting, surrounded by other large houses, was considered eminently suitable and it was close to where the charity had found a temporary home in rented accommodation. None the less, by the time of his death Reed had ensured that the Hospital for Incurables was firmly established, and some 150 patients were comfortably housed in Putney House, receiving the highest standards of care.[45]

As with the Asylum for Idiots, the charity Reed had established was at the leading edge of caring for some of the most vulnerable and needy individuals in society. The nineteenth century saw an increasing trend towards specialization in health care. Reed opted to fill a gap in the existing medical provision, taking up a cause that had little glamour and outward popularity attached to it, as evidenced by the difficulties in obtaining royal patronage. As usual he showed great foresight in aiming for the highest standards of palliative care and rehabilitation, and through great skill and personal charm he drew about him not only leading donors, but medical experts.

The charity was also a tribute to Christian compassion — it was not simply to be a hospital, but a permanent home and a family. As one visitor reported, 'It would be impossible for any stranger to visit the Hospital and not be struck by the cheerfulness and contentment that prevail amongst the family, arising from the knowledge that they are permanently released from worldly cares and anxieties, and from all unnecessary and hurtful exertion.'[46] The inspiration for the project was the example of Jesus Christ, who turned away none of the suffering and infirm who came to him. With his remaining strength Reed drove the plan, the child of his declining years, through to completion, hoping that one day the Hospital for Incurables would be able to say that nobody in need was ever turned away. Such hopes pre-dated the creation of the National Health Service by almost a century.

22.
Ready for the harvest

'I have never met a man of
such business capacity as
Dr Reed ... by God's
help, he has been permitted
to do, perhaps, more good
than any other man of the
present day'
(A speaker at the service
to mark Reed's golden
jubilee in the ministry).

22.
Ready for the harvest

The physical and mental strain placed on Andrew Reed's constitution by his ceaseless round of charitable work, together with pastoral and preaching labours, took its toll. As he approached his mid-sixties, when many would have considered retirement, his schedule was as punishing as ever. His hair was passing from grey to white, and at times he was very tired, but his cry to God was: 'Forsake me not, until I have showed Thy strength to this generation, and Thy power to every one that is to come.'

The demands he made on himself were bound to have consequences. In 1851 when he had suffered a slight stroke, which affected his right side, his cry had been that God might spare his life, for the work at Earlswood and the Asylum for Fatherless Children was at a critical phase. If he was spared, he resolved to be 'more diligent in my work, more faithful in my trust, and more cheerful beneath the burdens and trials of my service'. His priority was clear: 'There remains before me, if God will, the *Triumph* of the *Pulpit*, the *Triumph of Grace* over flesh, sense, and time, to a glorious immortality.'[1] He believed that prayer was answered with a further ten years of useful service.

Bust of Andrew Reed

The final decade

November 1851 brought the fortieth anniversary of his ministry at Wycliffe Chapel. The congregation desired to mark the event with a gift, but he refused the usual tokens of money, or silver plate. Finally he consented to a marble bust of himself being made, by which he might be remembered. Reed was deeply grateful for what he had been able to achieve, but he acknowledged it was God's work, and remained painfully aware of his own shortcomings: 'O God, Thou hast been my helper from infancy to youth, to manhood, and to age! Be my helper still! Spare my mind! Spare my affections! Spare to me the means of glorifying Thy name and of serving my generation! O Lord, I am anything rather than the wise, the strong, the virtuous, the important being I sometimes think myself... Alas! ... I am more unworthy than others.'[2]

In 1852 he was still, as ever, full of plans — to complete the building work for the Earlswood Asylum and the Asylum for Fatherless Children, to write a book on revival, to complete another on the proper care of people suffering from mental disability, to publish a volume of sermons. The list stretched on, but paramount was his resolve to 'sustain my life — *this year* — by prayer'. He wrote to his congregation urging them to 'place me by your prayers, in the hands of *God*'.

The work of the church continued to flourish — in October 1852 nineteen new members were received, and every evening for a fortnight Reed was at the church, meeting with enquirers. Late into Saturday evenings, and sometimes in his wakeful hours during the night, he could be found wrestling in prayer for his congregation, that he might be more effective and helpful in the pulpit. There seems to have been little diminishing in his preaching ministry in the 1850s, and to his zeal was added an impressiveness that sprang from age and mature experience.

He continued to read widely, keeping himself abreast of the latest trends in theology. After reading *Essays and Reviews*, one of the early flowerings of theologically liberal academic scholarship from the British universities, Reed preached a sermon to his congregation carefully setting out what he believed were the dangers of such developments.[3] Above all, his longing was to remain useful in some way for God: 'I would like anything, decline anything, be anything, bear anything, if I might become a prepared vessel meet for the Master's service. My hope, my boundless hope, is in Thee!'[4]

The year 1854 brought further reminders of the terrible problems of urban living in nineteenth-century London. Sewers had been built to improve the sanitation of the great city, but they still discharged into the River Thames and its adjacent streams, which also served as London's drinking-water supply. It was a disaster waiting to happen. In late summer cholera broke out again. One week in September saw 3,413 deaths. The suddenness of its onset, and its rapid progress, horrified the population. In one night in a small district of the capital, 150 people were carried away and buried. Most of them had been alive and well the previous morning. The epidemic of 1854 did bring a major breakthrough in knowledge about the spread of cholera, when Dr John Snow was able to prove his theory that the disease was spread through polluted water, by showing that it was worst in areas where the water supply was contaminated by sewage. By stopping people drinking from pumps connected to the polluted water sources, the outbreak was contained in some neighbourhoods.[5] None the less, such a discovery was too late for most of the victims of the cholera epidemic.

Reed stood steadfast to his pastoral responsibilities at this time; he simply recorded in his journal: 'Just returned to my duty, and do not mean to run from it.' Aware of the dangers to his health to which he was exposing himself, he found the urgent pastoral needs all around him were too pressing to ignore. Yet he was honest enough to acknowledge: 'It is very fearful.'[6] Across the Thames in South London that September, the young Baptist pastor C. H. Spurgeon was just beginning his ministry. As the tired and apprehensive young minister walked along similar cholera-ridden streets, he came across a note pasted in a shoemaker's window, containing words from Psalm 91: 'Because thou hast made the LORD, which is my refuge, even the most High, thy habitation; there shall no evil befall thee, neither shall any plague come nigh thy dwelling.' Spurgeon took the message as an encouragement from God to press on in the work, and he won many over to his ministry through being faithful to the pastoral task in dangerous times.[7] Reed was similarly faithful to his calling.

The last decade of Reed's life brought only a slight slowing of his ministry. There were periods of illness, a little more frequent than before, but none that kept him from his work for too long. Through it all, the longing of his heart grew stronger, to be nearer to God, to be more like Christ, to be more ready for heaven. He maintained the same balanced desire to preach the gospel and to offer compassionate care for those in need that had motivated him from his early years of ministry at the New Road Chapel when the London Orphan Asylum first started: 'For my occupation, I had rather not be engaged in any other pursuit; and for my recreation, I prefer to relieve the miseries of the wretched above all other pleasures.' He acknowledged that he had begged hundreds of thousands of pounds for those who could not plead for themselves, but confessed how difficult he had found this, and how he would 'much rather give a sovereign than ask a shilling. I deeply feel the sublime truth of Him who says, "It is more blessed to give than to receive".' Yet, for all the difficulty of this work, he acknowledged a deep conviction that 'The very thing I am doing, is the very thing I ought to do.'[8]

Family life remained a constant delight to Andrew and Elizabeth. Over time their children married and moved away to rear their own families. The house at Cambridge Heath was often filled with the sound of children laughing and playing as their grandchildren came to visit or stay. Andrew Reed lived to see his oldest grandchild make a profession of conversion and be accepted into church membership. In 1857 he recalled how in over fifty years of preaching, often going to church in pain and weakness, or returning home to his sickbed, he had never found himself unable to finish a sermon, for which he gave great thanks.[9] His diary for a week at the close of July and into early August 1860 shows what was required of the then seventy-two-year-old: on successive days from the 30th July he was at the Hospital for Incurables in Putney, the London office of the Earlswood Asylum, the London office of the Asylum for Fatherless Children and the Eastern Counties Asylum in Colchester, while on the 4th August he was at the central London office of the Hospital for Incurables.[10]

His ministry draws to a close

Sadly, he could not sustain this pace indefinitely. On the last Sunday of 1860, as he left his home for the chapel service, he slipped on an icy path outside and fell heavily. From that time on his mobility was increasingly impaired and throughout 1861 his strength began to fail. He travelled down to the regular board meetings at Earlswood as often as he could until April 1861, but in August of that year he tendered his resignation as secretary of the Asylum for Idiots on the grounds of his failing health. Aware of how he was so closely associated with the charity, Reed allowed his name to remain on its publicity, but he was no longer an active participant in its workings. Similarly he tendered his resignation from the Asylum for Fatherless Children, but again he met with a refusal to accept it. He was relieved of the duties of visiting the London office, but still attended the elections of children and the anniversary meeting. His presence at meetings was greatly missed, but he continued to send the children regular expressions of his love.

In a manner fitting for one becoming increasingly infirm, he sought to focus his remaining energies on the establishment of the Hospital for Incurables, and also on his preaching work: 'My days are few; I will lose no opportunity for preaching the gospel.' His voice began to lose its old power, but was all the more filled with emotion. His beloved congregation still listened with rapt attention, but his closing thoughts at the end of a sermon were often words of tender parting as he feared each service might be the last opportunity he had of pointing them to the Saviour. The last baptismal service he was to take was for one of his own grandchildren and, as he stood before the congregation with the infant in his arms, the 2,094th that he had baptized, he wept with joy as he prayed for a future work of God in the life of the child.[11]

And then he could preach no more; his voice was too weak for such a large church building as Wycliffe Chapel. His last sermons were delivered on 21 July 1861. In the morning he preached on Ephesians 1:3: 'Blessed be the God and Father of our Lord Jesus Christ, who hath blessed us with all spiritual blessings in heavenly places in Christ,' and in the evening on 2 Corinthians 5:19: 'God was in Christ, reconciling the world to himself.' For the last time he preached the same age-old gospel he had proclaimed for the previous fifty years. The effort was huge. Overwhelmed with weakness, he brought the sermon to a close before he had finished all he had intended to say, and he had to be helped in the short walk back to the vestry. Reed knew his life's preaching work was done, and he told the deacons he would formally resign from the pastorate on the 27th November, his birthday and the anniversary of his induction, resisting any pleas that he might reconsider his decision.[12]

No longer able to speak in public, he continued to receive many visitors at his home. He loved to explain the purpose for which the various charities had been set up, and spoke fondly of the Earlswood Asylum, dedicated to those with learning disabilities, remembering that 'I have always had their souls in view.' He recalled sadly those who had questioned whether children with mental disabilities even had souls, and then remembered the little boy at Highgate who had decisively declared, 'I love God.' Reed declared his firm conviction that together they would share the presence of God in the eternal future: 'Nothing that loves Him shall perish... I shall meet them soon in heaven.'[13]

His strength failing, he made farewell visits to Cheshunt, a place rich in associations with his family, to Ponders End, where he had begun his Christian work as a Sunday school teacher, to the London Orphan and Infant Orphan Asylums and to the grave of his father and mother.[14] His last visit to the board meeting of the Hospital for Incurables came on the 24th October, and then he became too weak to travel any more. Slowly there came the realization that the charities he had set up were no longer to be his daily responsibility. With this came both sadness and hope: 'I must leave them all; but my country will care for them.' He inspected the plans for the long-hoped-for building for the Hospital for Incurables, and stressed the importance of using lifts and ramps for the severely disabled patients, making the gardens as accessible as possible and windows low enough for patients to be able to see out from their beds.[15]

He still prayed with those who came to see him, and offered words of pastoral counsel: 'To live for this world only, were to live for nothing'; 'Let the line of separation between the Christian and the Christian be less and less, and the line between the Church and the World greater and stronger'; 'Nothing can lift me up, for I am the chief of sinners; nothing shall cast me down, for God is the rock of my salvation. If I perish, I perish there.'[16]

The golden jubilee

On 27 November 1861, the church celebrated the golden jubilee of his induction as minister, and his retirement, but he was too ill to attend. Ministerial friends, colleagues from the charities, those who had been converted or blessed under his ministry, those called into Christian service, visitors and ordinary chapel members all thronged the building and publicly paid tribute to his influence. Messages of love and affection flowed in from around the world. Many were the expressions of esteem. A ministerial colleague remembered how, in the midst of shifting theological opinion over fifty years, Reed had been renowned for his 'unflinching adherence to the truth as it is in Jesus'. Another remembered how he had been converted while hearing Reed deliver the funeral sermon for Rev. Mathew Wilks, and Reed had subsequently preached at the same man's ordination. One participant recalled sitting in many committees associated with Reed's charities, and remarked, 'I have never met a man of such business capacity as Dr Reed ... by God's help, he has been permitted to do, perhaps, more good than any other man of the present day. His name will go down in posterity with those of John Howard and Elizabeth Fry.' Another, who was an orphan, had been cared for by the London Orphan Asylum and had gone on to join Wycliffe Chapel. He declared he owed almost everything to Andrew Reed, as did so many others. He noted how many who had been cared for by the orphanages were now members of churches, and were actively involved in religious and charitable work. To him, Andrew Reed was simply 'The Orphan's Friend'.[17]

Sadly, Reed was unable to hear such moving testimony to the fruit of his life's work but, as one who shunned personal acclaim, had he been present such public sentiments would have made him feel uneasy. His loving congregation presented him with a farewell gift of £500, which, with his characteristic generosity, he promptly handed over to the Asylum for Fatherless Children. It was a fitting close to a long and generous ministry.

The final days

The decision to step back from charities and church work had come at the right time. A gentle peacefulness fell upon him; he sent letters and books to ministerial colleagues who had disagreed with him in previous years — no savour of previous discord was allowed to remain at the end. His strength failed rapidly, but he continued to read, loving the old works of divinity that had been his strength for so long. Whenever he took up a biography to read, his first question became: 'Let me know, not what men did, but how they died.'

Outside his room the world went on its sad, distressing way. In 1861 America, the country he had visited and loved, descended into a bitter Civil War. Nearer home, on the 14th December, the nation was stunned by the sudden death, at the age of only forty-two, of Prince Albert, whom Reed knew so well. His lament was heartfelt: 'Charity will weep for him.'

The winter wore on, and Reed no longer had the strength to leave his room and go into his study. For the last time he wound up the study-room clock given to him by his congregation, and put his writing things away neatly in their places. Soon he was confined to bed, lovingly tended by his wife and children, who read to him the Scriptures and hymns that were so dear to him. There was no sadness as the end neared, as he prayed, 'Let me indulge no wrong thought, do no wrong thing, entertain no wrong fear; but let me nestle down in the lap of Providence, and be warm, and safe, and happy.'[18]

In his last days of frailty his mind began to wander, yet he spoke often of his Saviour and of heaven, of the children in the orphanages and of his concern for the welfare of his congregation when he had gone. And then, after a succession of long days and nights of restlessness and pain, the seventy-four-year-old Andrew Reed quietly said, 'Now we will sleep.' A little while later he slipped into unconsciousness, his breathing stilled and, in the early hours of 24 February 1862, he gently passed into the presence of his Saviour.[19]

The funeral

His body was taken to Wycliffe Chapel on the Sunday before his funeral, where members of the church and supporters of the charity were able to pay their respects. On the coffin was a last message from the pastor to his congregation: 'I have lived, and laboured and prayed for your salvation.' That Sunday the services at Wycliffe Chapel were taken by Dr Robert Halley of Cheshunt College, reflecting Reed's deep concern for training ministers, and in the evening by Robert Milne, the orphaned son of the missionary William Milne, to whom Andrew and Elizabeth Reed had given a home. The funeral was held the following morning, taken by Thomas Binney of the King's Weigh House Chapel and Arthur Tidman of the London Missionary Society (the disagreements of the 1840s over the running of the missionary society now long forgotten). The participants recalled the remarkable events of Reed's life — how he had been converted in the same church that he was later to pastor for fifty years. The root of Reed's success was attributed to his confidence in the grace of God for the salvation of men, the centrality of the cross in his preaching and his reliance on the work of the Holy Spirit to bring life to his gospel message.[20]

The body of Andrew Reed was then taken the three miles to Abney Park Cemetery. Following the coffin were carriages containing members of the family and representatives from the church and the charities Reed had founded. Hundreds of others walked behind. The funeral cortege made its way through Bethnal Green and Hackney to Clapton, where it paused outside the gates of the London Orphan Asylum. Here the orphan children lined up outside to honour the 'Orphan's Friend', founder of the charity to which they owed so much. At Abney Park children from the Reedham orphanage led the way to the graveside. Then Andrew Reed was laid to rest amidst the graves of many of the leading Nonconformists of his day. His obituary in the *Congregational Year Book* summed up the scene: 'Thus lived and died Andrew Reed, who having "served his generation according to the will of God — fell on sleep, and was gathered to his fathers".'[21]

23.
Conclusion

'I give, not because I have great means, but because I have few wants... If rich in no other sense, I would be rich in mercy... Verily I share my daily bread with the orphan...'

(Andrew Reed).

23.
Conclusion

The death of Andrew Reed on 25 February 1862 was greeted with great sorrow by the five charities he had done so much to establish.

The board of the Hospital for Incurables recorded their belief that his name should be 'cherished and respected as long as public philanthropy and private virtue continue to command the reverence of men'. The Annual Report of the hospital for 1862 continued this theme: 'His praises shall not be wanting till the sick and helpless need charity no more.' The board members pledged themselves to carry out to the best of their ability the 'noble objects of the institution, according to the spirit and design of its Author'.[1]

At Earlswood, the flag flew at half mast, the staff wore mourning for six weeks and the board recorded that their 'Founder, Munificent Supporter, and gratuitous Secretary' was indeed a 'generous, large-hearted friend of suffering humanity' and 'a Christian Philanthropist'.[2] The anniversary dinner of the Earlswood Asylum fell a week after Reed's death, but his family would not countenance such an important event being cancelled. Those present stood in silence to remember the founder, and the board inscribed a scroll recording their gratitude for Reed's work, and their 'admiration of his long-continued and arduous exertions in promoting the success of this and other benevolent institutions, and their reverence for his character as a Christian Philanthropist'. The Eastern Counties Asylum in

Colchester similarly added their deep thanks for the valuable services and generosity Reed had shown to it.

The Managers of the Asylum for Fatherless Children recorded the debt so many owed to the founder of the charity: 'In the hearts of widowed mothers who have found in the Asylum a home for their fatherless ones, and in those of the orphans blessed with its privileges, his name will be embalmed in hallowed remembrance.'

Even the charities from which sad breaches had occurred in 1843 and 1844 were unstinting in their praise. With gratitude the London Orphan Asylum remembered him as their founder, acknowledged their debt to him for his thirty years of involvement as honorary secretary, and acclaimed his 'conspicuous example and matchless benevolence, based as they were on the principle of love to his God'. The Infant Orphan Asylum placed on record their sincere thanks for Andrew Reed's active exertions towards the foundation and development of the orphanage.[3]

The charities continued to have cause to bless his memory, for in his will Reed was typically generous. To the Earlswood Asylum he left £1,000, and a further £1,000 was bequeathed to the Asylum for Fatherless Children, in addition to the 500 guineas testimonial he received from his church in 1861. To the London Orphan Asylum Andrew Reed left £300, requesting that it be used in the education of the children in the natural sciences, and to the Infant Orphan Asylum he gave £100, with a stipulation characteristic of the founder — that it should be spent on toys to be given to the children at Christmas.[4]

A life of extraordinary achievement

By the time of their founder's death, what had been achieved by the charities was enormous.

From its formal commencement in 1813 to Reed's death in 1862, the London Orphan Asylum had provided care for 2,757 children, and had seen £407,128 raised on its behalf; its work was firmly established in its impressive building in Clapton. The Infant Orphan Asylum, in the years from 1827, had admitted 1,918 children, and had raised £302,611, and was flourishing in its semi-rural location at Wanstead.

The more recent foundation of the Asylum for Fatherless Children had, in just under twenty years of existence, been able to raise £62,821 and provide care for 468 orphans, and was well established on its Surrey hillside site at Reedham.

The Asylum for Idiots had completed the Earlswood Hospital project and, since its foundation in 1847, the charity had cared for 920 patients and raised £210,000, with a further £17,133 being raised after 1859 for the smaller Eastern Counties Asylum in Colchester, which had cared for 102 patients.

The most recent of the projects, the Hospital for Incurables, which had been begun in 1854, had admitted 258 patients and raised £43,871. Plans for a permanent hospital at Reedham had been drawn up by the time of Reed's death, although the charity later decided to stay in Putney and purchase an estate at Putney Heath.

In total, the charities Reed established had provided care for 6,423 individuals, with a continuing capacity to care for 2,110 needy people. Between them, by the time of his death, they had raised £1,043,566, of which Reed had personally contributed £4,540. In years when a good salary was around £200 per year, this was an astonishing amount.[5] The religious paper the *Patriot* believed he was rightly to be called 'The Orphan's Friend', and added, 'Who could covet a higher eulogy?'[6]

Andrew Reed was a man who through his organizational and business capacity could have made a million pounds for himself, but instead he gave his all to help raise that sum for some of the most vulnerable members of society. He turned the guinea subscriptions of supporters — some wealthy, some far less so — into clothes and food, and wheelchair-friendly slopes, into the work of supporting and caring for people who had suffered much and were often desperately unhappy. Upon each

of the charities, as they began, developed and became established with major building projects, he bestowed the utmost of
his creative energies. From the laying of the foundation stone to
the opening of each building, Reed's was the guiding hand that
presided over operations. He resolved to 'know no weariness,
and to refuse to be discouraged';[7] he was possessed of indomi-
table perseverance and capacity for great attention to detail.

There is no doubt that Andrew Reed's life was one of
extraordinary achievement. He was responsible for starting not
just one major charity, but five. The first was begun when he
was only twenty-four years old, fresh from college, newly
ordained as minister of a small congregation struggling in a
large building with a huge debt. He was a man of extraordinary
vision and courage. When he found that provision for orphans
in the East of London was utterly inadequate, he set about
beginning his own orphanage. When religious controversy
brought a parting of the ways from the Infant Orphan and the
London Orphan Asylums, deep sadness was not allowed to
become festering bitterness, but was instead channelled cre-
atively into the formation of the Asylum for Fatherless Children.

Perhaps he was at his most visionary in his care for children
with severe learning disabilities. He was convinced that they
were people made in the image of God, that they had souls,
that they had an inherent dignity and deserved care and
respect. His researches also put him at the leading edge of
thinking as to their proper care and support, especially his belief
that education should be an essential part of what the asylum
offered. He was convinced that children with severe learning
difficulties could make progress, intellectually and physically,
under enlightened, humanitarian, Christian care. In that education, simple religious instruction was to take an important
place, and he was thrilled to see the children developing
spiritually.

The pioneering theme continued with the Hospital for
Incurables, in which his thinking pre-dated by many years the
modern concept of long-term palliative medical care and the

contemporary hospice movement. In the orphanages, the needs of the child were to be paramount. None was to cry without the reason why being ascertained and appropriate help being offered; food was to be of the best quality and not limited; education was to be of the highest standard and with the whole of life in view. Those in the homes were to be a family.

The preacher and pastor

Andrew Reed's background gave little indication of what was to follow, being of solid, respectable artisan stock, but no more. Through the sacrifice of his parents and his own personal abilities and efforts he rose from humble beginnings. His abilities and earnestness attracted the interest and support of Matthew Wilks, who encouraged him. On grounds of conscience he turned his back on Cambridge and instead he settled for the solid, but limited, theological education available at Hackney College. Of this opportunity he made the most. After his call to the New Road Chapel, news of his preaching and pastoral work spread through the crowded streets of East London, and people came in steadily increasing numbers to hear his vigorous, eloquent but practical sermons.

The prime motive force of his life remained his call to be a preacher of the gospel. He saw great success in this, but constantly felt that he had not done enough. His preaching style was clear and simple, accessible enough for a child, yet sufficiently challenging for the mature believer. Reed loved the Bible, and delighted to share its riches with his congregation. He read widely and deeply, and ensured that his sermons were a distillation of what he had read into a form suitable for the urban dwellers of the East End of London. Although he believed that the preacher should prepare extensively, he was still convinced that the message of the Bible remained accessible to all: 'The best interpreter of Scripture is a humble spirit; and nigh to it is common sense.'[8]

In his theology Andrew Reed was strongly evangelical — marrying the evangelical urgency of the Evangelical Revival with the certainties of Calvinism. He emphasized the importance of Christian experience, both of salvation and of ongoing knowledge and experience of the presence of God in a person's life.

The calm, slightly reserved manner with which Reed delivered his sermons charged them with an energy which, by being slightly suppressed, made them deeper and more intensely powerful. As a preacher Andrew Reed stands amongst the front rank of his generation. His invariable habit was to give the first part of each day to preparation for his pulpit ministry, reading widely and praying deeply before writing each sermon. His messages were warmly pastoral and thoroughly evangelistic. Under his ministry nearly 2,500 new members joined his church, the majority of whom were converts through his preaching.

Andrew Reed was also an important thinker in the field of revival, and in his time helped promote a Calvinistic antidote to Charles Finney's teaching. Under his ministry Wycliffe Chapel enjoyed a period of revival, and other shorter periods of spiritual awakening.

Reed was also a man of great pastoral sensitivity, spending much time with those in need, especially in matters of spiritual concern, although his extensive philanthropic commitments precluded much time being spent on routine pastoral visitation.

His burden for those who had never heard the gospel was very great, particularly in the newly developing mission-fields. His longing to be a missionary was strong, but despite several attempts to offer his services, it was to remain unfulfilled. Others realized that his work in Britain was too important to be given up. It was sad that mission agencies could not use his enormous gifts to promote and develop their work, and his often well-founded criticisms were received badly and brought upon him a storm of protest. What he could have achieved as the inspirational leader of a group of younger missionaries will never be known, but he certainly inspired many others into ministry both at home and abroad. By the time of Reed's death there were very deep social needs surrounding Wycliffe Chapel — the East End of London had become a mission-field in its own right. To develop and sustain a congregation of up to 2,000 over several decades in such an environment was a huge achievement.

A holistic ministry

Andrew Reed did not simply believe in institutional charity. His personal benevolence, often spontaneous and financially costly, was immense. When a labourer fell from the scaffolding surrounding a building upon which he was working in the East End of London, he was killed instantly. Reed was distressed to hear of the accident, especially when it was revealed that the labourer had left eight children fatherless. The tragedy was compounded when, after hearing news of her husband's death, his grief-stricken wife, who was heavily pregnant, went into labour but died in giving birth. Another little orphan was left to add to the eight other children. Reed was immediately moved to action by what he heard and, without telling anyone but close members of his family, he decided to pay personally for a nurse to look after the baby in the village of Hendon, near to the residence of his daughter Elizabeth, who could oversee the care of the child. When the girl was a little older, after Reed's death, she was welcomed into the Asylum for Fatherless Children.[9]

The ministry of Andrew Reed was truly holistic — between the responsibility urgently to proclaim the message of salvation and the need to care for those with profound social needs there was 'perfect harmony'. Both were part of the gospel of compassion that he believed should motivate the true Christian. In 1828, speaking at the induction of a fellow-minister, he justified this approach: 'Whatever has a tendency to meliorate the sufferings of humanity, to disperse the darkness of the mind, to subdue the vices of society, to restore man to a divine obedience, and to attach his hopes and his thoughts to an unseen eternity, you will see as in perfect harmony with the spirit and the letter of your commission.'[10] To Andrew Reed, this was the epitome of true faith: 'the best evidence and surest nourisher of life' was 'action, action — holy and benevolent action! Exercise is at once the cure and the preventative of a thousand religious aliments.' The Christian was to be benevolent in the practical and the devotional realm. Spiritual riches or earthly wealth — these were to be freely shared: 'All that you have you have received; all that you have received, you are freely to bestow. It were a robbery to retain what is given to ourselves... You lose what you selfishly keep; you multiply the treasure you generously bestow.'[11]

This compassion was directed particularly at the most needy, and is summed up in a memorial tablet placed in the London Orphan Asylum in 1863. It depicts Andrew Reed bending down and reaching out towards three little children: in one hand he holds a plate of bread, and in the other a Bible. That was the heart of his Christian compassion — the Bread of Life and bread for life, both offered together, each as necessary as the other. This was the compassion of Christ, and in this Andrew Reed wanted to imitate his Master.[12] The impulse to charity and compassion was the hallmark of the true Christian. As his own life drew to a close, this thought filled him with great consolation: 'While Christianity lives, charity cannot die.'[13]

Giving to those in need

Through his charitable work Reed also believed he had a ministry to those who were wealthy. The vast majority of donors and subscribers to the charity were of modest means, but some were very affluent. How were they to spend their money? Reed courteously, but effectively, pricked their consciences. He boldly presented the needs of the less fortunate

THIS TABLET WAS ERECTED
IN GRATEFUL MEMORY
OF
THE REV? ANDREW REED.D.D.
THE FOUNDER OF THE
LONDON ORPHAN ASYLUM
BY
THOSE WHO HAVE BEEN EDUCATED IN THE INSTITUTION.
A.D. 1863.

Memorial tablet to Andrew Reed,
London Orphan Asylum

before their eyes and challenged them to respond. In the
busyness of business life, the needs of their fellow creatures
were easily forgotten. By awakening in them a charitable
impulse, and opening their eyes to the reality of a suffering
humanity all around them, Reed hoped that wealthy donors to
a strongly Christian charity would also be awakened to their
own spiritual need. In this he was lifting two burdens of oppression. The poor and needy were being delivered from the

burden of their suffering, and the wealthy from the oppression of not being charitable with their God-given wealth.

Andrew's marriage to Elizabeth certainly brought an improvement in his financial status. After the early years, in which his salary from New Road was low, and Andrew and his sister Martha struggled to provide for the two orphan children they had offered to care for, his rate of pay improved. As the congregation of the chapel grew, his salary increased, and at Wycliffe Chapel this peaked at £500, a comfortable, but not particularly large, sum in comparison with other leading Independent ministers. Elizabeth's money allowed them to become financially more independent, and Andrew's salary was reduced to £400 in 1855 and then halved to £200 in 1859. Increasingly frail, in 1861, the last full year of active ministry, he received just £100.[14] Reed lived comfortably but modestly, as he remembered after his retirement: 'I give, not because I have great means, but because I have few wants. My tendencies have been to economy, as to the wise and upright course. If I have deviated, it has been in charity. If rich in no other sense, I would be rich in mercy... Verily I share my daily bread with the orphan ... they get the half of my salary.'[15] Much of what he earned he invested in his church and charities, preferring to lay up treasures in heaven.

Working with others

His business capacity was prodigious — his sons described him as 'decisive in all his acts, punctual to all engagements, and methodical in the conduct of his many enterprises. He performed with comparative ease, as those who knew him best are well aware, a daily pressure of work wonderful to contemplate.'[16] Proficiency in the business realm was a mixed blessing, and led to some of the mistakes he made. Reed himself was the first to recognize this, and in his journal he lamented his weaknesses and failings and begged forgiveness of God. At times he was prone to press ahead in independent fashion, not taking time to consult and bring gently along those who wished to move more slowly. At times he could be guilty of a lack of foresight, as in failing to see the likely repercussions of his only thinly disguising the character of Francis Barnett in a 'novel', or of taking his criticisms of the London Missionary Society to the public. But, in his defence, his motives were always honourable and he never acted out of self-interest.

On first acquaintance Reed could appear quiet, a little reserved — some initially thought his manner cold. This was born of a tendency to shyness coupled with an undemonstrative manner and a quiet decision of purpose. To those who knew him away from the public arena, he was filled with affection and warmth, deep and lasting thoughtfulness, and love and compassion, but he was uncomfortable when people sought to laud him on public occasions.

Some complained that he could be inflexible, unwilling to adapt his views. Certainly he was tenacious of purpose, but what he resolved upon was born of great thought and widespread research. He had a deeply retentive memory and an exceptional grasp of the details of projects on which he was embarked. He was able to present his ideas and plans with great lucidity and authority. With remarkable frequency he showed himself a man of great vision and foresight, and some of the conflicts he faced came because he could see further than many others.

Not willing to see any of his time wasted, he often acted on the axiom that, if you wanted a thing done, you were best to do it yourself. But he also wanted to be sure others around him did not waste their time. With mighty projects to accomplish, and limited time available, it was easier to dictate than consult when a quick decision was required. This could leave colleagues presented with a fait accompli when they might have preferred to debate and discuss their way to a policy. Such is often the way with pioneers and leaders. To those who knew, loved and trusted him this was not a problem, but those newer to his charitable work were sometimes less understanding. Yet the outcome was always positive: all the philanthropic projects in which he was engaged were a success. His record stands as second to none.

Although consultation in crucial matters did not always come easily, Reed was no lone maverick. As one obituary notice of his life observed, 'Personally he was active, he enlisted the efforts of hundreds in his undertakings; and personally self-denying and generous, he never failed in securing from a benevolent public the funds necessary to carry out his projects.'[17] He was a skilled administrator, delegating areas of responsibility to others and managing teams of workers well. In the charities hugely successful committees and sub-committees were established, and agents and staff were appointed. In his choice of co-workers Reed frequently demonstrated great sagacity. Without their dedicated efforts, the charitable work would have failed. Similarly, in his church work, Andrew Reed gathered around him a very large and loyal band of workers. If he did not accept the services of an assistant minister, he instead mobilized dozens of willingly active lay people, to whom was entrusted the work of Sunday school teaching, local visitation, conducting preaching meetings and services in cottages and halls. To their heroic work in the increasingly deteriorating environmental conditions of the East End of London, much of the success of Wycliffe Chapel was owing.

Champion of the most vulnerable

Reed was once quoted as saying, 'I sprang from the people; I have lived for the people — the most for the most unhappy.'[18] The suffering he sought to counteract was indeed that experienced by the most unhappy — that of children, those with severe learning difficulties and those suffering from incurable disease. He championed the cause of those who had no voice of their own.

As a Nonconformist, suffering serious discrimination in many areas of social and religious life, he was also deeply opposed to any project, be it educational, social, or religious, that allowed for the dominance of one religious grouping above others. He argued for liberty of opinion in matters not fundamental to the gospel, of which church order was one. The events of 1843 and the fight for religious liberty on behalf of Nonconformist parents show how deeply Reed felt about the cause, and also how bitterly such views were opposed, especially by many Anglican clergy, who were unyielding in seeking to retain every vestige of their religious dominance of national life. Reed was shocked when some were utterly inflexible in their adherence to their position, even when dealing with those who were the most vulnerable in society and the least capable of understanding the significance of such matters — orphan children. Reed did all he could to oppose this: from the project for the Hackney Grammar School to the Asylum for Fatherless Children, religion was clearly to be taught, with a distinctively evangelical emphasis, but without favouring any denomination. It was a far-sighted policy, which many in those days were unwilling, or unable, to comprehend.

'The greatest is charity'

With such a record of achievement — from his church work, to his large, lasting and successful philanthropic work — why, we may ask, is Andrew Reed largely forgotten today? An obituary in the *Patriot* of February 1862 suggested that he had done more in the work of Christian charity 'than any other man or woman of his own time'. The editions of the *Illustrated London News* printed in the two weeks after his death included a portrait and a memoir, and details relating to the charities he founded. The *Gentleman's Magazine* included a lengthy obituary, in which it was declared that the growth of voluntary charity in the previous fifty years 'has been very much owing to the personal effort and powerful example in the cause of true philanthropy of the late Andrew Reed'.[19]

In part the lack of widespread awareness of Reed's work is due to his modesty — his charities never bore his name, but were rather a description of what they were formed to accomplish. Although the founder of the charities, he would often modestly assume a minor office, such as secretary or sub-treasurer — to the casual observer a minor functionary; but to those who attended the committee meetings, or read the minutes, he was the initiator and overseer of most of what was accomplished. Those who joined the charities once they were well established did not always appreciate the foundational role he had played, and sometimes showed a lack of respect for his achievement. He made it a point of principle never to receive financial reward for his labours with the charities. When, at the annual dinners of the charities, friends sought to propose a toast to him, he would decline, and ask for a toast 'to charity'. He wanted the glory to go to God, not himself. When asked by his sons to help them with a memoir of his life, he was reluctant to comply, replying, 'I was born *yesterday*, I shall die *tomorrow*. I must not spend *today* in telling what I have done, but in doing what I can for Him who has done all for me.'[20]

Self-denying and generous, with unwavering success he was able to move others to give to his charitable work. His charm and persuasiveness were irresistible — as the aged Duke of Wellington said, after finally agreeing to attend the anniversary of the London Orphan Asylum: 'I am here tonight at the request of that great man [pointing to Dr Reed], whose wishes are to me law, and, whose entreaties I felt as a command it was impossible to resist.'[21] His own giving freely and fully of his money to his charities encouraged others to have *every* confidence in his work, and to do the same. In his will he bequeathed the charities he had done so much to found to the care and regard of the British nation. The obituaries that appeared after Reed's death stressed his philanthropic and benevolent works, likening his achievement to that of John

Finally
I bequeath the four Asylums to my
beloved country with an earnest
prayer that they may be watched over
with wisdom & benevolence; that they
may be kept free from abuse; preserved
in efficiency & remain; as oft as ye
Memorial of that divine charity
which erecteth & glorifyeth a people.
Tottenham
Oct. 3, 1850.   Andrew Reed

Facsimile of the last sentence of Andrew Reed's will, in which he bequeaths the charities to the nation

Howard, upon whose statue in St Paul's Cathedral he had gazed when he was a boy.

The proclamation of the gospel, the compassionate support of the weak, vulnerable and needy — these were part of being Christlike in every dimension. In a library archive in Surrey can be found the last words Andrew Reed ever wrote. They sum up his philosophy, that true gospel compassion, true gospel charity should look to the needs of the whole person; that individuals should be cared for holistically, both body and soul. They are words of Scripture written in a spidery hand with failing strength, but then underlined with a firmness and resolve showing that in his dying days his conviction and spirit were undimmed: 'The greatest is charity.'[22]

24.
Epilogue

The charities that
survived over the past
150 years or more have
... continued to help
meet the type of needs
Andrew Reed originally
identified. They have
changed with the times,
but his legacy lives on.

24.
Epilogue

The work established by Andrew Reed continued after his death. *Wycliffe Chapel* found him difficult to replace. His successor Walter Hardie struggled to maintain the congregation Reed had built up; he also battled with ill health and died after only five years in the post. Hardie was succeeded by Reuen Thomas, who was a very gifted preacher and did something to reverse the decline in the size of the congregation. However, after seven years at Wycliffe Chapel he accepted a call to a Congregational church in Boston, in the United States, where he was highly successful. From the time of Thomas's resignation, numbers in the congregation began to decrease steadily. Many who attended the chapel began to move into suburbs beyond Stepney, and large numbers of Jewish families moved into the immediate area. The fifty-year ministry of Andrew Reed was superseded by a series of ministers each of whom only stayed for a short period. In 1906, with very few members still living in Stepney, it was decided to transfer the church to Ilford, where increasing numbers of the congregation were now resident.[1]

The philanthropic work of Andrew Reed left a deep and lasting legacy for good. Of the five charities he founded, four survive to this day, although in changed form.[2] *The London Orphan Asylum* remained at Clapton until 1871. By that time the area was becoming increasingly crowded, and an outbreak of typhoid encouraged the charity to move to a healthier

location. In 1871 a new building on the outskirts of Watford was
opened for the orphanage. The school became the London
Orphan School in 1915, and in 1939 it was renamed Reed's
School in honour of its founder. During the Second World War
the children were evacuated from the school, and the buildings
became a war hospital. After the war, the government continued to use the site at Watford, and so property at Dogmersfield
Park in Hampshire was obtained for a girls' school, and at
Cobham in Surrey for a boys' school. By the 1950s state
support for families which had lost father or mother was greatly
improved and the nature of the orphanage needed to change.
The school took some hard decisions, the first of which was to
close the girls' school at Dogmersfield Park and the second to
admit fee-paying boarders, with full bursaries for those in
particular need. Reed's School continues today as an independent school, with a significant number of places available
paid for by the Reedonian Foundation, which was set up to
continue the support of children who had suffered major family
trauma, in continuity with the ideas of Andrew Reed.[3]

The *Infant Orphan Asylum* became the Royal Infant Orphanage, and then the Royal Wanstead School. The post-war
improvements in state provision for families who had suffered
from bereavement similarly affected intake. The Royal Wanstead School finally closed in 1971, the building becoming
Snaresbrook Crown Courts. Its funds were vested in trust for
the support of children whose home circumstances were,
through factors such as the death, illness, or separation of their
parents, seriously prejudicial to their normal development. In
1998 the Royal Wanstead Children's Foundation was helping
354 children.

The *Asylum for Fatherless Children*, which became known
simply as the Reedham Orphanage, then Reedham School,
suffered in the second half of the twentieth century from declining numbers of children needing the special care the orphanage
provided. It eventually closed in 1980, its land sold for building,
and the proceeds vested in trust to become the Reedham Trust,

which supports children from tragic or deprived home back-grounds through funding their education in appropriate schools. In the year 2000 the trust was supporting 181 children.[4]

The *Asylum for Idiots* became the Earlswood Asylum, and in 1914 permission was granted by the Crown for the hospital to take on the name Royal, so that it became the 'Royal Earlswood Institution for Mental Defectives', and eventually the Royal Earlswood Hospital. In 1948 it became part of the post-war National Health Service, retaining its high reputation for care in the following decades. In the years after the passing of the Community Care Act of 1991 the numbers of patients declined, and the hospital was closed.

The *Hospital for Incurables*, which in 1919 formally became the Royal Hospital and Home for Incurables, settled firmly at Putney in the years after Andrew Reed's death. It steadfastly and successfully resisted efforts in the years after 1946 to draw it into the National Health Service, claiming that the charity was a home offering palliative care for those suffering from chronic illness, rather than a hospital, and that it should retain its independence as a centre for teaching and research. As the work of the hospital developed in more recent years, the title 'Incurables' became increasingly inappropriate. The hospital changed its name in the 1980s to the Royal Hospital and Home, Putney, and then in 1995 it became the Royal Hospital for Neuro-disability. It now undertakes specialist work in assess-ing and rehabilitating adults with traumatic brain injuries incurred through strokes or accidents (including pioneering work with those who have lapsed into the persistent vegetative state). It also provides long-term care for patients with severe and complex neurological conditions, including Huntingdon's Disease, multiple sclerosis and cerebral palsy.[5]

The charities that survived over the past 150 years or more have, therefore, continued to help meet the type of needs Andrew Reed originally identified. They have changed with the times, but his legacy lives on.[6] Some of the specific problems he laboured so hard to meet are less pressing than before, but others have arisen in their place. The charities have sought to adapt to these changed circumstances, while seeking to remain true to Andrew Reed's vision.

Many of the needs identified and addressed by Andrew Reed have now diminished, or are met by government agencies. Yet the world remains a world of need. In Africa, there are now around eleven million AIDS orphans, calling for vast philanthropic work by enlightened individuals to provide orphanages for their care. Across other continents, millions of orphaned, unwanted or abandoned children live on the streets of major cities, prey to hunger, disease and exploitation for sexual purposes. Around the world, the need for enlightened, compassionate care for those with severe learning disabilities is as great as ever, as are the needs of those suffering from severe physical disabilities, or degenerative and terminal illness. In the face of such needs, moved by his Christian compassion, Andrew Reed would not have stood idly by.

Notes

Chapter 1 — Beginnings

1. The Howard League for Penal Reform, founded in 1866, is named after John Howard. Devoted to his cause, John Howard's life had been cut tragically short in 1790 when he caught typhus while visiting a Russian military hospital.

2. A. Reed and C. Reed, *Memoirs of the Life and Philanthropic Labours of Andrew Reed, D. D., With Selections from His Journals* (London: Strahan and Co., 1863), pp.1-6.

3. *Ibid.,* pp.5-7.

4. *Wycliffe Chapel Burial Ground Register Book 1849-1902,* London Metropolitan Archive, N/C/40/25.

5. A. Reed, *Martha: A Memorial of an Only and Beloved Sister* (London: F. Westley, 1823, 2 vols.), p.3.

6. The catechism is dated 3 May 1795. It was given by Andrew Reed in 1844 to Sarah Jolly, one of the leading Sunday school teachers at Wycliffe Chapel, as a token of his esteem for her work.

7. Reed, *Martha,* p.30.

8. *Memoirs of Reed,* pp.7-14.

9. *Ibid.,* pp.14-15.

10. *Ibid.,* pp.15-17.

11. *Ibid.,* pp.17-19.

12. *Ibid.,* p.19.

13. *Ibid.,* p.20.

14. *Ibid.,* pp.21-2.

15. *Ibid.,* pp.22-3.

16. *Ibid.,* pp.25-6.

Chapter 2 — The call to the ministry

1. *Memoirs of Reed,* p.29.

2. *Ibid.,* pp.31-2.

3. Quoted in *Memoirs of Reed,* p.33.

4. *Ibid.*

5. *Ibid.,* p.34.

6. *Congregational Yearbook 1847,* pp.142-3.

7. T. Steadman, *Memoirs of the Rev. William Steadman D.D.* (London: Thomas Ward, 1838), pp.227-8, quoted in D. A. Johnson, *The Changing Shape of English Nonconformity, 1825-1925* (Oxford: Oxford University Press, 1999), p.19. Johnson provides a helpful survey of Nonconformist training in the early nineteenth century, especially pp.1-32.

8. *Memoirs of Reed,* p.35.

9. Many manual workers earned between £25 and £50 per year, so this was a large sum even for a craftsman like Andrew Reed senior.

10. *Memoirs of Reed,* p.37.

11. On the difference between high and evangelical Calvinism see I. J. Shaw, *High Calvinists in Action* (Oxford: Oxford University Press, 2002), especially pp.10-36.

12. 'The Work and Reward of the Christian Minister. A Charge delivered at the Ordination of the Rev. Andrew Reed, A.B., over the Church Assembling in the Old Meeting, Norwich, March 2, 1841' (London, 1841).

13. *Congregational Yearbook 1847,* pp.142-3.

14. *Memoirs of Reed,* pp.38-40.

15. *Ibid.,* pp.42-3.

16. *Ibid.,* p.44.

17. 'The Ordination Service of the Rev. Andrew Reed, to the Pastoral Office, over the Congregational Church of Christ, Assembling in the New Road Meeting, St George's-in-the East, on Wednesday, November 27th, 1811' (London, 1812).

18. Quoted in *Memoirs of Reed,* pp.45, 46.

Chapter 3 — Stepney

1. New Road is variously named. The 1809 map published by Laurie and Whittle gives its name as New Road, the appellation consistently employed by Reed's sons in their *Memoir*. On *Cross's New Plan of London*, 1847, it is called Cannon Street New Road. The road is now once again called New Road. It extends from Whitechapel Road down to the Commercial Road.

2. Lease No. 6567, New Road, St. George's, 26 December 1815, in Bancroft Library, East London.

3. Toilets which were without running water, with an earth pit or collecting receptacle underneath the seat. They were infrequently emptied, and were often in a revolting condition.

4. 'Report to the Council of the Statistical Society of London from a Committee of its Fellows Appointed to Make an Investigation into the State of the Poorer Classes in St. George's in the East', in *Quarterly Journal of the Statistical Society of London,* 11/2, August 1848, pp.193-210, and G. S. Jones, *Outcast London* (Oxford: Clarendon Press, 1971), pp.85-6, 91.

5. H. Gavin, *Sanitary Ramblings: Being Sketches and Illustrations of Bethnal Green, A Type of the Conditions of the Metropolis and Other Large Towns* (London, 1848), pp.9-11, 66, 79-80.

6. E. Chadwick, *Report on the Sanitary Condition of the Labouring Population of Great Britain, 1842* (Edinburgh: Edinburgh University Press, 1965 [first published 1842]), ed. M. W. Flinn; and Gavin, *Sanitary Ramblings,* pp.98-105.

7. *East London Advertiser,* 16 February 1907; R. J. W. Crabbe, 'Wycliffe Chapel: Notes Prepared by a Member of the Church,' 12 February 1964, unpublished manuscript in Surrey Record Office; *Archives of London Orphan Asylum,* 3719/15/8, and *Memoirs of Reed,* p.43.

Charles Lodemore, a local historian, has been unable to trace a direct link between the Minories Chapel and the New Road Chapel, see C. Lodemore, 'Wycliffe Chapel, Philpot Street, Stepney', *Cockney Ancestor,* No. 83, Summer 1999, pp.8-9.

8. *Religious Worship (England and Wales), Parliamentary Papers 1852-3,* vol. lxxxix, *Census of Great Britain, 1851* (London, 1853), pp.cclxxviii, 5-7; M. Watts, *The Dissenters,* vol. 2 (Oxford: Clarendon Press, 1995), p.682.

9. Quoted in H. McLeod, *Class and Religion in the Late Victorian City* (London: Croom Helm, 1974), p.104.

10. Reed, *Martha,* vol. I, p.51.

11. *Ibid.,* p.76.

12. *Ibid.,* pp.220-22.

13. *Memoirs of Reed,* pp.52-3.

14. *Ibid.,* p.48; Crabbe, 'Wycliffe Chapel,' section III.

15. Reed, *Martha,* vol. I, pp.294-8, 306.

16. *Ibid.,* vol. II, p.34.

17. On Champneys see D. B. McIlhiney, *A Gentleman in Every Slum: Church of England Missions in East London, 1837-1914* (Allison Park, PA: Pickwick, 1988), pp.74-6.

18. *Memoirs of Reed,* p.49.

19. R. J. Helmstadter, 'The Reverend Andrew Reed (1787–1862): Evangelical Pastor as Entrepreneur', in R. W. Davies and R. J. Helmstadter (eds.), *Religion and Irreligion in Victorian Society* (Essays in Honour of R. K. Webb), (London: Routledge, 1992), pp.12-13.

At the height of his ministry in the 1830s, Reed's salary reached £500 — just above the average for Congregational ministers at the time, but considerably less than that of some of his local colleagues. The average salary for Independent ministers was between £200 and £400 per annum at this period. George Ford, at Stepney Old Meeting, a local Independent chapel, was reckoned to receive £1,500 per year at the time of Reed's ministry. Reed received nothing by way of reimbursement for his work with the charities he was to establish, and he frequently refused even expenses when invited to preach in different churches around the country.

20. *Memoirs of Reed,* p.56.
21. *Ibid.,* pp.57-8.
22. *Ibid.,* p.55.

Chapter 4 — The cry of the children
1. *Memoirs of Reed,* pp.86-7.
2. *Ibid.,* p.88.
3. K. Heasman, *Evangelicals in Action: An Appraisal of their Social Work* (London: Geoffrey Bles, 1962), p.89.
4. *Memoirs of Reed,* pp.88-9.
5. *Ibid.,* pp 88-9; and 'Appeal', in *Annual Report of the London Orphan Asylum, 1815* (London), pp.5-7.
6. 'Pauper' was the term given to those who were dependent for their subsistence on poor relief given by the local parish. At a time when many saw poverty as attributable to personal failings, such as immorality, improvidence, or recklessness, to be labelled a 'pauper' was a significant social stigma.
7. 'Address' in *Annual Report LOA, 1815,* pp.6-8; and *Memoirs of Reed,* p.89.
8. *Annual Report LOA, 1815,* pp.7-8; 11-12.
9. *Memoirs of Reed,* p.90.
10. *Ibid.,* p.91.
11. *Ibid.,* p.92.
12. *Ibid.,* pp.92-3.
13. *Annual Report LOA, 1815,* pp.8-9.
14. A guinea was one pound and one shilling (i.e., twenty-one shillings) in value.
15. *Memoirs of Reed,* pp.92-3: N. Alvey, *Education by Election: Reed's School, Clapton and Watford* (St Albans: St Albans and Hertfordshire Architectural and Archaeological Society, 1990), pp.4-5.
16. G. Holden Pike, *The Life and Work of Charles Haddon Spurgeon* (London: Cassell and Co., 1894), vol. IV, pp.194, 354; vol. V, p.51.
17. London Orphan Asylum, Ladies' Committee Meeting Minutes, 18 October 1814; 14 December 1814, Surrey History Centre, Woking, 3719/3/33.
18. Ladies' Committee Minutes, 18 October 1814; 5 July 1814; 30 August 1815; 27 July 1815.
19. *Memoirs of Reed,* p.93.
20. *Ibid.,* pp.95, 99; also Materials and Artefacts from London Orphan Asylum in Surrey History Centre, Woking, 3719/8/10.
21. *Memoirs of Reed,* p.95.
22. *Ibid.,* p.95; Ladies' Committee Minutes, 4 November 1816.
23. *Memoirs of Reed,* p.97.
24. *Ibid.,* p.96.

Chapter 5 — Joy, trial and sorrow

1. *Memoirs of Reed,* p.53.
2. Reed, *Martha,* vol. 1, p.306.
3. *Ibid.,* vol. 2, p.38.
4. *Ibid.,* pp.124-211; *Memoirs of Reed,* pp.60-61.
5. Reed, *Martha,* vol. 2, p.326.
6. The subject is thoroughly explored in D. Rosman, *Evangelicals and Culture,* (Beckenham: Croom Helm, 1984), pp.174-93.
7. A. Reed, *A Letter to the Editor of the 'British Review', Occasioned by the Notice of 'No Fiction' and 'Martha' in the Last Number of that Work* (London, 1823), pp.60-73.
8. *Memoirs of Reed,* pp.28, 69.
9. *Ibid.,* pp.70-72.
10. A. Reed, *No Fiction: A Narrative Founded on Recent and Interesting Facts,* vol. 1 (2nd edition, London, 1820), Dedication and Preface, pp.viii-xi.
11. F. Barnett, *Memoirs of Francis Barnett, the Lefevre of 'No Fiction', and a Review of that Work with Letters and Authentic Documents* (London, 1823), vol. 1, pp.viii-xxii, 120-41, 145-217. See also F. Barnett, *A Threatening Letter from Douglas, (the Self-Acknowledged Author of 'No Fiction'), to Lefevre: With Lefevre's Reply* (London, 1822); *Reply to Mr Reed's Advertisement to the Seventh Edition of 'No Fiction', with a review of 'Martha',* and *A Reply to the Reverend Andrew Reed's Promised 'Full Justification', Consisting of Four Pages, as an Advertisement to the Seventh Edition of 'No Fiction'* (London, 1823).
12. Reed, *Letter to the 'British Review',* pp.6-7.
13. *Memoirs of Reed,* pp.83-4.
14. *Ibid.,* pp.78-80.
15. *Ibid.,* pp.76-7.
16. *Ibid.,* p.72.
17. Reed, *Martha* (see chapter 1, note 5 for full publication details).
18. *Lectures on Some of the Principal Evidences of Revelation: Delivered at the Monthly Meetings of the Associated Ministers and Churches of the London Congregational Union* (London, 1827).

Chapter 6 — A home for the helpless

1. *London Orphan Asylum, Annual Report, 1820* (London, 1820).
2. *Memoirs of Reed,* pp.97-8.
3. G. Müller, *Narrative of Some of the Lord's Dealings with George Müller, Written by Himself* (London: J. Nisbet, 1855), pp.159, 181; and M. Gorsky, *Patterns of Philanthropy: Charity and Society in Nineteenth-Century Bristol* (Woodbridge: Boydell, 1999), pp.108-9.
4. Holden Pike, *Spurgeon,* vol. IV, p.221; vol. V, p.41; vol. IV, p.219.
5. F. Booth-Tucker, *General William Booth* (New York, 1898), p.105.

6. *Memoirs of Reed,* p.98.

7. *Ibid.,* p.100.

8. *Ibid.,* pp.100-103.

9. *Ibid.,* pp.104-7.

10. Board Minutes, London Orphan Asylum, Surrey History Centre, Woking, SHC 3719/3/3, Board Meeting 15 May 1824, p.75.

11. *Memoirs of Reed,* p.107.

12. *Ibid.,* p.110.

13. *Ibid.,* p.110.

14. *Ibid.,* p.113.

15. *Annual Report of LOA, 1815,* p.6.

16. C. M. Cipolla, *Literacy and Development in the West* (Harmondsworth: Penguin, 1969), p.62; and R. K. Webb, *The British Working Class Reader 1790-1840* (London: Allen and Unwin, 1955), p.22.

17. *Annual Report of LOA, 1815,* p.11.

18. *Ibid.,* pp.12-22.

19. R. K. McClure, *Coram's Children: The London Foundling Hospital in the Eighteenth Century* (London: Yale University Press, 1981), pp.150-53.

20. R. H. Nichols and F. A. Wray, *History of the Foundling Hospital* (London: Oxford University Press, 1935), pp.196-9.

21. Müller, *Narrative of the Lord's Dealings with George Müller,* p.164.

22. *Annual Report, London Orphan Asylum, 1818* (London, 1818), pp.21-4.

23. *Memoirs of Reed,* p.112.

24. The average was 5.27 children per family, based on figures from 1833. Of the 384 orphaned children resident in 1833, the largest group of fathers of any single occupation was that of clerk, numbering twenty-three, followed by eighteen master mariners, and thirteen each of farmers and carpenters. In all, most fathers were from the artisan and 'respectable' working classes. *Annual Report, London Orphan Asylum, 1833* (London, 1833), Surrey History Centre, Woking, 3719/1/7.

25. R. Steer, *George Müller: Delighted in God* (London: Hodder and Stoughton, 1975), p.60.

26. *Memoirs of Reed,* p.112.

27. *Ibid.,* p.114.

Chapter 7 — Wycliffe Chapel

1. *Memoirs of Reed,* p.63. Historians of Nonconformity have suggested that for every chapel member, there were between three and seven non-members in attendance in the early nineteenth century (see M. Watts, *The Dissenters* (Oxford: Clarendon Press, 1995), vol. II, pp.680-81; and D. Lovegrove, *Established Church, Sectarian People: Itinerancy and the Transformation of English Dissent, 1780-1830* (Cambridge: Cambridge University Press, 1988), p.149.

2. *Memoirs of Reed,* pp.147-8.
3. *Ibid.,* p.152.
4. A. Reed, *The Revival of Religion: A Narrative of the State of Religion at Wycliffe Chapel During the Year 1839* (6th edition, London, 1840) p.4; Minutes of Deacons' Meetings and Church Meetings, 1849–1851, Wycliffe Chapel, Reverse, Deacons Meeting 1 June 1849, GLRO N/C/40/3 Reverse; Minutes of Deacons' Meetings and Church Meetings Commencing 27 November 1861, Wycliffe Chapel, Deacons' Meeting, 27 November 1861, GLRO N/C/40/3/ Front.
5. Deacons' Minutes, Wycliffe Chapel, 1849-50; Reed, *Revival of Religion,* pp.5-6.
6. *Memoirs of Reed,* pp.149-53.
7. *Ibid.,* pp.316-17.
8. *Ibid.,* p.153.
9. Reed, *The Revival of Religion,* pp.5-6.
10. *Memoirs of Reed,* pp.149-53.
11. *Ibid.,* pp.154-7.
12. *Ibid,* pp.155-7.
13. New Road and Wycliffe Chapel Members' Roll, 1822-67, London Metropolitan Archive, N/C/40/10.
14. *Memoirs of Reed,* p.158.

Chapter 8 — Suffer the little children

1. *Memoirs of Reed,* pp.115-16.
2. *Ibid.,* p.117.
3. *Ibid.,* pp.117-19.
4. *First Report of the Infant Orphan Asylum, for the Reception of Bereaved and Destitute Children Under Seven Years of Age* (London, 1827), pp.4-12.
5. *Memoirs of Reed,* p.119, quoting *The New Times,* 4 July 1827.
6. *First Report Infant Orphan Asylum,* General Regulations, pp.13-15.
7. Minutes of the Infant Orphan Asylum, Infant Orphan Asylum Archives, in Royal Wanstead Collection, Redbridge Library, Ilford, 13 September 1827; 4 October 1827.
8. Minutes of Infant Orphan Asylum, 25 October 1827.
9. *First Annual Report,* Rule V, p.14.
10. Minutes of Infant Orphan Asylum, 15 November 1827; 22 November 1827; 6 December 1827.
11. *Ibid.,* 22 November 1827.
12. *Ibid.,* 10 February 1827.
13. *Ibid.,* 27 March 1828.
14. *Memoirs of Reed,* p.121.
15. *Ibid.,* pp.121-2.
16. Minutes of Infant Orphan Asylum, 22 September 1832.

17. *Memoirs of Reed,* p.123.

18. *Ibid.,* pp.124-5.

19. Stewards' Committee Meetings, Infant Orphan Asylum, in Infant Orphan Asylum Archives, Royal Wanstead Collection, Redbridge Library, Ilford, Book 1, March 29 1831 to 30 March 1840; and Minutes of the General Meetings of the Infant Orphan Asylum, in Infant Orphan Asylum Archives, Royal Wanstead Collection, Redbridge Library, Ilford, p.4.

20. Minutes of Infant Orphan Asylum, 24 December 1835.

21. *Ibid.,* 10 April 1828.

22. *Ibid.,* 20 February 1833.

23. Ladies' Visitors Book (bound as House Committee Minutes 1), Infant Orphan Asylum Archives, Royal Wanstead Collection, Redbridge Library, Ilford, 1829-1843.

24. Annual Reports of the Infant Orphan Asylum, 1830, 1840.

25. Poll Books, Infant Orphan Asylum 1827-43, in Infant Orphan Asylum Archives, Royal Wanstead Collection, Redbridge Library, Ilford.

26. *Memoirs of Reed,* p.128.

27. *Annual Reports of the Infant Orphan Asylum* (London, 1827-40).

28. *Memoirs of Reed,* p.126.

Chapter 9 — Delegate to America

1. *Tenth Annual Report of Home Missionary Society* (London, 1829).

2. R. W. Dale, *History of English Congregationalism,* completed and edited by A. W. W. Dale (2nd edition, London: Hodder and Stoughton, 1907), pp.688-95

3. A. Reed, 'The Day of Pentecost. A Sermon Preached at Leeds Before the West Riding Auxiliary Missionary Society, 6 June 1839; and Published by Request,' in *Charges and Sermons,* pp.448-9.

4. A. Reed, 'Eminent Piety Essential to Eminent Usefulness: A Discourse Preached at the Anniversary of the London Missionary Society, May 11, 1831, at Surrey Chapel' (London, 1831), p.15.

5. *Memoirs of Reed,* pp.225-31.

6. *Ibid.,* pp.162-4.

7. A. Reed and J. Matheson, *Narrative of the Visit to the American Churches* (London: Jackson and Walford, 1835), vol. II, p.299.

8. *Ibid.,* vol. II, pp.3-4.

9. *Ibid.,* vol. I, p.93.

10. *Ibid.,* vol. I, pp.118-28.

11. *Ibid.,* vol. I, pp.156, 148.

12. *Ibid.,* vol. I, pp.182-6.

13. *Ibid.,* vol. I, pp.201-4.

14. *Ibid.,* vol. I, pp.182-4.

15. *Ibid.,* vol. I, p.262.

16. *Ibid.*, vol. II, pp.242-8.
17. *Ibid.*, vol. I, p.309.
18. *Ibid.*, vol. II, p.256.
19. *Ibid.*, vol. II, pp.268-9.
20. *Ibid.*, vol. II, pp.269-71.
21. *Ibid.*, vol. II, p.163.
22. *Ibid.*, vol. I, pp.296-7 (see also chapter 12 below).
23. W. B. Sprague, *Lectures on Revival* (Albany, New York, 1832, pp.12-14, 129-48, 258-86).
24. Reed and Matheson, *Narrative of American Visit,* vol. I, p.373.
25. *Ibid.*, vol. II, pp.376-83.
26. *Ibid.*, vol. I, pp.391-401, 351, 427, 467.
27. *Ibid.*, vol. I, pp.436-7.
28. *Ibid.*, vol. I, p.481.
29. *Ibid.*, vol. I, pp.497-8.
30. *Memoirs of Reed,* pp.182-5.

Chapter 10 — A house by the forest

1. Minutes of Infant Orphan Asylum, 27 March 1834.
2. *Ibid.*, 25 September 1834; 23 April 1835; 22 October 1835.
3. *Memoirs of Andrew Reed,* p.126.
4. *Ibid.*, p.127.
5. Building Committee Minutes, Infant Orphan Asylum, Book 1, Infant Orphan Asylum Archives, Royal Wanstead Collection, Redbridge Library, Ilford, Meetings 14 May 1840; 25 June 1840.
6. *Memoirs of Andrew Reed,* pp.128-31.
7. *Ibid.*, p.133.
8. I am grateful to Mrs Marianne Thorne, Honorary Archivist to the Royal Wanstead Children's Foundation, for drawing my attention to the connection between James Edmeston, Gilbert Scott and William Moffatt.
9. *The Builder,* 1844, pp.459-60.
10. Building Committee Minutes, Meetings 3 August 1841 to 7 February 1843.
11. *Memoirs of Andrew Reed,* pp.134-5.

Chapter 11 — Politics

1. 'Ordination Service of Reverend Andrew Reed', p.36 (italics original).
2. A. Reed, ' "The Trophies of Death!" A Sermon Occasioned by the Death of Her Royal Highness the Princess Charlotte Augusta, etc, Delivered at the New Road Meeting House, St-George's-in-the-East, 16 November 1817' (London, 1817), pp.6, 30-31.
3. A. Reed, ' "Lamentations for the Dead!" A Sermon Occasioned by the Death of His Royal Highness Edward, Duke of Kent; and of His Most Gracious

Majesty George the Third: Delivered at Cannon Street Road Chapel, St George's-in-the-East, February 16, 1820' (London, 1820), pp.12-16, 23, 29.

4. A. Reed, ' "A Voice from the Tomb." A Sermon Occasioned by the Death of the Rev. Matthew Wilks, Delivered at the Tabernacle, on Sunday, 8 February 1829' (London, 1829), p.34; *Memoirs of Andrew Reed,* pp.192-3.

5. A. Miall, *The Life of Edward Miall* (London: Macmillan, 1884), p.42.

6. *Memoirs of Andrew Reed,* pp.193-5; A. Reed, ' "The Case of the Dissenters", in a Letter Addressed to the Lord Chancellor, 5th edition (with a Postscript Addressed to the Editor of *The Times*)', (London, 1834), pp.7-23 (italics and capitals original), 33-44, 47-61.

7. 'Postscript to the Editor of *The Times*', in' Case of the Dissenters', p 65.

8. E.g., 'An Answer to a Letter Addressed to the Lord Chancellor on the Case of the Dissenters in a Letter to the Same. By a Clergyman' (London, 1834); 'The Case of the Church of England', reprinted from *Fraser's Magazine* for February 1834; 'The Designs of the Dissenters. A Letter to the King, By a Protestant Dissenter' (London, 1834); Rev. W. Sewell (Fellow and Tutor of Exeter College, Oxford), 'Thoughts on the Admission of Dissenters to the University of Oxford; and on the Establishment of a State Religion; in a Letter to a Dissenter' (Oxford and London, 1834); T. Turton, D.D. (Regius Professor of Divinity, University of Cambridge), 'Thoughts on the Admission of Persons without Regard to their Religious Opinions to Certain Degrees in the Universities of England' (Cambridge and London, 1834).

9. Reed, Ordination Service, p.25.

10. Quoted in E. Kaye, *The History of the King's Weigh House Church* (London: Allen and Unwin, 1968), pp.66-7.

11. *Memoirs of Andrew Reed,* pp.196-8.

12. *Ibid.,* pp.215-21.

13. *Ibid.,* pp.342-3; Reed and Matheson, *Narrative of American Visit,* vol. II, p.267. The bill to emancipate the slaves passed through the House of Commons in 1833, and finally became law in 1834.

14. Reed and Matheson, *Narrative of American Visit,* vol. II, pp.268-9, 243-5, 255.

Chapter 12 — Educational matters

1. Minute Book of Wycliffe Chapel Sabbath School, October 1882 onwards, Jubilee Services, 21 October 1883; and Public Meeting, 24 October 1883.

2. Reed and Matheson, *Narrative of American Visit,* vol. 1, p.389.

3. Wycliffe Chapel Girls' Sunday School, Minutes of Meetings of Teachers 1849-1868, Metropolitan Archive, N/C/40/16, Quarterly Meeting, 28 October 1862.

4. Sabbath School Minute Book, 21 October 1883; 24 October 1883; Reed, *Revival of Religion,* p.47.

5. *Memoirs of Andrew Reed,* p.308; Minute Book of Wycliffe Chapel Sabbath School, 1882 onwards, 21 October 1883; 24 October 1883.

6. Committee Minutes, Boys' School, 1843-67, Annual Public Meetings, 26 October 1859; 29 October 1861.

7. Wycliffe Chapel Girls' Sunday School, Minutes of Meetings of Teachers, Quarterly Meetings and Sub-Committee Meetings, 1849-68, Quarterly Meetings, 8 September 1850; 28 February 1861, GLRO, N/C/40/16.

8. Minute Book of Girls' Sunday School, Quarterly Meetings, 18 September 1850; 6 October 1853; 28 February 1861.

9. Minute Book of Girls' Sunday School, Quarterly Meeting, 15 June 1858; 18 September 1850.

10. Minute Book of Girls' Sunday School, Quarterly Meetings, 18 December 1854; 12 June 1856; 11 June 1857.

11. Reed, *Revival of Religion,* p.47.

12. Letter from Stephen Curtis to Hackney Grammar School, 5 May 1830, in Guildhall Library, London, Pamphlet 1839, pp.1-9. Curtis wrote complaining that the teaching of Christianity played too much of a role in the operation of the school, which is ironic in the light of the opposition to the project of the local Anglican vicar, H. H. Norris.

13. *Memoirs of Andrew Reed,* pp.332-8. H. H. Norris was a leading High Churchman — see P. Nockles, 'Church Parties in the pre-Tractarian Church of England, 1750-1833: the "Orthodox" — Some Problems of Definition and Identity', in *The Church of England c. 1689 – c. 1833: From Toleration to Tractarianism,* ed. J. Walsh, C. Haydon and S. Taylor (Cambridge: Cambridge University Press, 1993), p.340.

14. *Wycliffe Year Book, 1863,* pp.15-16.

15. *Memoirs of Andrew Reed,* pp.203-4.

16. E. Baines, '"A New Danger to Religious Liberty, Lord John Russell's Resolutions." A Letter to the Rev. Andrew Reed, D.D., Chairman of the London Central Committee for Opposing the Factories' Educational Bill by Edward Baines Junior (from the *Leeds Mercury)*', (London, 1843), pp.4-9. The campaign against Graham's bill is fully discussed in J. T. Ward and J. H. Treble, 'Religion and Education in 1843: Reaction to the "Factory Education Bill",' *Journal of Ecclesiastical History,* 20/1 (April 1969), pp.79-110.

17. These included the Protestant Society for the Protection of Religious Liberty, the Committee of Deputies, the Protestant Dissenting Ministers of the Three Denominations, the Wesleyan Committee of Privileges, the Society of Friends, The British and Foreign Schools Society, the Sunday School Union, the Religious Freedom Society, the Congregational Union, the Baptist Union, the Methodist New Connexion and the Wesleyan Association (E. Baines, *Letter to Andrew Reed,* p.3).

18. *Memoirs of Andrew Reed,* pp.204-7.

19. Committee Meetings of Wycliffe Chapel Boys' Sabbath School, 1843-67, Committee Meeting, 22 March 1843; Minutes of Teachers' Meetings, Boys' Sabbath School 1843-49, Teachers' Meeting, 11 April 1843; *Memoirs of Andrew Reed,* pp.203-7.
20. Baines, *Letter to Andrew Reed,* pp.4-9.
21. *Memoirs of Andrew Reed,* pp.208-12.
22. *Ibid.,* pp.213-17.
23. Reed and Matheson, *Narrative of American Visit,* vol. II, pp.219-39.

Chapter 13 — Parting from friends
1. Infant Orphan Asylum Minute Book, 28 February 1839.
2. *Memoirs of Andrew Reed,* pp.135-7.
3. Baptismal regeneration is the teaching that children are spiritually regenerated (born anew to spiritual life) and adopted into the church as children of God through the sacrament of baptism. Evangelicals who practised infant baptism saw it as an important sign, but spiritual regeneration only took place when an individual responded to the Christian message with a personal act of repentance and faith. It was only then that they were adopted as children of God and promises made on their behalf at their baptism became true for them personally.
4. *Memoirs of Andrew Reed,* pp.138-42; Minutes of Infant Orphan Asylum, 23 February 1843; 2 March 1843; 9 March 1843; 23 March 1843; 30 March 1843.
5. Minutes of the General Meetings of the Infant Orphan Asylum, Annual Meeting, 14 April 1843, p.95.
6. *Memoirs of Andrew Reed,* pp.138-9.
7. *Ibid.,* pp.140-41.
8. *Ibid.,* pp.238-9.
9. *Ibid.,* pp.237-9.
10. *Ibid.,* p.240.
11. *Ibid.*
12. A. Reed, *A Brief and Final Appeal to the Constituents of the London Missionary Society;* London, 1847, p.42.

Chapter 14 — Pastoral labours
1. *Memoirs of Andrew Reed,* p.285.
2. *Ibid.,* pp.287-8.
3. *Ibid.,* p.289.
4. *Ibid.,* pp.290-91.
5. *Ibid.,* p.297.
6. *Ibid.,* p.298.
7. *Ibid.,* p.320.
8. Reed, *The Hope and Duty of the Church,* pp.21-2.

9. A. Reed, 'Ministerial Perseverance, A Charge Delivered at the Settlement of Rev. Arthur Tidman, over the Church Assembling in Barbican, London, on the 8th of January, 1829' (London, 1829), pp 10-11, 16.

10. *Ibid.,* pp.21, 24, 27-8.

11. *Memoirs of Andrew Reed,* pp.158-9.

12. A. Reed, 'The Pastor's Acknowledgements. A Sermon Occasioned by the Occurrence of the Ninth Anniversary: On Sunday November 26, 1820' (London, 1820).

13. *Memoirs of Andrew Reed,* pp.292-4, 315-16.

14. Reed, 'Eminent Piety', pp.40-43.

15. A. Reed, *Personal Effort for the Salvation of Men: A Manual for Christians,* pp.3-53.

16. Reed issues strong warnings against such behaviour in an ordination sermon he delivered in 1833, 'Discourses Delivered at the Ordination of the Rev. Thomas Hughes to the Pastoral Office over the Congregational Church at Marlborough Chapel, Kent Road, November 27, 1833' (London, 1834).

17. New Road and Wycliffe Chapel Members' Roll, 1822-1867, in Metropolitan Archive, London, N/C/40/10.

18. *Memoirs of Andrew Reed,* pp.64, 144-8, 370.

19. *Ibid.,* pp.371-5.

20. *Ibid.,* p.290.

21. Reed, *The Revival of Religion,* pp.47, 43. In 1863, the year after Reed's death, the church was still continuing evangelism in the area round the church through supporting three city missionaries, one of whom was attached to the London City Mission.

22. C. D. Field, 'Adam and Eve: Gender in the English Free Church Constituency', *Journal of Ecclesiastical History,* 44, 1993, p.78.

23. *The Wycliffe Year Book, 1863* (London, 1863), pp.9-15.

24. Wycliffe Chapel Balance Sheets, 1848-1907, London Metropolitan Archive, N/C/40/13.

25. The evidence comes from the early years of Reed's ministry. Baptismal Register, New Road Meeting, 1811-17, Metropolitan Archive, N/C/23/1.

26. *Memoirs of Andrew Reed,* pp.339-41; *Wycliffe Year Book 1863,* p.11.

27. Wycliffe Chapel Members Roll, 1822-36, in London Metropolitan Archive, N/C/40/10.

28. *Memoirs of Andrew Reed,* p.381.

Chapter 15 — Revival

1. Reed and Matheson, *Narrative of American Visit,* vol. II, pp.2-3.

2. *Ibid.,* vol. I, p.250.

3. *Ibid.,* vol. II, p.12.

4. *Ibid.,* pp.12-13.

5. *Ibid.,* pp.3, 30.

6. Finney's views were published as *Revivals of Religion, Lectures by Charles Grandison Finney*, in 1835, but were the fruit of ten years of practical work. On this see also R. Carwardine, *Transatlantic Revivalism: Popular Evangelicalism in Britain and America, 1790-1865* (Westport, Connecticut: Greenwood Press, 1978), p.6.

7. Reed and Matheson, *Narrative of American Visit*, vol. II, pp.35-55.

8. *Ibid.*, vol. II, pp.59-60.

9. *Ibid.*, vol. I, pp.272-97.

10. *Memoirs of Andrew Reed*, pp.295-6.

11. *Ibid.*, pp.301-3.

12. Reed, *Revival of Religion*, pp.6-7.

13. *Ibid.*, pp.8-9.

14. *Ibid.*, pp.10-11.

15. *Ibid.*, p.16.

16. *Ibid.*, pp.12, 16.

17. *Ibid.*, p.15.

18. *Ibid.*, pp.17-18.

19. *Ibid.*, pp.29-43; Members' Roll, 1822-67, New Road and Wycliffe Chapel, N/C/40/10.

When revival came to Jonathan Edwards' church in Northampton, Massachusetts in 1735, around 300 members were added to the church, of 'all sorts, sober and vicious, high and low, rich and poor, wise and unwise' (G. M. Marsden, *Jonathan Edwards: A Life,* New Haven: Yale University Press, 2003, p.160).

20. Wycliffe Chapel Members' Roll, 1822-67.

21. Reed, *Revival of Religion*, pp.29-98.

22. *Ibid.*, pp.26-8.

23. The nature and changing meaning of revival at this time of flux is discussed in Iain Murray's *Revival and Revivalism: The Making and Marring of American Evangelicalism, 1750-1858* (Edinburgh: Banner of Truth, 1994), pp.12-17.

24. *Memoirs of Andrew Reed*, pp.321-2, 330.

25. *Ibid.*, pp.307-8, 321.

Chapter 16 — Preacher of the Word

1. A. Reed, 'The Pastor's Acknowledgements, A Sermon Occasioned by the Occurrence of the Ninth Anniversary, on Sunday November 25, 1820' (London, 1820).

2. A. Reed, 'The Sacred Trust, A Charge Delivered at the Ordination of the Rev. T. Atkinson over the Church Assembling at Hounslow, Middlesex, on the Second of October, 1832' (London, 1832), pp.10,14.

3. A. Reed, 'Ministerial Perseverance, A Charge Delivered at the Settlement of Rev. Arthur Tidman, over the Church Assembling in Barbican, London, on the 8th of January, 1829' (London, 1829), pp.27-8; A. Reed, ' "The Man of God":

A Charge Delivered at the Ordination of Rev. Ebenezer Miller, M.A., over the Church Assembling at Old Gravel Lane, on the Twenty-Second of February, 1828' (London, 1829), p.43.
4. *Memoirs of Andrew Reed,* pp.44-6.
5. A Reed, 'The Man of God', p.27.
6. A. Reed, 'The Sacred Trust: A Charge Delivered at the Ordination of the Rev. T. Atkinson, over the Church Assembling at Hounslow, Middlesex, on the 2nd of October, 1832' (London, 1832), pp.11-12.
7. *Memoirs of Andrew Reed,* pp.48-9.
8. *Ibid.,* pp.306-7.
9. *Ibid.,* p.480.
10. A. Reed, 'An Efficient Ministry — A Charge Delivered at the Ordination of Rev. Joseph Elliott, and over the Congregational Church, Bury St Edmonds, London, 1837', in *Charges and Sermons During a Ministry of Fifty Years* (London, 1861), p.153.
11. Reed, 'Ministerial Perseverance', p.8.
12. *Memoirs of Andrew Reed,* p.297.
13. *Ibid.,* p.319.
14. *Ibid.,* p.327.
15. 'The Pastor's Acknowledgements' in Reed, *Charges and Sermons,* pp.614-15.
16. Unnamed article in *The Sacred Star,* January-June 1838, pp.145-8.
17. Pocket Book 1846-51 of Richard Jolly (1784–1872), the manuscript in possession of Richard Link, Kensington, who kindly made it available for the purposes of this study.
18. *Memoirs of Andrew Reed,* pp.470-71.
19. Reed, 'Eminent Piety', pp.37-8.
20. Jolly, Pocket Book.
21. Wycliffe Chapel Members' Roll, 1822-67; *Memoirs of Andrew Reed,* pp.547, 308.
22. *Memoirs of Andrew Reed,* pp.64, 290-91; *Revival of Religion,* p.47.
23. Reed. 'The Sacred Trust', p.5.
24. Reed, *The Advancement of Religion the Claim of the Times* (London, 1843).
25. Reed, 'Ministerial Perseverance', pp.47-8.
26. *Memoirs of Andrew Reed,* pp.14-15; *Memoirs of Francis Barnett,* vol. I, p.7.
27. Reed and Matheson, *Narrative of American Visit,* vol. II, pp.72-4.
28. Reed, 'The Sacred Trust', p.19.
29. Reed, 'The Man of God', pp.20-22.
30. A. Reed, 'The Ordination Service of the Rev. Andrew Reed' (London, 1812), p.34.
31. Reed, 'The Sacred Trust', p.7.

32. Reed, *The Revival of Religion*, pp.21-2.

33. A. Reed, 'The Extension of the Messiah's Kingdom. A Sermon Preached at the Opening of the Independent Chapel, St Mary's Street, Portsmouth, on Tuesday Morning, August 30th, 1842' (Portsea, 1842), pp.8-9.

Chapter 17 — Starting again

1. Holden Pike, *Life and Labours of C. H. Spurgeon*, vol. IV, pp.354-5.

2. *The Asylum for Fatherless Children, Reedham, Near Croydon, Late at Stamford Hill, Designed to Receive and Educate the Orphan, Through the Whole Period of Infancy and Childhood, Annual Report* (London, 1868), p.ix.

3. *Memoirs of Andrew Reed*, p.234.

4. Minutes of Asylum for Fatherless Children 1844-1883, held at the Reedham Trust Offices, The Lodge, 23 Old Lodge Lane, Purley. These were badly damaged by a fire and are incomplete; *Memoirs of Andrew Reed*, pp.235-6.

5. *Memoirs of Andrew Reed*, p.237.

6. *Ibid.,* pp.241-2.

7. Asylum for Fatherless Children, Minutes (date has been destroyed, but in sequence lies between 1845 and 1849); 20 December 1849.

8. *Asylum for Fatherless Children, Annual Report 1868*, pp.vii-xx.

9. *Ibid.,* pp.xii-xv.

10. *Memoirs of Andrew Reed*, pp.245-6; H. E. Rolph, *The Home on the Hill: The Story of Reedham* (Coulsdon: Reedham Old Scholars' Association, 1981), pp.16, 19.

11. *Memoirs of Andrew Reed*, pp.245-6.

12. Minutes of Asylum for Fatherless Children, 11 November 1852.

13. Coulsden was Andrew Reed's spelling of the name of the estate. Local maps and other contemporary sources prefer the spelling Coulsdon.

14. Extracts from Queen Victoria's Patronage Book, at Reedham Trust office, Old Lodge Lane, Reedham, Purley.

15. *Asylum for Fatherless Children, Annual Report 1868*, pp.xlv-xlvi.

16. *Memoirs of Andrew Reed*, p.248.

17. Asylum for Fatherless Children, Minutes, 29 February 1856.

18. *Ibid.,* 23 June 1858.

19. *Croydon Chronicle,* 17 July 1858; Asylum for Fatherless Children Minutes, 29 July 1858.

20. Asylum for Fatherless Children Minutes, 5 February 1859; 8 February 1859; *Memoirs of Andrew Reed*, p.251; *Asylum for Fatherless Children, Annual Report 1868*, p.xix.

21. Minutes of Infant Orphan Asylum, 4 December 1851.

22. *Ibid.,* 5 February 1852.

23. *Asylum for Fatherless Children Annual Report 1868*, p.xxviii.

24. *Ibid.,* pp.xi, xxviii- xxxv.

25. Asylum for Fatherless Children Minutes, 20 October 1854; 17 November 1854; 15 January 1857.
26. Report of Robert Saunders, of British and Foreign Bible Society to Board of Asylum for Fatherless Children, in *Asylum for Fatherless Children Annual Report 1868*, pp.xxi-xxii.
27. Masters' Report of Boys' School, Midsummer 1868, in *Asylum for Fatherless Children Annual Report 1868*, pp.xxiii-iv.
28. *Asylum for Fatherless Children Annual Report 1868*, p.xxvi.
29. *Ibid.*, p.xxi.
30. *Ibid.*, pp.xxvi-ii.
31. *Ibid.*, p.xix.
32. *Memoirs of Andrew Reed*, pp.252-3.
33. *Ibid.*, p.252.

Chapter 18 — The missionary call
1. A. Reed, 'The Hope and Duty of the Church. A Sermon Delivered in Grosvenor Street Chapel, Manchester, at the Annual Meeting of the East Lancashire Auxiliary Missionary Society, June 18th, 1833' (London, 1833), pp.19-20.
2. *Memoirs of Andrew Reed*, pp.257-8.
3. A. C. Ross, *David Livingstone: Mission and Empire* (London: Hambledon and London, 2002), pp.17, 25, 33-35; A. C. Ross, *John Philip (1775-1851): Missions, Race and Politics in South Africa* (Aberdeen: Aberdeen University Press, 1986), pp.105-11; B. Stanley, *The Bible and the Flag* (Leicester: Apollos, 1990), pp.93-8.
4. *Memoirs of Andrew Reed*, pp.260-61.
5. *Ibid.*, pp.370-71.
6. *Ibid.*, pp.262-6.
7. Reed, 'Eminent Piety' (see chapter 9, note 4 for full publication details).
8. *Memoirs of Andrew Reed*, pp.266-9.
9. *Ibid.*, pp.271-2.
10. Reed, 'The Hope and Duty of the Church', p.50.
11. *Memoirs of Andrew Reed*, pp.259-60.
12. *Ibid.*, pp.269-70.
13. *Ibid.*, pp.275.
14. *Ibid.*, p.276.
15. *Ibid.*, pp.277-9.
16. *Tenth Annual Report of the Home Missionary Society* (London, 1829).
17. *Memoirs of Andrew Reed*, p.326.
18. A. Reed, Preface to C. Gutzlaff, *China Opened* (London, 1838), pp.iii-iv.
19. *LMS Annual Report for 1842-43*, pp.xciv-xcv, quoted in Stanley, *Bible and Flag*, p.106.
20. *Memoirs of Andrew Reed*, pp.273-82.

21. The following account is based on the pamphlets relating to the contro-
versy, which are to be found in the British Library, including A. Reed, *The
Case of Tahiti: An Appeal to the Constituents of the London Missionary
Society, In Reply to the 'Statement of the Directors'* (London, 1847); *A Brief
and Final Appeal to the Constituents of the London Missionary Society*
(London, 1847); *The Case of the London Missionary Society Containing the
Appeals to the Constituency on the State of the Society, Together with Two
Letters on the Case of Tahiti, Revised from the 'Patriot' Newspaper* (London,
1847). The LMS replies included: *A Short Answer to the Enquiry of the Rev.
Dr Reed 'Where lies the Truth?'* By the Directors of the London Missionary
Society (London, 1847); *A Reply to the Animadversions of the Rev. Dr Reed
in his Appeal to the Constituents of the London Missionary Society, by the
Directors of the Society* (London, 1847); *Strictures on the Brief and Final
Appeal of Rev. Dr Reed, to the Constituents of the London Missionary Society*
(London, 1847). Others joined the debate, including 'Luther and Melanch-
thon', *The Marrow of the Controversy: The Facts and Figures Between the
Rev. Dr Reed and the Directors of the London Missionary Society* (London,
1847); 'Simon Fairplay', *A Peep at the Controversy Between Rev. Dr Andrew
Reed and the Directors of the London Missionary Society* (London, 1847).
See also C. S. Horne, *The Story of the London Missionary Society* (London,
1908), pp.23-55, 201-3, and *Memoirs of Andrew Reed*, pp.372-6. The
relevant pages in the minutes of the London Missionary Society have been
removed, probably at a later date by the committee wishing to draw a line
under the unseemly controversy.

22. 'Luther and Melanchthon', *The Marrow of the Controversy'*, pp.9-10.

23. *Strictures on the Brief and Final Appeal of Dr Reed*, pp.9, 11, 30.

24. *Memoirs of Andrew Reed*, pp.373-4.

25. *Ibid.,* p.375.

26. Stanley, *Bible and Flag*, p.98.

27. *Memoirs of Andrew Reed*, p.378.

28. *Ibid.,* p.376.

Chapter 19 — Caring for the most needy

1. *Memoirs of Andrew Reed*, p.384.

2. K. Day and J. Jancar, 'Mental Handicap and the Royal Medico-
Psychological Association: A Historical Association, 1841-1991', in G. E.
Berrios and H. Freeman, *150 Years of British Psychiatry, 1841-1991* (London:
Gaskell, 1991), pp.268-70; *Memoirs of Andrew Reed*, pp.386-7.

3. D. Wright, *Mental Disability in Victorian England: The Earlswood Asylum,
1847-1901* (Oxford: Clarendon Press, 2001), pp.20-32. On the Plumbe family
see chapter 20. Anne Plumbe was almost certainly the widow of Samuel
Plumbe, who had so ably assisted Reed as a deacon for several years.

4. *Memoirs of Andrew Reed*, pp.383-9.

5. *Ibid.,* p.390.

6. W. A. F. Browne, *What Asylums Were, Are, and Ought to be: Being the Substance of Five Lectures Delivered Before the Managers of the Montrose Royal Lunatic Asylum* (Edinburgh, 1837). 'Insanity' (or lunacy) was perceived to be a quite different condition, described at the time as the 'irregular or impaired action of the mind, instincts, sentiments or perceptive powers'. The work of the White sisters in Bath was with 'imbecile' children. 'Cretin' was the term used to describe a person suffering from disability created by a defective thyroid gland. The work of Guggenbühl at Abendberg focused on such cases, who were at the time ranked among the mentally handicapped; sadly, many of his exaggerated claims were later discredited.

7. Andrew Reed's leading role is acknowledged in histories of the care of those with mental handicap — e.g., Berrios and Freeman (eds.), *One Hundred and Fifty Years of British Psychiatry.*

8. *Memoirs of Andrew Reed,* p.391; Annual Reports of Asylum for Idiots, 1849 Report, in Royal Earlswood Hospital Archives, Surrey History Centre, Woking, 392/1/ 4/1.

9. Minutes of Board Meetings of Asylum for Idiots, Book I, 1847-1852, in Royal Earlswood Hospital Archives, Surrey History Centre, Woking, 392/2/1/1, Report of Public Meeting, 27 October 1847.

10. 1849 Asylum for Idiots' Annual Report, Constitution, pp.11-15. £50 was the full annual charge for payment cases; others paid a subsidized rate of £15-45 (Wright, *Mental Disability,* p.123).

11. Asylum Board Minutes, Book I, 1847-1852, Board Meetings 1847-48.

12. *Memoirs of Andrew Reed,* pp.392-3.

13. Asylum Board Minutes, 22 March 1849; 26 February 1850; 6 March 1850.

14. *Ibid.,* 16 June 1848.

15. *Ibid.,* 3 November 1848; 9 June 1848.

16. *Ibid.,* 22 November 1848.

17. *Ibid.,* 29 December 1848; M. A. Crowther, *The Workhouse System 1834-1929* (London: Batsford, 1981), pp.214-18.

18. Asylum Board Minutes, 29 September 1848.

19. *Memoirs of Andrew Reed,* p.394.

20. *Ibid.,* pp.396-7.

21. *Ibid.,* pp.397-8.

22. *Ibid.,* p.400.

23. Asylum Visitors' Books, in Royal Earlswood Hospital Archives, Surrey History Centre, Woking, 392/10/1/1, Visits of Commissioners in Lunacy, 6 June 1850; 30 June 1851.

24. Asylum Board Minutes, 26 February 1849; 26 September 1849.

25. Asylum Board Minutes, 17 April 1850; 24 April 1850. The role of doctors in medical charities and the workhouse system is discussed Crowther, *The Workhouse System 1834-1929*, pp.157-60.

26. J. Conolly, *Inquiry Concerning Insanity* (London, 1830), pp.4-5, 17.

27. A. Scull, *The Most Solitary of Afflictions: Madness and Society in Britain 1700-1900* (New Haven: Yale University Press, 1993), pp.290, 377. Much of the inspiration for Conolly's approach came from the pioneering work of the Quaker William Tuke at his asylum in York for 'Friends Deprived of their Reason'.

28. Day and Jancar, 'Mental Handicap', p.287.

29. Scull, *Madness and Society*, pp.89-101, 140-46, 226-8, 251-2, 268-9.

30. P. McCandless, 'Liberty and Lunacy: The Victorians and Wrongful Confinement', in A. Scull (ed.), *Madhouses, Mad-Doctors, and Madmen: The Social History of Psychiatry in the Victorian Era* (London: Athlone, 1981), pp.343-5.

31. Asylum Board Minutes, 1 August 1849; 21 November 1849; 12 December 1849. In 1855, Peto turned the loan into a gift.

32. *Memoirs of Andrew Reed*, p.399.

33. Asylum Board Minutes, 21 March 1850.

34. *Memoirs of Andrew Reed*, pp.408-9.

35. Asylum Board Minutes, 18 December 1850.

36. *Ibid.*, 26 March 1851.

37. *Memoirs of Andrew Reed*, p.410.

38. See chapter 21.

39. *Memoirs of Andrew Reed*, pp.416-19.

40. *Ibid.*, pp.417-18.

41. Correspondence with William Moffatt, and Contracts, for the Building of the Earlswood Asylum, Royal Earlswood Hospital Archives, Surrey History Centre, Woking, 392/16/1.

42. Lunacy Commissioners Reports, 1858, 1859, 1860, in Visitors' Books, Royal Earlswood Hospital, Surrey History Centre, 392 / 10/ 1/ 1; and Medical Officers' Reports, Surrey History Centre, 392/10/3/1, 25 September 1861.

43. *Memoirs of Andrew Reed*, p.423.

44. House Committee Minutes, Eastern Counties Branch Asylum. Surrey History Centre, Woking, 392/3/5, Meetings 20 November 1855.

45. By 1866 this hope was being fulfilled, with asylums at Exeter, Lancaster and near Birmingham being established after the pattern set by Andrew Reed at Earlswood.

46. Down's categorization system placed types of mental disabilities into groups, which he labelled according to what he believed were racial character-istics, the largest being 'Mongolian', or 'Mongol'. This system, and the terminology, is no longer acceptable today. The term 'Down's syndrome' (or

with some authorities 'Down Syndrome') is now normally preferred (D. Wright, *Mental Disability*, Clarendon, pp.155-76).

47. Day and Jancar, 'Mental Handicap', p.270.

48. *Memoirs of Andrew Reed*, p.423.

49. Girls' School Case Books, Royal Earlswood Hospital, Royal Earlswood Archives, Surrey History Centre, 392/11/5/1.

50. Letters of thanks to the Board of the Asylum for Idiots, 1849-87, Royal Earlswood Archives, Surrey History Centre, Woking, 392/2/8/2, letters dated 1849 to 1862.

51. *Memoirs of Andrew Reed*, pp.423-4.

Chapter 20 — Family and friends

1. E. Reed, *Swiss Tracts by Rev. Caesar Malan* (London, 1822). Helmstadter, 'The Reverend Andrew Reed (1787-1862): Evangelical Pastor as Entrepreneur', p.18.

2. Reed and Matheson, *Narrative of American Visit*, vol. II, p.114.

3. *Memoirs of Andrew Reed*, p.511.

4. A. Reed (ed.), *The Hymn* Book (London, 1841), with further editions, *The Hymn Book, 1860* (London, 1860); The *Wycliffe Chapel Supplement, Original Hymns by Rev. Andrew Reed D.D. and Mrs Reed* (London, 1872).

5. C. E. B. Reed, *Memoir of Sir Charles Reed* (London, 1883), p.9.

6. *Memoirs of Andrew Reed*, pp.159-60.

7. Wycliffe Chapel Balance Sheets, 1848-1907, London Metropolitan Archive, N/C/40/13; *Memoirs of Andrew Reed*, pp.538-9.

8. *Memoirs of Andrew Reed*, p.317.

9. *Ibid.*, p.329.

10. *Memoir of Sir Charles Reed*, p.70.

11. *Memoirs of Andrew Reed*, p.160.

12. *Congregational Yearbook, 1900*, pp.211-12.

13. *Memoir of Sir Charles Reed; Dictionary of National Biography*, vol. xvi (London, 1909), p.831.

14. Minutes of Quarterly Meetings of Teachers, 1849-62, Girls' Sunday School, London Metropolitan Archive, Meetings 18 September 1850; 13 December 1855; 28 February 1861; *Wycliffe Year Book, 1863*, p.11.

15. Both items are in the possession of Mr Richard Link, a relative of the Jolly family.

16. *Memoirs of Andrew Reed*, p.510.

17. *Ibid.*, p.316.

18. A. Reed, *Rolls Plumbe: An Authentic Memoir of a Child, in a Series of Letters to a Child* (London, 1832), pp.36,49. A copy of the tract, in the edition published by the American Tract Society, is in the archives of the Reedham Trust, Purley, Surrey.

19. *Memoirs of Andrew Reed*, pp.313-16.

Chapter 21 — A home for the incurable

1. G. Rivett, *The Development of the London Hospital System 1823-1982* (London: King Edward's Hospital Fund for London, 1986), pp.24-9.

2, *The Lancet*, 1865, I, p.410, quoted in Rivett, *London Hospital System,* p.68. Florence Nightingale was a leading campaigner to improve standards in the workhouses. Her demands included separation of medical from pauper cases, and training for medical staff. By the 1880s standards were significantly improved.

3. Crowther, *The Workhouse System 1834-1929,* pp.239, 224-6.

4. *Ibid.,* pp.160-66.

5. *Memoirs of Andrew Reed,* p.427.

6. *Ibid.,* p.429. Similar figures are found in J. Woodward, *To do the Sick No Harm: A Study of the British Voluntary Hospital System to 1875* (London: Routledge and Kegan Paul, 1974), especially pp.159-65. In 1855, the Glasgow Royal Infirmary admitted 3,416 patients, of whom 283 were discharged as not cured (p.159).

7. C. Dickens, *Household Words* (1850), cited in *Memoirs of Andrew Reed,* p.430.

8. *Memoirs of Andrew Reed,* p.430.

9. *Ibid.,* p.431.

10. *Ibid.,* p.432.

11. Appeal No. 1, in Royal Hospital for Incurables Minute Book 1, 1854, pp.9-15, at Royal Hospital for Neuro-disability, Putney, London. The Bible passage is Luke 16:9-12.

12. Report of Preliminary Meeting, 13 July 1854, in Minute Book 1, pp.1-3; *Memoirs of Andrew Reed,* p.435.

13. It was 1919 before the hospital was granted its Royal Charter of Incorporation, and formally became the Royal Hospital and Home for Incurables, Putney (L. French, *The Royal Hospital and Home for Incurables, Putney, and its Founder: A Short History of the Parent Institution for Incurables Until its Completion in 1918, with a Biography of its Founder, Andrew Reed, D.D,* London: Royal Hospital and Home for Incurables, 1936, p.38f.)

14. 'Report of the Public Meeting Held July 31 1854 at the Mansion House', in Royal Hospital, Minute Book 1, pp.27-32.

15. Rivett, *London Hospital System,* p.32.

16. Constitution and Bye-Laws of The Royal Hospital; and Report of First Annual Meeting, 26 November 1855, in Royal Hospital Minute Book 1, pp.19-27.

17. Constitution and Bye-Laws, pp.36, 105; G. C. Cook, *Victorian Incurables: A History of the Royal Hospital for Neuro-Disability, Putney* (Spennymoor: Memoir Club, 2004), p.58.

18. Rivett, *London Hospital System,* p.32.

19. Woodward, *To Do the Sick No Harm,* pp.36-49.

20. Rivett, *London Hospital System*, p.29.
21. A. E. Clark-Kennedy, *The London: A Study in the Voluntary Hospital System, Vol. 1, The First Hundred Years 1740-1840* (London: Pitman, 1962), pp.222-6.
22. Rivett, *London Hospital System*, p.31.
23. *Ibid.*, p.213.
24. Appeal No. 2, Royal Hospital Minute Book 1, pp.16-19.
25. *Memoirs of Andrew Reed*, pp.437-40; *The Royal Hospital for Incurables, designed for the permanent care and comfort of those who by Disease, Accident, or Deformity, are hopelessly disqualified for the duties of life* (London, 1868), pp.11-14, cited in Cook, *Victorian Incurables*, pp.45-8.
26. *Memoirs of Andrew Reed*, pp.440-42.
27. Board Meetings, 9 November 1854; 14 December 1854, Royal Hospital Minute Book 1, pp.40-42.
28. First Case Book, Royal Hospital, at Royal Hospital for Neuro-disability, Putney, London, cited in Cook, *Victorian Incurables*, pp.59-62.
29. Board Meeting, Royal Hospital Minute Book 1, 25 October 1855; 26 November 1855 ; 29 November 1855, pp.101-11.
30. Minutes of Asylum for Fatherless Children, 20 December 1855; 3 January 1856; *Memoirs of Andrew Reed*, pp.251-2.
31. *Memoirs of Andrew Reed*, pp.443-6.
32. Board Meetings 23 May 1857; 11 June 1857; 23 July 1857, Royal Hospital Minute Book, pp.307, 318, 323-4.
33. Rivett, *London Hospital System*, pp.32-3.
34. Board Meetings, 24 February 1859; 24 March 1859; 12 May 1859; 10 November 1859; Royal Hospital Minute Book 2, pp.185, 200, 228-9, 331.
35. Annual Report, 10 October 1861; 14 November 1861, in Royal Hospital Minute Book 4, pp.19, 42.
36. *Memoirs of Andrew Reed*, p.450.
37. F. Nightingale, *Suggestions on the Subject of Providing, Training, and Organising Nurses for the Sick Poor in Workhouse Infirmaries* (London, 1867), p.1, quoted in J. Woodward, *To Do the Sick No Harm*, p.32.
38. Rivett, *London Hospital System*, pp.36-8.
39. French, *The Royal Hospital and Home for Incurables*, p.25; and Letters from Florence Nightingale to F. Andrew (Secretary), 4 September 1861; 10 September 1861, in Archives, Royal Hospital for Neuro-disability, Putney.
40. Rivett, *London Hospital System*, pp.39-41.
41. Board Meetings, 10 December 1857; 31 December 1857, Royal Hospital Minute Book 1, pp.384, 392; and Board Meeting, Royal Hospital Minute Book 2, 23 Dec. 1858, p.148.
42. Special Board Meetings 9 February 1860; 8 March 1860, Royal Hospital Minute Book 2, pp.386-8, 416-18; 16 April 1860, Royal Hospital Minute Book 3, pp.1-12.

43. French, *Royal Hospital For Incurables,* p.23. The new charity established, The British Home for Incurables, still exists.
44. Board Meeting, 14 May 1861, Royal Hospital Minute Book 3, pp.360-61.
45. Board Meetings, 22 October 1863; 12 November 1863, Royal Hospital Minute Book 4, pp.100, 107, 111-120. The sale of the Coulsdon land was not finally agreed until 1867, and the land only conveyed in 1870. The hospital received £2,000, which was £500 less than the original purchase price.
46. Reported at Board Meeting, 27 November 1862, Royal Hospital Minute Book 4, pp.323-4.

Chapter 22 — Ready for the harvest
1. *Memoirs of Andrew Reed,* p.382.
2. *Ibid.,* p.461.
3. *Ibid.,* pp.461-8.
4. *Ibid.,* p.469.
5. J. Snow, *On the Mode of Communication of Cholera* (London, 2nd edition, 1855).
6. *Memoirs of Andrew Reed,* p.469.
7. I. Murray, ed., *The Autobiography of Charles Haddon Spurgeon: vol. I, The Early Years* (London: Banner of Truth, 1962), p.272.
8. *Memoirs of Andrew Reed,* p.473.
9. *Ibid.,* pp.474-6.
10. *Ibid.,* p.423.
11. *Ibid.,* pp.476-8.
12. *Ibid.,* p.484.
13. *Ibid.,* p.424.
14. *Ibid.,* pp.482-3.
15. *Ibid.,* pp.500, 515.
16. *Ibid.,* pp.478-80.
17. *Ibid.,* pp.493-4.
18. *Ibid.,* p.505.
19. *Ibid.,* p.518.
20. *Ibid.,* p.523.
21. *Congregational Year Book,* 1863, pp.255-6.

Chapter 23 — Conclusion
1. Board Meeting, 27 February 1862; Annual Report 1862, in Royal Hospital Minute Book 4, pp.139-40, 322-3.
2. Board Minutes, Royal Earlswood Hospital, Royal Earlswood Archives, Surrey History Centre, Woking, 392/2/1/4, Board Meetings 7 August 1861; 27 February 1862; 5 March 1862.
3. *Memoirs of Andrew Reed,* pp.535-45.
4. *Ibid.,* pp.535-7.

5. *Ibid.,* pp.538-9.
6. *Ibid.,* pp.549-50.
7. *First Annual Report, Asylum for Idiots,* p.6.
8. *Memoirs of Andrew Reed,* p.480.
9. *Ibid.,* pp.253-4.
10. Reed, 'The Man of God,' p.23.
11. Reed, *Personal Efforts for the Salvation of Men,* p.53.
12. *Memoirs of Andrew Reed,* p.528.
13. *Ibid.,* p.515.
14. Wycliffe Chapel Balance Sheets, 1848-1907, London Metropolitan Archive N/C/40/13.
15. *Memoirs of Andrew Reed,* p.480.
16. *Ibid.,* p.377.
17. Quoted in *Memoirs of Andrew Reed,* pp.548-9.
18. Quoted in *East London Congregationalist,* vol. 1874-7 (London), p.86.
19. *Illustrated London News,* 1 March 1862; *Gentleman's Magazine,* 1862, quoted in *Memoirs of Andrew Reed,* pp.548-9.
20. C. E. B. Reed, *Memoir of Charles Reed,* p.92.
21. *Memoirs of Andrew Reed,* p.495.
22. Last Words of Andrew Reed, in London Orphan Asylum Archives, Surrey History Centre, Woking, 3719/8/2.

Chapter 24 — Epilogue

1. R. J. W. Crabbe, Notes on the History of Wycliffe Chapel, unpublished manuscript in Surrey History Centre, 3719/15/8.
2. The subsequent history of all the charities is told in J. McMillan and N. Alvey, *Faith is the Spur: Andrew Reed and the Schools and Hospitals he Founded,* Reed's School (Cobham: MCB University Press, 1993).
3. The history of the school is told in Alvey, *Education by Election — Reed's School, Clapton and Watford.*
4. The story of Reedham is told in H. E. Rolph, *The Home on the Hill* (Coulsdon, 1981).
5. G. C. Cook's, *Victorian Incurables: A History of the Royal Hospital for Neuro-Disability* recounts the story of the charity, as does *A Short History of the Royal Hospital for Neuro-disability* (Putney, 2004).
6. The Reed family have retained an active involvement in the charities since Andrew Reed's death. Members of the family still serve on the boards of three out of the four remaining charities.

Index